Psychodynamic and Cognitive Behavioral Theory and Practice

Psychodynamic and Cognitive Behavioral Theory and Practice

Talking Across the Divide

TERRY B. NORTHCUT
SHVETA KUMARIA

OXFORD
UNIVERSITY PRESS

OXFORD
UNIVERSITY PRESS

Oxford University Press is a department of the University of Oxford.
It furthers the University's objective of excellence in research, scholarship,
and education by publishing worldwide. Oxford is a registered trade mark of
Oxford University Press in the UK and in certain other countries.

Published in the United States of America by Oxford University Press
198 Madison Avenue, New York, NY 10016, United States of America.

CIP data is on file at the Library of Congress

ISBN 9780197508398

DOI: 10.1093/9780197508404.001.0001

Printed by Marquis Book Printing, Canada

The manufacturer's authorized representative in the EU for product safety is
Oxford University Press España S.A., of Parque Empresarial San Fernando de Henares,
Avenida de Castilla, 2 – 28830 Madrid (www.oup.es/en or product.safety@oup.com).
OUP España S.A. also acts as importer into Spain of products made by the manufacturer.

FSC www.fsc.org MIX Paper | Supporting responsible forestry FSC® C103567

In loving memory of my husband Greg (TBN)

To all who have taught me important lessons in life and learning (SK)

Contents

Preface

Nothing is as compelling or instructive for a clinician as a good story or a well-conceptualized case. From childhood, all of us are soothed, supported, and excited by stories that bridge our fantasy world with what we are experiencing in the "real world." Sometimes we choose narratives that provide us with a complete escape from the day-to-day life, and sometimes we feel a kinship with hearing about people experiencing situations similar to our own. For clients and clinicians, we feel the most understood when our listeners reflect that they understand our attempts to negotiate the internal world and external world on a day-to-day basis, including our wishes and desires and our pragmatic accommodations to what we perceive is reality. Part of that understanding requires an acknowledgment of the external world that imposes significant and real obstacles, or advantages that impede or accelerate our progression in this world. This is a great deal to juggle in our own lives, and as clinicians confronting clients overwhelmed by their experiences in the world they live in. Many clinicians respond to these always present and varied perspectives by embracing eclecticism without understanding how changing approaches or frameworks impact the therapeutic process. The different approaches often feel disconnected for client and therapist, and perhaps even more alarming may seem or reflect that we don't know what we are doing. Consequently, misunderstandings, failures in empathy, and an unnecessary extension of symptoms can result.

It would seem to make the most sense then—that mental health providers are more effective when they consider the client from a framework that acknowledges that the "whole is more than the sum of its parts." For example, social workers have historically and ideologically operated from a framework that acknowledged what affects one part of a client system affects all parts of the system. Unfortunately, with the social, economic, and physical difficulties in the mental health world in which all disciplines practice, this biopsychosocial spiritual framework, while important and meaningful, gets reduced to the most immediate, observable problem that can be "solved" in the quickest, most overtly verifiable manner. Little time or resources are available to preserve a focus on the entire system(s) with all of its components, which will be discussed further in Chapter 1.

One solution to this dilemma has been a "common factors" approach that examines the qualities and/or techniques that appear to transcend theoretical parties and yield positive outcomes in practice. Evidence-informed practice provides yet another umbrella for selecting the common factors. However, what often gets left out in this "evidence" is the dynamic process that facilitates understanding of underlying issues as well as overt symptomatology. The creative part of our therapeutic work is the "weaving of the tapestry" of internal and external worlds. It is rare and usually contraindicated to focus on only one explanatory model to guide clinical interventions for the duration of the therapeutic relationship, just as it is rare for the weaver to be satisfied with one color of wool or one weaving pattern for the finished product. But how the choices are made and when to change techniques or patterns by the therapist or the artist are often difficult to articulate.

One common denominator to all modes of practice is the importance of the therapeutic relationship. The field of interpersonal neurobiology has confirmed the importance of sustained relationships in shaping and altering brain functioning over the course of the lifespan (Siegel, 2012). Psychodynamic theory has traditionally provided a conceptual framework that has been found to be clinically useful and qualitatively effective in understanding relationship patterns (Brandell, 2013; Ornstein & Ganzer, 2000). Likewise, psychodynamic theory has provided a means to understand clients' internal, subjective worlds and the resulting therapeutic alliance or relationship. For this reason, and our experiences as clinicians and educators, psychodynamic theory and its many permutations, will provide one foundation for guiding treatment in this textbook. In a similar fashion, cognitive behavioral therapy (CBT) has provided empirical support for its use with certain clinical syndromes and presenting problems while also empowering clients in their sense of mastery. Examining the rationale for the choice of these two schools of treatment will be considered and supported. In addition, examining how to bridge the two theoretical frameworks will enhance clinical usefulness and allow for the utilization of common factors with the necessary theoretical scaffolding.

While the case can be made that psychodynamic theory and cognitive behavioral interventions are two theoretical frameworks and methods of intervention that have consistently been found to have therapeutic value, albeit with different symptoms and/or presenting problems, it is critical to continue to try to determine why and how to combine these two frameworks with an ongoing focus on the impact on the client of when and how to change techniques. No therapy method or model suits all clients during all phases of their treatment or their life. Therefore, the assimilation of CBT in psychodynamic practice will be examined in relation to different phases of treatment and for a variety of intrapsychic and interpersonal difficulties. We are fortunate in this time period of examining mental health and functioning in the United States and around the world—that we have access to an amazing amount of research that ranges from discoveries in neurobiology from developed countries to emerging data on mental health patterns and behavior in low-income and middle-income non-industrialized countries around the world. There is some comfort in knowing we cannot "resolve" or "solve" the mysterious synergy that produces private troubles and public issues because it is a misnomer that problems can be classified as either/or. We will never be able to use our human minds to comprehend all human behavior as we are always being influenced by the dynamic process between our internal and external worlds and the "gray" area between in which we live. Recognizing that "truth"—that we will never get it all "right"—relieves us of the burden to find the best and perfect approach to help others, which also means that we can rest in being "good enough" and allow our rationality and our creativity to influence our clinical theorizing and practice. Consequently, we can continually be open to revising our ideas and not be troubled by "hardening of the categories" (Kelly, 1963) of classification or treatment modules or manuals as if problems lend themselves to step-by-step dismantling and then resolving. This text will try to hold in tension the need to present the most up-to-date research and clinical interventions and illustrations with the recognition that this text won't have all of the answers, yet can still offer some possibilities for future directions and ways to capitalize on our clients' similarities and idiosyncrasies in meanings and experiences.

A few words about what this book is NOT: This book is not a manualized treatment approach to working with clients with certain characteristics or demographic variables. Nor is this a beginner's guide to understanding psychodynamic theory and practice or CBT theory and practice. There are numerous volumes that provide those important contributions that will be drawn upon and referred to in the text for readers to pursue as needed or interest dictates. What this book does provide is an emphasis on the treatment relationship, the professional use of the therapist's self in practice, and the use of theories of understanding to provide a window into the subjective world of clients and consequently to guide the choice of when and how CBT interventions might be warranted. As many writers have acknowledged and emphasized, clinical work is an art and a science (Hofmann & Weinberger, 2007; Schore, 2012; Soldz & McCullough, 2000). We have lost our way in proposing guidelines to interventions when we have lost sight of the need to recognize both art and science in our work. Out of the urgent and pressing problems of vulnerable populations in our society, we need to act swiftly and effectively, however, that urgency can sometimes do more harm than good if it perpetuates the myth that clinical work is only a science. As Keats reminds us, we need to "abide in uncertainties, mysteries, and doubts" and allow ourselves to rest in "negative capability" without "irritably reaching for fact and reason" (Bates, 1963, p. 249; Weingarten, 2009, p. 246). However, it is a misunderstanding of Keats if we only offer a "warm and fuzzy" view of clinical work as "creative" meanderings through our clients' lives. Our personal and social problems in the world are too serious to minimize the need and progress made with scientific positivistic knowledge. There are serious social problems and fundamental philosophical differences that continue to keep particular groups in society vulnerable to changing economic practices (Klein, 2007). But we cannot assume that positivistic science has the sole answer to today's social and psychological problems. The key to solving private troubles and public issues cannot be in a singular focus on a short-term or a long-term approach. Nor can clients be considered as only consumers, without consideration of the personhood of each system. It would be too simplistic to think that psychodynamic theory has the corner on understanding what is meant by empathy and CBT has the empirically "proven" excellence in problem-solving. However, they are often presenting as "two minds" as if one must always make a clear choice between these methodologies. Instead of fighting each other, Keats suggested that the idea of "doubt" (Latin, 'dubitare') or "two minds" to be most facilitative for creativity. Psychotherapy and decisions effecting public policy in the twenty-first century require enormous knowledge and the ability to think creatively, which also requires a healthy dose of doubt, and an ability to talk to each other. There are many perspectives essential to pragmatically facilitate growth and change for clients and communities. It is the intention of this text to juxtapose two historically different perspectives and encourage readers to utilize their own informed creativity to grapple with the many problems facing the mental health field.

For greater flexibility in this text, we use terms such as clinical, treatment, interventions, and so on, while still very aware that terminology matters and reflects a historical and value base. As clinical social workers and academics, our job is to understand the context of clients, students, our profession, and the society in which we exist, which is the focus in this text. Focusing on context allows us to discriminate between which theories and techniques are most helpful to clients and their cultural surround at different points in time.

Both psychodynamic theory and cognitive behavioral theory will be examined to summarize the status of the theories at this point in time, particularly strengths and weaknesses. A common factors approach will then be considered as one of a number of attempts to integrate a variety of guidelines for practice; however, the limitations with that perspective as it impacts psychotherapy research and practice will also be considered. The common factors considered relevant for this text are articulated and organized somewhat differently than the generally accepted focus of "common factors" (Cameron & Keenan, 2010; Stricker, 2010). In this text, the therapeutic relationship, findings from research and clinical practice, problem-solving skills, and the tincture of time are considered the most essential common factors, the rationale being elaborated in Chapters 1–5. Chapter 6 provides our synthesis of early chapters paving the way for the remaining two chapters (7 and 8) of case composites, which demonstrate theoretical and technical practice integration. These cases will emphasize building therapeutic relationships as well as the management of symptoms, developing enhanced affect regulation, facilitating identity development or expansion, and negotiating loss as an essential component of developmental tasks in living. Both of these cases demonstrate as well how the tincture of time played an important role in the dynamics of the therapeutic relationship.

As Segalo, Kruger, Fourie, & Terre Blanche (2007) envision community psychology, the adage "approach with an open mind but not empty handed" (p.11) applies to our clinical work. We are not without knowledge, but we have to remember that evidence-based strategies may not allow for the fullest understanding of the clients and communities we work with, depending on how that evidence is solicited and recorded. How we interpret the "clinical expertise" emphasized in Evidence-Based Practice (Thyer & Pignotti, 2011) leaves room to hold onto what others have learned ahead of us, as well as consider the multiple ways of clinical knowing (Drisko, 2011). We have to be open to learning from each other while holding onto the wisdom of historical clinical experience guiding the way for possibilities in understanding and helping (Downes, 2011; Fynn, Terre Blanche, Fourie, & Kruger, 2012).

References

Bates, W. J. (1963). *John Keats*. Harvard University Press.

Brandell, J. R. (2013). Psychoanalysis in the halls of social work academe: Can this patient be saved? *Journal of Social Work Practice*, 27(3), 235–248.

Downes, S. (2011, October). *Connectivism and Personal Learning*. Keynote presentation delivered to Charles University, Prague, Czech Republic.

Drisko, J. (2011). A clinician-researcher's understanding of "The Effectiveness of Long-Term Psychodynamic Psychotherapy." *Clinical Social Work Journal*, 39, 334–339.

Fynn, A., Terre Blanche, M., Fourie, E., & Kruger, J. (2012). Teaching community psychology as community engagement. *Journal of Psychology in Africa*, 22(4), 573–578.

Hofmann, S. G. & Weinberger, J. (Eds.) (2014). *The art and science of psychotherapy*. Routledge.

Cameron, M., & Keenan, E. K. (2010). The common factors model: Implications for transtheoretical clinical social work practice. *Social Work*, 55(1), 63–73.

Kelly, George. (1963). *A theory of personality*. W.W. Norton & Co.

Klein, N. (2007). The shock doctrine. Picador.

Ornstein, E. & Ganzer, C. (2000). Strengthening the strengths perspective: An integrative relational approach. *Psychoanalytic Social Work*, 7, 57–78.

Segalo, P., Kruger, D. J., Fourie, E., & Terre Blanche, M. (2007). Re-imagining community: The Unisa community psychology experience. In M. Anderson (Ed.), *Journey to freedom narratives* (41–53). Unisa Press.

Schore, A. N. (2012). *The science of the art of psychotherapy*. Norton Series on Interpersonal Neurobiology.

Siegel, D. (2012). *The developing mind*, 2nd ed. Guilford Press.

Soldz, S. & McCullough, L. (Eds.). (2000). *Reconciling empirical knowledge and clinical experience: The art and science of psychotherapy*. American Psychological Association Books.

Stricker, G. (2010). *Psychotherapy integration*. American Psychological Association Books.

Thyer, B. & Pignotti, M. (2011). Evidence-based practices do not exist. *Clinical Social Work Journal*, 39, 328–333.

Weingarten, K. (2009). Stretching to meet what's given: Opportunities for a spiritual practice. In F. Walsh (Ed.), Spiritual resources in family therapy (340–358). Guilford Press.

Acknowledgments

Many people have contributed to this text, through love and support and with tangible help on finding the oft-misplaced reference. We specifically want to thank Nuri Kim, Francesca Castelli, and Ian M. Rogers for their editorial assistance. Our respective deans, Patricia Findley and Marianne Yoshioka, encouraged us in this endeavor and tried not to load us up with too many committee responsibilities. Friends, families, partners, and canine companions were patient, loving, and continued to provide sustenance and important doses of reality throughout the process. We feel privileged to be able to work together in reflecting on our clinical work, teaching, research, and challenging each other to finish the next chapter.

1
Contextualizing private troubles and public issues

Introduction

C. Wright Mills (1959) stressed the importance of understanding both the individual and society by contemplating what constitutes a "private trouble" versus a "public issue." Never has the line between the two been less clear than currently with a rapidly changing sociological, cultural, economic, political, and technological world. Practitioners are often in the position of trying to treat clients as independent entities distinct from the world around them or as only social products of the environment in which we all reside. Sadly, reality (if we can use such a term in these "fake news" and postmodern days) involves an oft-subtle interface that requires not only an understanding of both the internal world and the external world but also an appreciation of the dynamism that occurs at their points of intersection. This dynamism defies simple explanations or simple solutions when problems or conflicts occur. Our human nature seems to cry for simple and clear answers that will be reinforced by our economic and social policies, despite our knowledge that private troubles or public issues seldom have simple explanations.

Mental health providers are not exempt from this craving for clarity. While we like to think that we are choosing a theoretical framework for its utility and efficacy, as well as for our personal comfort and sense of its applicability, we are swayed by economic and sociological factors. Charlotte Towle commented in 1935:

> The field of social casework is swept almost annually with a hue and cry of new methods, new approaches, new emphases. Every national conference has its keynote of this or that emphasis or over emphasis. Avid and needful for a solution, social workers respond with a hectic pursuit of the last word in a reaction so widespread and so compulsive that one is reminded of the

Psychodynamic and Cognitive Behavioral Theory and Practice. Terry B. Northcut and Shveta Kumaria, Oxford University Press. © Oxford University Press (2025). DOI: 10.1093/9780197508404.003.0001

sweep of flames through dry grass, only to experience again the acrid smoke of frustration and disillusionment.

(Towle, 1935; quoted in Cooper, 1977)

It is striking that the field of mental health still seems to experience the same "hectic pursuit" for answers and, of course, funding. At times these pursuits reflect the economic and the political landscape, which is necessary for accountability in our professions. However, there is often a push that places expediency above what we know is clinically sound practice. Astounding technological advances have reshaped accessibility to mental health in important and positive ways. However, these advances are not all positive. Clients, therapists, and society at large forget that what gets defined as mental illness and who are the appropriate providers are subject to interpretation based on the time and place in which we live. We are familiar with the historical description of the "schizophrenigenic mother" or the "refrigerator mothers" blamed for schizophrenia and autism, respectively. Likewise, sexual orientation and gender classifications have suffered through decades of pathologizing. Economic factors often decide which treatment is preferred and provided by managed care, insurance companies, and governmental programs even going so far as to regulate what kind of problems warrant a specified length and type of treatment. As Foucault aptly emphasized, those who get to decide how problems are defined and treated hold a great deal of power in society (Martin & Sugarman, 1999).

One of the most glaring examples of the impact of social, political, and economic factors on mental health treatment is the consideration of Axis II or Personality disorders in DSM history. Because of the difficulty in establishing reliability of these diagnostic categories and for the lack of a quick treatment effect, insurance companies elected to not fund mental health treatment for personality disorders. With the lack of funding for treatment in the past, we then didn't have accurate recording of the incidence of these diagnoses, nor did we have sufficient culturally appropriate scholarship on this seemingly elusive diagnostic category despite the clinical experience routinely challenging clinicians. Research currently has attempted to correct these previous gaps (Choi-Kain et al., 2021) yet still struggle with the complexity of the disorders in terms of controversy about diagnosis and best practices. Of particular concern in our diverse society, clients may appear "personality disordered," which takes the focus away from the cultural and contextual factors that have contributed to, caused, and labeled this clinical presentation. Also of critical importance is the context of the clinician assigning this diagnosis. We will discuss more of the clinicians' contextual factors and their role in practice in later chapters.

This interface between subjective experience of clients and clinicians and the external impingements that impact both is often unwieldy and elusive. The choice of theory and the type of research funded and administered may not take into account the important qualitative factors in therapy (Drisko, 2011). For example, currently clinical work in Veterans Hospitals requires the knowledge and ability to use prolonged exposure therapy to treat PTSD (www.va.gov/). There is an important research that has supported that decision; however, other factors make that choice problematic when considering the type of trauma, the length of treatment funded, the stage of reintegration back home, and the types of social supports available to the veteran following treatment (Basham, 2013; Northcut & Kienow, 2014). In addition, there are the practical constraints of negotiating the Veteran Affairs (VA) system that is heavily burdened with the quantity of veterans needing services. How do the budgetary needs of the VA impact the type of training for mental health personnel and the type of treatment that is provided? How is therapeutic "success" measured for Post-traumatic Stress Disorder (PTSD) with veterans? How are clients' personal experiences factored into the treatment within an organization as large as VA? What if the trauma was perpetrated by the veteran's superiors as is the case with Military Sexual Trauma? All these questions and their answers must be considered when negotiating the tightrope that is clinical practice in this type of setting. A guiding principle of any form of therapy should be knowledge of results from qualitative and quantitative research on human behavior and the effects of trauma which can safely and effectively help veterans readjust to their homeland in a manner that isn't "one size fits all." This knowledge requires us to examine multiple therapeutic models to determine which models, in what way, and under what circumstances are the "best practices" for clinicians engaged in practice in diverse settings.

Two of the most studied and enduring therapeutic theories and techniques are psychodynamic and cognitive behavior. Both schools have developed over the years since their inception, each factoring in changes in knowledge about human behavior. Unfortunately, these theoretical frameworks are often reduced to caricatures of themselves; psychodynamic as navel-gazing and CBT as too rational or symptom-focused. Both frameworks have evolved substantially to defy such characterizations. One example of how psychodynamic theory has evolved is the consideration of results from neurobiological research. The field of interpersonal neurobiology has confirmed the importance of human relationships in forming and changing brain patterns that influence present and future behavior emphasizing the continuing relevance of the therapeutic alliance (Cozolino, 2010; Schore, 2012; Siegel, 1999). Likewise, cognitive behavioral therapy moved years ago to considering more than just cognitive distortions to allow for consideration of schemas, meaning, emotions, and the therapeutic relationship (Granvold, 1999; Mahoney, 1993; Suveg et al., 2006; Wright et al., 2006) and have folded in these considerations to extensive research and practice. Treatment process and outcome studies also have confirmed the relevance and primacy of the therapeutic relationship for all kinds of therapy (Crits-Christoph et al., 2013; Rubel et al., 2019). As a result, both psychodynamic and cognitive behavior treatments value the therapeutic relationship and the impact on treatment. Barth (2014) concluded that "insight-oriented psychotherapy as well as developmental, cognitive behavioral, neuropsychological, symptom-focused and affect regulative approaches ... are in one way or another, relational" (p. 23).

A focus on the relational factors in psychotherapy cannot be managed or maintained without a clear understanding of contextual factors impacting and shaping our identities and our experiences and those of our clients. For this reason, we begin this text on bridging psychodynamic and CBT with a closer look at these factors. "Knowing about the factors that influence the development of legislation, policies, program services, and funding at all levels of our political system is an essential component of (practice) competency" (Singer et al., 2012, p. 461). These factors compel us to rethink our assumptions about clients within the therapy space and make room for the clients' subjective experiences with these factors and form more effective therapeutic relationships.

Philosophical factors

Questions about the nature of our existence and what constitutes mind and reality may not seem relevant when you are trying to figure out what to do with a client in pain in front of you. Or if you are trying to figure out what kind of treatment program would be best suited for a particular symptom or a large-scale social problem. However, it is extremely critical as the underlying philosophy shapes what we even consider problems and whether we think we can get to the root of the problem. Western culture, in particular, has struggled with how to understand the relationship between mind, body, and spirit. The current increase in clients' request for, and the demand by, the general public for the inclusion of spirituality in understanding and promoting health care, reflects a cultural pendulum swinging from viewing mind and body as separate entities to recognizing the inescapable intertwining of mind, body, and spirit. Victoria Sweet (2012) reviewed the medical progress patients made in the historic Laguna Honda Hospital and attributed it to the critical importance of community and the soul of medicine, rather than economics, politics, and even science. In a similar vein, Oliver Sacks promoted the idea of there being more to medical care than an appreciation of the science behind diagnoses.

> The emergent field of narrative medicine, in which a patient's life story is elicited in order that his immediate health crisis may be addressed, in many ways reflects Sack's belief that a patient may know more about his condition than those treating him do, and that doctors' ability to listen can therefore outrank technical erudition .... Patients want coherence, which can be achieved only when the contradictory essentials of experience are assembled into a fluid account. The doctor must not only listen but also process what he has heard.
>
> The formation of our individual health and mental health narratives requires theoretical frameworks that make room for more than symptom relief, rather allow for subjective experiences that cannot be divorced from a presenting focal problem, nor reduced to a quantitative algorithm.
>
> (Solomon, 2015)

Harrington (2008) traced the evolution of medical care in the Western world, which provides one perspective in our struggle to understand the mind–body conundrum. She proposed that the relationship between mind and body in medicine represents a complex myriad of stories woven together across time. Such narratives are formed, edited, and influenced by scientific and humanistic disciplines, as well as by economic, political, religious, secular, and historical factors. There have been points where the science of psychotherapy has embraced empirical proof as the path forward and minimized the narrative shifts over time. This distancing of the mind and body stems from the historical roots of the field in medicine and the aspirational desire to be seen as prestigious as medicine. Unfortunately, what was left out of "treatment" were the social and personal narratives influencing private troubles and public issues. Consequently, examining results of empirical study *and* the narratives surrounding the study of both mind and body is warranted in order to gain a more complete understanding of how to best intervene clinically (Northcut, 2017). In this text, the narratives surrounding psychodynamic theory and CBT and our evolving ideas about mind and body are considered.

Biological factors

Every culture has had elements of trauma, violence, and/or war of some kind. However, the confluence of technological advances and effective, efficient global communication (including social media) and the staggering social problems that maintain a strong foothold in our world have created a melting pot of trauma whether from natural or man-made disasters. We are simultaneously reminded of how far-reaching our impact is and how personal and embodied our experience is of "glocalized trauma," to borrow the phrase from Hong & Song (2010), "thinking globally and acting locally." Shifting to use "glocalized trauma" helps us think of how we experience trauma socially, politically, economically, psychologically, and physiologically, whether it is trauma inflicted by nature, such as devastating hurricanes and extreme temperatures, acts of domestic and international terrorism, medical procedures, and/or interpersonal violence. The effects cannot be isolated to some social system "over there." We experience PTSD, whatever the cause, within our national borders and within our individual bodies.

Neurobiological research and study of trauma survivors has done much to illuminate the impact of trauma, and specifically what kinds of conceptual models help to explain how to facilitate the process of healing. Reaching back in history to Helen Flanders Dunbar (1902–1959), who founded the American Psychosomatic Society, she and her colleagues:

> saw patients first as human beings who were dynamically involved in an environment in which they were formed and transformed.... And her concern with seeing patients and disease in terms of a patterned, organic whole anticipates what came to be formally called by the 1960s the 'biopsychosocial model.'
>
> (Hart, 2014, p. 784)

The patient began to be viewed as a combination of the psych and soma, body, and soul. We also owe credit to Walter Cannon for linking the impact of trauma to physiological reactions in the body (Harrington, 2008). Hans Selye and his colleagues also examined how the body processes negative emotions, including the severe trauma experienced by military personnel (Harrington, 2008). Historical champions of the linkage between mind and body have contemporary advocates, including authors and researchers such as Bessel van der Kolk (2014) and Bruce Perry (2007) (discussed further in the next chapter and throughout this book), who reconcile neurological advances with the impact of developmental, psychological, and sociological trauma. Their work connects physiological indicators and reactions with an understanding of how the brain functions to generate treatment models that benefit from the best of a number of theoretical frameworks. In a similar way, Fonagy (2015) focuses on the ability to mentalize as essential for interpersonal development and to potentially mediate the impact of stress (Jansen et al., 2023). Theorists and practitioners are also incorporating sensory awareness to further help clients not necessarily traumatized by war, but who nevertheless experience a disconnect from their bodies in ways that interfere with optimal mental and physical functioning (Ogden, 2021; Ogden & Fisher, 2015; Levine, 1997). Any integration of theoretical frameworks must also reconcile our understandings about how trauma has been recorded in the body and thereby disrupts or shapes treatment responses. Rightly so, the World Health Organization (WHO) advocates that "there can be no health without mental health." Likewise, there can be no mental health without an understanding of the physical and sociological conditions shaping our minds and bodies.

Sociological factors

Technological advances have improved medical care globally but have accentuated a sociological and psychological sense of ennui and perhaps even alexithymia (Barth, 2014), in which emoticons substitute for an in-depth experiencing of feelings. COVID-19 has intensified anxiety, lethargy, sense of isolation, and despair across the world. A pervasive sense of isolation leads to an increase in online use of social media, which then can lead to the perception that we have many contacts (or "hits") and more social support than we have actual healthy relationships. Burgeoning research considering the types of young adults utilizing social media to cope with ongoing health or common mental health disorders indicates that online support has a significant role to play. However, concerns about privacy and how adolescents and young adults present themselves persist despite any potential positive impact of the production and consumption of social media (Fergie et al., 2016). Furthermore, contradictory reports scramble the perceived benefits of social media with chronic disease in providing social, emotional, or experiential support (Patel et al., 2015; Turner & Lefevre, 2017). To date, the use of social media has also been associated with poor sleep quality, anxiety, depression, and low self-esteem when routinely utilized at night; a convenient, prevalent time of usage for teenagers and adults (Woods & Scott, 2016). Multiple social media sites/venues, as well as general usage, are also correlated with increased symptoms of depression and anxiety for young adults regardless of time spent on social media (Farquhar & Davidson, 2014; Lin et al., 2016; Primack et al., 2017; Vannucci et al., 2017). Technology-based social comparisons and attempts to receive feedback and reassurance are also associated with depressive symptoms particularly with girls reporting low popularity offline (Nesi & Prinstein, 2015). A recent report in *Wall Street Journal* highlighted how Instagram and Facebook hid data for three years that showed how their algorithms exacerbate teen girls' dissatisfaction with their own bodies that lead to sadness and linked it to eating disorders (Perrigo, 2021). Needless to say, results are mixed and much more study is needed to investigate the different intervening individual factors that can impact self-harming behavior, suicidal ideations, and management of psychotic symptoms (Alvarez-Jimenez et al., 2014; Dyson et al., 2016). Technology itself is not the problem; rather it is problematic depending on who is using it, who controls it, and who has access to monitor it, that is key to determining its benefits and drawbacks.

Areas where the use of specific technologies such as Facebook with individuals with serious mental illness does have a positive impact is in the areas of weight loss, increased physical activity, and healthy eating. Most notable has been the perception of improved peer support (Naslund et al., 2016). Despite the unreliability of content advisory warnings, (Moreno et al., 2016), there is indication that particular usages of Facebook can be helpful with depression. In particular, using Facebook to seek social support, communicate, distract, recall positive memories, and reappraise negative thoughts are positive steps to reduce depression (Tran et al., 2015). Among older adults (age 50+), Internet use has a positive correlation post-retirement (Cotten et al., 2014) in terms of maintaining already-developed connections and establishing new support systems. The challenge is, once again, to determine in what way individuals are using social media. If Facebook, for example, is used for ruminating, making damaging social comparisons, and recalling negative memories, its use can obviously exacerbate depressive symptoms. If Facebook is also being used to "light a match" to accentuate polarizing views, interpersonal and societal safety are compromised. Clinicians must be up to date on the wide-ranging impact of the usage of social media on themselves and on their clients.

Technological advances combined with the impact of pandemic restrictions have also impacted the mode and venue for mental health services delivery. The extended length of time before a vaccine was developed increased stress for everyone, especially mental health providers and other essential workers. Telehealth became and continues to be an essential component of health care provision. Certainly, the possibility of Skype, Facetime, Zoom, Teletherapy, and so on enhances the ability of clients to connect with therapists, friends, and families during illness, a pandemic, or prolonged absences, but research is early about its benefits and drawbacks. These benefits of accessibility are limited in terms of populations at risk such as with poorer and/or elderly clients, and clients in developing countries with limited access to high-speed Internet. While teletherapy has shown promise, comparison studies with in-person treatment are not conclusive. Several problematic issues also have been found to exist with telehealth: a lack of access to nonverbal cues particularly with certain populations, disorders, and treatment models (e.g., Emotion Focused Therapy); therapist burnout from ongoing screen usage and limited movement; distractions of all kinds for clients and clinicians; and technical difficulties interrupting sessions, derailing clarity, and posing potential confidentiality risks. These drawbacks have raised important questions about the use of telehealth for use with assessments, interventions, and evaluations of short- and long-term therapies (Markowitz et al., 2021).

The role of artificial intelligence in the provision of human responses also is critical for further research, particularly the use of AI-generated empathy (Perry, 2023). Testing of an online emotional-support chat showed the ability of GPT-3 to craft "human responses" relationally superior to human-only responses. However, once participants learned that the responses were AI-generated, any gains were diminished. Human empathy is comprised of a cognitive recognition of the emotional states of others, an emotional component that involves sharing the affective states of another, and a motivational or caring aspect that requires an investment of time and energy of the empathizer. AI advancements are most deficient in the ability to share the pains and feelings of others, which allows a "joining-with" the other so essential in clinical work. Infant and early childhood researchers have long emphasized the importance of shared affective states between caregiver and child as a way for children to regulate emotions. We have yet to see the impact psychologically of this sociological revolution toward AI-generated empathy.

Economic factors

In addition to philosophical, biological, and sociological factors, clinical research and therapeutic services cannot be conducted or provided without recognition of the economic factors that shape the funding and determine access to care. Of grave concern in the current economic climate are the short- and long-term effects the global pandemic has had on developing and developed countries. The pandemic has had disproportional longer-term effects on the most economically vulnerable segments of the population in most countries.

> The COVID-19 shock affected workers and labour income differently, depending on the composition of the workforce in terms of skills, occupation types, infrastructure (particularly, but not exclusively, those lacking connectivity), and type of contractual relations (particularly, informal and self-employed workers).
>
> (Yeyati & Filippini, 2021, p. 14)

Job losses over the past few years have also disproportionately impacted individuals from lower-income communities, communities of color, and communities where the populations have lower education. These are communities that may have less savings and less external support to weather the challenge of sustained unemployment. Lower-income minorities are far more likely to experience ongoing exposure and health complications from COVID-19 and other viruses and suffer the economic effects (Smialek & Tankersley, 2020). They are also more likely to live in food deserts, face discrimination, and lack access to quality care. Before the pandemic, African

American workers had higher unemployment rates (6.1%) as compared to their Asian (3%) and White counterparts (3%); during the pandemic, Black workers' unemployment rates rose to 16.7% and as of July 2021 it still remains higher than White workers (Falk et al., 2021, August 20).

Within these changing fiscal realities, despite the increase in medical and mental health needs, government funding and the social support infrastructure are and will continue to be stretched beyond capacity. A particular area of concern is the impact of the pandemic on the future labor market. "On average, school closures induced by COVID-19 led to a learning loss of 0.17 of a standard deviation—that is, at least one-third of a year's worth of learning" (Jakubowski et al., 2024, p. 2; Patrinos, 2023). Additionally, "Azevedo et al. (2021) estimate the lifetime loss in labour earnings for the affected cohort at $10 trillion—around 12% of global GDP" (Yeyati & Filippini, 2021, p. 34). These factors in determining the economic impact of the pandemic indicate an uncertain future for the provision of local and national funds for treatment of any kind as well as the labor force to provide the services.

The history of the National Institute for Mental Health (NIMH) and their priorities for funding is another prime example of the influence of the economy on what kinds of mental health treatment gets funded. Depending on the prevalent political, social, and economic issues confronting the United States, NIMH has moved through a variety of phases of interest: focusing on deinstitutionalization from asylums when NIMH was created (1949), establishing community mental health centers (1960s); examining the needed social supports for the large increase of mentally ill in the criminal justice system and increased homelessness as a result of deinstitutionalization (1970s and 1980s); and researching neurobiology in the "decade of the brain"(1990s), studying treatment models based on the diagnostic categories of the Diagnostic and Statistical Manual (DSM) (2000s), and currently the shift away from funding research based on these categories (Winerman, 2013). NIMH is now funding Research Domain Criteria (RDoC) instead of using the DSM as a guide, in order to "transform diagnosis by incorporating genetics, imaging, cognitive science, and other levels of information to lay the foundation for a new classification system" (Insel, 2013). In addition to the focus on RDoC, Markowitz & Friedman (2020) caution that "since 2002, the NIMH has funded neuroscience at the expense of clinical and services research, putting all its eggs in one biologic basket, envisioning a breakthrough that may not arrive for decades" (p. 1096). Specifically, only

10% of the research funding went to fund clinical trials in 2015 with only 5.4% of those funds supporting clinical research (ibid.)

All of these changes in funding emphasis may have been necessary in response to research findings at points in time, but have also been heavily influenced by advances in psychopharmacology as well as bureaucratic bickering "between successive (political) administrations, tensions and rivalries within the mental health professions, and the difficulties of distinguishing the roles played by social issues such as poverty, racism, stigmatization, and unemployment" (Sundararaman, 2009). The deep pockets of psychopharmacology and the politicization of understanding the effects of social problems has skewed focus to efficiency and/or negotiable pawns of lobbying parties. A more hopeful avenue to factor in a more complex understanding of mental health problems around the world is to increase focus on interdisciplinary research and integrative treatment models. In addition, it is important to recognize that these same economic factors influence funding, and act to maintain the sociological landscape of who has access to care and who can deliver that care.

An even more concerning trend running parallel with the advancements in technology is the commodification of mental health care. Online therapists and applications available via phone have become big businesses offering immediate, accessible care for little investment. On the surface this provides much-needed care to a wider audience; however, little appreciation for sustained depth psychotherapy is evident particularly when examining the scripted solutions offered, particularly utilized by some insurance companies under the heading of "wellness" resources. Delboy & Michaels (2023) found that in addition to "feeling heard," the "general public" wants the results of psychotherapy to produce change and greater choices in their lives but that it is also critical to "get to the root" (p. 233) of their problems necessitating greater depth in their treatment. The organization Psychotherapy Action Network (PsIAN) was created to advocate for greater awareness, policies, and access for psychotherapies that can create lasting change. In addition, they have continued to focus on having an impact on the economic factors that influence marketing of varied brands of psychotherapy, the development and utilization of mental health apps and technology, and the biases of insurance companies regarding whose treatment is covered and which providers can be reimbursed.

Despite these problems of bias in the funding of mental health studies and treatment, and the proliferation of technologically enhanced clinical services, the need for accountability in mental health treatment remains an essential focus in service delivery. For too long the field has been and continues to be subjected to the misappropriation of funds, whether through "fraud, waste, and excess profits to for-profit managed care companies" (Torrey, 2015; Torrey, et al., 2015). There have also been extended treatments that lack apparent benefits to the populations the programs were designed to serve. Additionally, competitive insurance markets have functioned especially poorly in providing coverage to people at elevated risk of mental health and substance abuse problems (Alakeson & Frank, 2010; McGuire & Sinaiko, 2010). Wrap-around services are still needed to provide critical social support to those experiencing mental health issues and lack coverage by private health insurance. Quality measures are also needed that balance an overemphasis on minimizing units of service at the expense of solidified gains in treatment. In other words, treatment cannot and should not be reduced to hours or units of treatment. Our best bet for effective and ultimately efficient treatment (services across a lifespan) is to integrate therapeutic models with proven effectiveness. Combining two theoretical approaches that have demonstrated effectiveness can broaden the type, quality, and effectiveness of mental health treatment without losing important accountability. The challenge remains in how to understand which theories and methods work best in which situations, given that the "client and clinician-in-situation" (Tosone, 2004, p. 483) may be the most critical factor, rather than an internalized, independent disorder divorced from its surroundings.

Empirical factors

There are hundreds, if not thousands, of research articles that demonstrate the effectiveness of CBT with an array of disorders, ranging from cessation of smoking to coping with depression. The relevant studies for this text's purposes will be reviewed and summarized in Chapter 4. However, it is important to step back and consider the context in which many of these studies have occurred. At present, the provision of mental health services in the United States is heavily influenced by the evidence-based practice (EBP) movement that began in the medical field in the early 1990s (Hammersley, 2005; Lambert, 2013; Satterfield et al., 2009). The emphasis was on creating standards by which clinical decisions could be made that relied on results of research studies that met specific established norms. The idea was sound in terms of eliminating improper or harmful medical practices. However, these "norms" disregarded theoretical and qualitative studies and considered quantitative studies, particularly randomly controlled trials (RCT), the "gold standard" for what constituted true evidence (Wachtel, 2010). If the criteria were not met, then studies were considered "research-based practice," a lower designation than "evidence-based practice" (Hjorland, 2011). Consequently, a hierarchy of "best practices" has resulted that prioritizes or idealizes EBP in the top two levels.

Level 1: (meaning most desired) practice guidelines and manuals; well supported, efficacious treatments established by Randomized Control Trials (RCTs)
Level 2: supported and efficacious treatment, based on positive outcomes of nonrandomized designs with some form of controls
Level 3: supported and acceptable treatment, including interventions supported by one controlled or uncontrolled study, or a series of single-subject studies, or by work with a different population than the one of interest
Level 4: promising and acceptable treatment, includes interventions that have no support except general acceptance and clinical anecdotal literature
Level 5: innovative and novel treatment, includes interventions that are not thought to be harmful, but are not widely used or discussed in the literature
Level 6: classification for treatments that have the possibility of doing harm, as well as having unknown or inappropriate theoretical foundations (Saunders et al., 2004).

Unfortunately, what has happened is a privileging of RCTs to the point that it is assumed that treatments that have not been researched through RCTs are not effective (an "incorrect rejection"). However, the reason some therapeutic approaches have not been subjected to this type of research may have more to do with the academic culture that rewards types of research that can generate income for the university. For example, peer or third-party payer perceptions have often equated efficiency with efficacy of certain treatments. In addition, RCTs are inappropriate in measuring effectiveness of some psychotherapy treatments as those may be more amenable to qualitative research (Fonagy, 2005). Westen et al. (2004) appropriately challenged the assumptions underlying RCTs methodology to psychotherapy research by pointing out that the viewpoint seems to be that

> (1) "psychopathology is so malleable that a brief intervention is likely to change it permanently, (2) most patients can be treated for a single disorder or problem, (3) psychiatric disorders can be treated with psychosocial interventions without regard to personality factors that are less likely to change with brief treatments, and (4) experimental methods provide a 'gold standard' for evaluation for these treatments. (p. 2)

Realistically, no human behavior can be isolated to a single symptom or type of intervention, and symptoms cannot usually be reduced to a single treatment intervention like a particular strain of bacteria can respond to a particular antibiotic. However, that fantasy persists among many private citizens, clinicians, administrators, and policymakers. Our mental health care system in this country continues to prioritize research that doesn't address clients' access to care, focus on internal experience, family patterns of interaction, or the completeness and coherence of one's narrative (Drisko, 2011). Consequently, when contemplating which theoretical models hold promise for integration in helping clients and therapists understand internal subjective experience as well as external influencing factors, we should not limit the search to just what has been "proven" effective in one form of research (Wachtel, 2010). Fortunately, evidence-informed practice does require "the integration of the best research evidence *with* our clinical expertise, and *with* our patient's unique values and circumstances" (Strauss et al., 2010; Thyer & Pignotti, 2011), which means we are not confined to data from RCT's alone. We can look further to include the subjective experiences of clients and clinicians essential to understanding how best to intervene therapeutically.

"*Local knowledge*" and "*experience-near wisdom*" (Weingarten, 1999, p. 245) are also valuable in considering the complexity of human behavior and interpersonal relationships. However, in terms of research funding, "best research evidence" in the past has superseded clinical expertise and patient's values as even irrelevant—so much so that there has had to be quite a bit of "consciousness raising" about the other two components (client's values and cultural contexts, and clinical wisdom) necessary to evaluate practice. Mullins-Sweatt et al. (2016) caution against relying too heavily on construct validity (how accurately any kind of diagnostic and treatment manual portrays the variables being studied) and focus more on clinical utility in developing and promulgating diagnostic manuals, a practice that unfortunately has been more common particularly in research. As Widiger (2012) summarizes, mental disorders are much more likely to be the result of complex dynamic interactions between biological predispositions and environment and psychosocial factors. Usefulness for a clinician relates to goodness of fit, ease of usage, and feasibility of theoretical approaches and interventions; not just how well the test measures reflect what you set out to measure (Reed, 2010).

Clinical research has made tremendous progress in operationalizing these interpersonal and intrapersonal variables which will be discussed further in Chapter 5. Psychodynamic theory and practice has demonstrated a persistent ability to conceptually describe and explain subjective experiences across gender, a variety of cultures, economic classes, and ages despite the stereotype of being suited best for White, upper class Westerners (Berzoff, & Drisko, 2015; Berzoff et al., 2016; Drisko, 2011, 2012; Fonagy, 2015; Glass, 2008; Leichsenring & Rabung, 2008; Lilliengren, 2023). Unfortunately, psychodynamic theory is sometimes interpreted as if it is still fixated in nineteenth-century Vienna, despite advances in theory and support in neurobiological research mentioned earlier and discussed further in the next chapter (Cozolino, 2010; Fonagy, 2005; Schore, 2012; Siegel, 1999). Likewise, CBT tends to be associated with scripted behavioral and cognitive interventions that discount the subjective experience of clients with those thoughts and behaviors, and has moved to incorporate emotions, images, values, and the body. When combined with clinical expertise and client's values, the usefulness of psychodynamic and cognitive behavioral theory and therapy as veterans in the mental health field offer ongoing relevance and utility for therapeutic gain. Integration of these two theoretical frameworks with results from quantitative and qualitative research, clinical experience, and client's values allow us to capitalize on the strengths and minimize the weaknesses of each variable.

Personal factors

The premise of this chapter and this book is that it is impossible to separate the personal context and that of the polis. Additionally, such a separation is not possible for mental health professionals as well. "Indeed, 'therapist effects' are much more important than 'method effects,' and therefore who the therapist is, is much more important than the therapeutic method used" (Rønnestaad & Skovholt, 2013, p. 7). These qualities include both what Orlinsky & Howard (1987) called the task-instrumental and the social-emotional aspects of therapy work. The social-emotional aspect refers to factors that help build the alliance and the therapeutic relationship. These social-emotional aspects are the therapist's relational manner, attachment style, and management of their own interpersonal issues. Of these characteristics, the therapist skillfulness and professional relational manner seem to be most related to client-rated alliance factors (Nissen-Lie et al., 2010). Studies across cultures on personal qualities of therapist who are good at what they do (master therapists) have also identified a warm relational style, self-reflection, empathy, humility, acceptance of ambiguity and human complexity, and ability to embrace paradox as critical to being effective clinicians (Hirai, 2010; Kwon & Kim, 2007; Rønnestaad & Skovholt, 2013).

However, these interlocking systems should include examining personal agency and the clinician's action, albeit also influenced by other factors (e.g., values, intersecting identities, culture, and class). Earlier psychotherapy researchers from the 1970s and 1980s attempted to look at what factors influence the personal theoretical choices of clinicians to determine what impact that may have on the therapeutic process and outcome. Prochaska & Norcross (1983) found that clinical experience, values and personal philosophy, and graduate training are strongly reported influences. The framework of the supervisor assigned in training is also heavily valued. In their view at that time, "the best current basis for choosing a theoretical orientation could be the degree to which it benefits or 'fits' the clinician rather than the client" (p, 205). In an earlier study, Strupp (1978) found that "reliance on a single theoretical technique is a product of inexperience, or conversely, with experience comes diversity" (Auerbach & Johnson, 1977; Norcross & Prochaska, 1983, p. 205; Strupp, 1978). In 2001, Arthur found an interesting comparison of psychodynamic-oriented therapist with cognitive behavioral-oriented clinicians in that psychodynamic therapists expressed a greater interest and investment in feelings and insight versus the cognitive behaviorists who preferred pragmatism and observable change (Arthur, 2001). Petko et al. (2016) conducted a study of masters' level students in a qualitative study and found participants emphasized compatibility of the theories with their personal value system and the logical connection between theory and practice learned in their educational program. What is most striking is Rasmussen's (2018) observation that Norcross (2005) reported that "in general the orientation chosen for the therapist's personal therapy has been psychoanalytic or psychodynamic" (p. 170). Given all the complex global, national, and local events in this decade, it will be interesting to see if that result early in this century will hold true in the future. Our post-positivist place in theory evolution has challenged linear, developmental models to keep pace with the nonlinear dynamic systems modeling influences of this era. Consequently, our treatment frameworks need to more effectively offer explanatory frameworks that provide flexible assessment and treatment tools as well as an ability to honor complexity while also including the personal experiences of clients *and* clinicians.

Conclusion

The philosophical, biological, sociological, economic, and personal factors interact at all levels with current political pressures which in turn shape how and when mental health is defined, studied, and treated. As a result of these contextual variables, we must examine closely our theories and interpretations of what is helpful, when, and with whom. As Horowitz (1998) exclaimed, "Social work theory has been cutting edge for eighty years without knowing it" (p. 369). We are at a point in history and theory development where psychodynamic and CBT are expanding to allow for the fuller conceptualization of what constitutes an individual, their social context, cognition, affect, behavior, and meaning. While the profession of social work has always been rooted in the biopsychosocial-spiritual approach to understanding private troubles and public issues (now being touted by other professions, for example, Engel, 1980), we have not always been able to sell the wisdom of this approach given the contextual factors that have dictated what gets emphasized in any time period. However, given the unfortunate prevalence of trauma around the world, and the interpersonal and communal perspectives we have learned from other cultures, we can continue to reunite the mind and the body in our understanding of human behavior and move to critical clinical integration—a reunion that both psychodynamic and cognitive behavioral theories and practices support, and we hope to demonstrate in this text.

References

Alakeson, V., & Frank, R. G. (2010). Health care reform and mental health care delivery. *Psychiatric Services (Washington, D.C.)*, *61*(11), 1063. https://doi.org/10.1176/ps.2010.61.11.1063

Alvarez-Jimenez, M., Alcazar-Corcoles, M. A., González-Blanch, C., Bendall, S., McGorry, P. D., Gleeson, J. F. (June 2014). Online, social media and mobile technologies for psychosis treatment: A systematic review on novel user-led interventions. *Schizophrenia Research*, *156*(1), 96–106. https://doi.org/10.1016/j.schres.2014.03.021. Epub 2014 April 17. PMID: 24746468.

Arthur, A. (2001). Personality, epistemology, and psychotherapists' choice of theoretical model: A review and analysis. *European Journal of Psychotherapy & Counselling*, *4*(1), 45–64.

Auerbach, A. H., & Johnson, M. (1977). Research on the therapist's level of experience. In A. S. Gurman & A. M. Razan (Eds.), *Effective psychotherapy*. 84–102. Pergamon Press.

Azevedo, J. P., Hasan, A., Goldemberg, D., Geven, K., & Iqbal, S. A. (2021). Simulating the Potential Impacts of COVID-19 School Closures on Schooling and Learning Outcomes: A Set of Global Estimates. *The World Bank Research Observer*, lkab003. https://doi.org/10.1093/wbro/lkab003

Barth, F. D. (2014). Integration, connection and individuation in Shaeffer's "transference, countertransference and mutuality in relational social work with college students." *Clinical Social Work Journal*, *42*, 22–26. https://doi.org/10.1007/s10615-014-0478-1

Basham, K. K. (2013). Facilitators and barriers in effective clinical practice with postdeployed military couples and families. *Military Behavioral Health*, *1*(1), 22–30,https://doi.org/10.1080/21635781.2012.721061

Berzoff, J., & Drisko, J. (2015). What clinical social workers need to know: Bio-psycho-social knowledge and skills for the twenty-first century. *Clinical Social Work Journal*, *43*, 263–273. https://doi.org/10.1007/s10615–015–0544–3

Berzoff, J., Flanagan, L., & Hertz, P. (2016). *Inside out and outside in: Psychodynamic theory and practice in multicultural contexts*. Bloomsbury Publishing.

Choi-Kain, L., Rodriguez-Villa, A., Ilagan, G., & Iliakis, E. (2021). Personality disorders. In A. Walker, S. Schlozman, & J. Alpert (Eds.), *Introduction to psychiatry: Preclinical foundations and clinical essentials* (pp. 233–262). Cambridge University Press. https://doi.org/10.1017/9780511846403.010

Cooper, S. (1977). Reflections on clinical social work. *Clinical Social Work Journal*, *5*(4), 303–315.

Cotten, S. R., Ford, G., Ford, S., Hale, T. M. (September 2014). Internet use and depression among retired older adults in the United States: A longitudinal analysis. *Journals Gerontology. Series B, Psychological Sciences Social Sciences*, *69*(5), 763–771. https://doi.org/10.1093/geronb/gbu018. Epub 2014 Mar 26. PMID: 24671896

Cozolino, L. (2010). *The neuroscience of psychotherapy: Building and rebuilding the human brain* (2nd ed.). Norton.

Crits-Christoph, P., Gibbons, M. B. C., & Mukherjee, D. (2013). Psychotherapy process-outcome research. In M. J. Lambert (Ed.), *Handbook of psychotherapy and behavior change (6th ed.)* (pp. 298–340). John Wiley & Sons.

Delboy, S., & Michaels, L. (2023). Going beneath the surface: What people want from therapy. In L. Michaels, T. Wooldridge, N. Burke, & J. R. Muhr (Eds.), *Advancing psychotherapy for the next generation* (211–239). Routledge.

Drisko, J. W. (2011). A clinician-researcher's understanding of "The effectiveness of long-term psychodynamic psychotherapy." *Clinical Social Work Journal*, *39*(4), 334–339.

Drisko, J. W. (2012). The evidence base for psychodynamic psychotherapy. *Smith college studies in social work*, *82*, 347–400.

Dyson, M. P., Hartling, L., Shulhan, J., Chisholm, A., Milne, A., Sundar, P., et al. (2016). A systematic review of social media use to discuss and view deliberate self-harm acts. PLoS ONE, *11*(5), e0155813. https://doi.org/10.1371/journal.pone.0155813

Engel, G. L. (1980). The clinical application of the biopsychosocial model. *American Journal of Psychiatry, 137*, 535–544.

Falk, G., Romero, P. D., Nicchitta, I. A., & Nyhof, E. C. (2021, August 20). *Unemployment rates during the COVID-19 pandemic* (CRS report no. R46554). https://crsreports.congress.gov/product/pdf/R/R46554/21

Farquhar, L., & Davidson, T. (2014). Facebook frets: The role of social media use in predicting social and Facebook-specific anxiety. *Journal of the Alabama Academy of Science, 85*(1), 8–25.

Fergie, G., Hunt, K., & Hilton, S. (2016). Social media as a space for support: Young adults' perspectives on producing and consuming user-generated content about diabetes and mental health. Social Science & Medicine, *170*, 46–54. https://doi.org/10.1016/j.socscimed.2016.10.006. Epub 2016 October 8. PMID: 27750067; PMCID: PMC5115652.

Fonagy, P. (2005). Psychodynamic psychotherapies: Evidence-based practice and clinical wisdom. *Bulletin of the Menninger Foundation, 69*(1), Winter, 1–58.

Fonagy, P. (2015). The effectiveness of psychodynamic psychotherapies: An update. *World Psychiatry, 14*(2), 137–150. https://doi.org/10.1002/wps.20235. PMID: 26043322; PMCID: PMC4471961.

Glass, R. M. (2008). Psychodynamic psychotherapy and research evidence: Bambi survives Godzilla? *Journal of American Medical Association, 300*(13), 1587–1589.

Granvold, D. K. (1999). Integrating cognitive and constructive psychotherapies: A cognitive perspective. In T. B. Northcut & N. R. Heller (Eds.), *Enhancing Psychodynamic Therapy with Cognitive Behavioral Techniques*. 55–93. Jason Aronson.

Hammersley, M. (2005). Is the evidence-based practice movement doing more good than harm? Reflections on Iain Chalmers' case for research-based policy making and practice. *Evidence & Policy, 1*(1), 85–100.

Harrington, A. (2008). *The cure within: A history of mind-body medicine*. W. W. Norton.

Hart, C. W. (2014). Biography as an art form: The story of Helen Flanders Dunbar, M.D., Ph.D., B.D., and Med. Sci. D. *Journal of Religion and Health, 53*(3), 778–788. https://doi.org/10.1007/s10943-013-9818-7. PMID: 24380971

Hirai, T. (2010). *Personal and professional characteristics of Japanese master therapists*: A qualitative investigation on expertise in psychotherapy and counseling in Japan (Unpublished doctoral dissertation). University of Minnesota, Minneapolis.

Hjorland, B. (2011). Evidence based practice: An analysis based on the philosophy of science. *Journal of the american society for information science and technology, 62*(7), 1301–1310.

Hong, P., & Song, I. H. (2010). Glocalization of social work practice: Global and local responses to globalization. *International Social Work, 53*(5), 656–670.

Horowitz, J. (1998). Contemporary psychoanalysis and social work theory. *Clinical Social Work Journal, 26*, 369–383. https://doi.org/10.1023/A:1022873920417

Insel, T. (2013). Post by former NIMH director Thomas Insel: Transforming diagnosis (blog post). https://www.nimh.nih.gov/about/directors/thomas-insel/blog/2013/transforming-diagnosis.shtml

Jakubowski, M., Gajderowica, T., & Patrinos, H. (2024). COVID-19, school closures, and student learning outcomes: New global evidence from PISA. https://documents1.worldbank.org/curated/en/099932301112496929/pdf/IDU16cf7d0801f2091478b1934914b47c3ab4027.pdf

Jansen, N., Kuhl, J., Eller, N., Kingdon, P., & Fink, C. (2023). Mentalizing capacity partially mediates the relationship between attachment and stress, depression, and anxiety in

social work. *Clinical Social Work Journal, 51*, 339–353. https://doi.org/10.1007/s10615-023-00882-2
Kwon, K., & Kim, C. (2007). Analysis on the characteristics of Korean master group counselor. *The Korean Journal of Counseling, 8*, 979–1010.
Lambert, M. J. (2013). Introduction and historical overview. In M. J. Lambert (Ed.), *Handbook of Psychotherapy and Behavior Change, (6th ed.)* (pp. 3–20). John Wiley & Sons.
Leichsenring, F., & Rabung, S. (2008). Effectiveness of long-term psychotherapy: A meta-analysis. *The Journal of the American Medical Association, 300*, 1551–1565.
Levine, P. (1997). *Waking the tiger: Healing trauma.* North Atlantic Press.
Lilliengren, P. (2023) A comprehensive overview of randomized controlled trials of psychodynamic psychotherapies. *Psychoanalytic Psychotherapy, 37*(2), 117–140. https://doi.org/10.1080/02668734.2023.2197617
Lin, L. Y., Sidani, J. E., Shensa, A. et al. (2016). Association between social media use and depression among U.S. young adults. *Depress Anxiety, 33*(4), 323–331. https://doi.org/10.1002/da.22466
Mahoney, M. J. (1993). Introduction to the special section: Theoretical developments in the cognitive psychotherapies. *Journal of Consulting and Clinical Psychology, 61*, 187–193.
Markowitz, J. C., & Friedman, R. A. (2020). NIMH's straight and neural path: The road to killing clinical psychiatric research. *Psychiatric Services, 71*(11), 1096–1097. https://doi.org/10.1176/appi.ps.202000057
Markowitz, J. C., Milrod, B., Heckman, T. G., Bergman, M., Amsalem, D., Zalman, H., Ballas, T., & Neria, Y. (2021). Psychotherapy at a distance. *American Journal of Psychiatry, 178*(3), 240–246. https://doi.org/10.1176/appi.ajp.2020.20050557
Martin, J., & Sugarman, J. (1999). *The possibility of human possibility and constraint.* SUNY.
McGuire, T. G., & Sinaiko, A. D. (2010). Regulating a health insurance exchange: Implications for individuals with mental illness. *Psychiatric Services (Washington, D.C.), 61*(11), 1074–1080. doi: 10.1176/ps.2010.61.11.1074. PMID: 21041344.
Mills, C. W. (1959). "The promise" and "private troubles, public issues," Introduction to *the Sociological Imagination.*
Moreno, M. A., Ton, A., Selkie, E., & Evans, Y. (2016). Secret society 123: Understanding the language of self-harm on Instagram. *Journal of Adolescent Health, 58*(1), 78–84. https://doi.org/10.1016/j.jadohealth.2015.09.015. PMID: 26707231; PMCID: PMC5322804.
Mullins-Sweatt, S. N., Lengel, G. J., & DeShong, H. L. (2016). The importance of considering clinical utility in the construction of a diagnostic manual. *Annual Review of Clinical Psychology, 12*, 133–155.
Naslund, J. A., Aschbrenner, K. A., Marsch, L. A., & Bartels, S. J. (2016). The future of mental health care: Peer-to-peer support and social media. *Epidemiology and Psychiatric Sciences, 25*(2), 113–122. https://doi.org/10.1017/S2045796015001067
Nesi, J., & Prinstein, M. J. (2015). Using social media for social comparison and feedback-seeking: Gender and popularity moderate associations with depressive symptoms. *Journal of Abnormal Child Psychology, 43*(8), 1427–1438. https://doi.org/10.1007/s10802-015-0020-0. PMID: 25899879; PMCID: PMC5985443.
Nissen-Lie, H. A., Monsen, J. T., & Rønnestad, M. H. (2010). Therapist predictors of early patient-rated working alliance: A multilevel approach. *Psychotherapy Research, 20*(6), 627–646.
Norcross, J. (2005). The psychotherapist's own psychotherapy: Educating and developing psychologists. *American Psychologist, 60*(8), 840–850.
Northcut, T. B. (2017). *Mindfulness in clinical social work practice.* Springer Publishing (Author and Editor).
Northcut, T. B., & Kienow, A. (2014). Trauma trifecta of military sexual trauma: A case study including mind and body in clinical social work treatment with a survivor of MST. In T.

Northcut & R. Strauss (Eds.), *Special issue: Integrating mind and body in clinical social work. Clinical Social Work Journal, 42*(3), 247–259.

Ogden, P. (2021). *The pocket guide to sensorimotor psychotherapy in context* (Norton series on interpersonal neurobiology). W. W. Norton.

Ogden, P., & Fisher, J. (2015). *Sensorimotor psychotherapy: Interventions for trauma and attachment.* W. W. Norton

Orlinsky, D. E., & Howard, K. (1987). A generic model of psychotherapy. *Journal of Integrative and Eclectic psychotherapy, 6*, 6–27.

Patel, R., Chang, T., Greysen, S. R., & Chopra, V. (2015). Social media use in chronic disease: A systematic review and novel taxonomy. *American Journal of Medicine, 128*(12), 1335–1350. https://doi.org/10.1016/j.amjmed.2015.06.015. Epub 2015 Jul 6. PMID: 26159633.

Patrinos, H. A. (2023). The longer students were out of school, the less they learned. *Journal of School Choice*, 17(2), 161–175. https://doi.org/10.1080/15582159.2023.2210941

Perrigo, B. (2021). Instagram makes teen girls hate themselves. Is that a bug or a feature? https://time.com/6098771/instagram-body-image-teen-girls/

Perry, A. (2023). AI will never convey the essence of human empathy. *Nature Human Behaviour, 7*, 1808–1809. https://doi.org/10.1038/s41562-023-01675-w

Perry, B. (2007). *The boy who was raised as a dog.* Basic Books.

Petko, J. T., Kendrick, E., & Young, M. E. (2016). Selecting a theory or counseling: What influences a counseling student to choose? *Universal Journal of Psychology*, 4(6), 285–291. https://doi.org/10.13189/ujp.2016.040606

Primack, B. A., Shensa, A., Escobar-Viera, C. G., Barrett, E. L., Sidani, J. E., Colditz, J. B., & James, A. E. (2017). Use of multiple social media platforms and symptoms of depression and anxiety: A nationally representative study among U.S. young adults. *Computers in Human Behavior, 69*, April 1–9. https://doi.org/10.1016/j.chb.2016.11.013

Prochaska, J. O., & Norcross, J. C. (1983). Contemporary psychotherapists: A national survey of characteristics, practices, orientations, and attitudes. *Psychotherapy: Theory, Research & Practice, 20*(2), 161–173. https://doi.org/10.1037/h0088487

Rasmussen, B. (2018). A critical examination of CBT in clinical social work practice. *Clinical Social Work Journal, 46*, 165–173. https://doi.org/10.1007/s10615-017-0632-7

Reed, G. M. (2010). Toward ICD-11: Improving the clinical utility of WHO's International Classification of Mental Disorders. *Professional Psychology, Research and Practice, 41*, 457–464.

Rønnestaad, M. H., & Skovholt, T. M. (2013). *The developing practitioner: Growth and stagnation of therapists and counselors.* Routledge.

Rubel, J. A., Hilpert, P., Wolfer, C., Held, J., Vîslă, A., & Flückiger, C. (2019). The working alliance in manualized CBT for generalized anxiety disorder: Does it lead to change and does the effect vary depending on manual implementation flexibility? *Journal of Consulting and Clinical Psychology, 87*(11), 989–1002. https://doi.org/10.1037/ccp0000433

Satterfield et al. (2009). Toward a transdisciplinary model of evidence-based practice. *Millbank Quarterly, 87*(2), 368–390.

Saunders, B. E., Berliner, L., & Hanson, R. F. (Eds.). (2004). *Child physical and sexual abuse: Guidelines for treatment (revised report: April 26, 2004).* National Crime Victims Research and Treatment Center. Retrieved October 29, 2013, from http://www.musc.edu/cvc/

Schore, A. N. (2012). *The science of the art of psychotherapy.* W.W. Norton

Siegel, D. (1999). *The developing mind.* Guilford.

Singer, J. B., Gray, S. W., & Miehls, D. (2012). An educator's guide to the development of advanced practice competencies in clinical social work. *Journal of Teaching in Social Work, 32*, 451–470.

Smialek, J., & Tankersley, J. (2020). Black workers, already lagging, face big economic risks. The New York Times. https://www.nytimes.com/2020/06/01/business/economy/blackworkers-inequality-economic-risks.html

Solomon, A. (2015). Book review of Oliver Sacks' biography "On the move" (NYTIMES Book Review, 5/17/15).

Strauss, S. E., Richardson, W. S., Glasziou, P., & Haynes, R. B. (2010). *Evidence-based medicine: How to practice and team EBM?* (4th ed.). Churchill-Livingstone.

Strupp, H. H. (1978). The therapist's theoretical orientation: An overrated variable. *Psychotherapy: Theory, Research & Practice, 15*(4), 314–317. https://doi.org/10.1037/h0086020

Sundararaman, R. (2009). The U.S. mental health delivery system infrastructure: A primer. Congressional Research Service, 7–5700, www.crs.gov R40536.

Suveg, C., Kendall, P. C., Comer, J. S., & Robin, J. (2006). Emotion-focused cognitive-behavioral therapy for anxious youth: A multiple-baseline evaluation. *Journal of Contemporary Psychotherapy, 36*, 77–85. https://doi.org/10.1007/s10879-006-9010-4

Sweet, V. (2012). *God's Hotel*. Riverhead Books.

Thyer, B., & Pignotti, M. (2011). Evidence-based ***practices*** do not exist. *Clinical Social Work Journal, 39*(4), 325–333.

Torrey, E. F. (2015). Fraud, waste and excess profits. *Psychiatric Times, 32*(11), https://www.psychiatrictimes.com/view/fraud-waste-and-excess-profits Accessed 12/11/21.

Torrey, E. F., Jaffe, D. J., Geller, J. L., & Lamb, R. (2015). Fraud, waste, and excess profits: The fate of money intended to treat people with serious mental illness. *Mental Illness Policy Org.* http://www.mentalillnesspolicy.org/national-studies/wastereport.pdf

Tosone, C. (2004). Relational social work: Honoring the tradition. *Smith College Studies in Social Work, 74*(3), 475–487.

Towle, C. (1935). Mental hygiene of the social worker. Reprinted in H. H. Perlman (Ed.) Helping. University of Chicago Press, 1969.

Tran, T., Collins, C., Broughton, M., Wenze, S., & Uebelacker, L. (2015). Adaptive and maladaptive means of using Facebook: A qualitative pilot study to inform development of a future intervention for depression. *Journal of Psychiatric Practice, 21*, 458–473. https://doi.org/10.1097/PRA.0000000000000109.

Turner, P. G., & Lefevre, C. E. (2017). Instagram use is linked to increased symptoms of orthorexia nervosa. Eating and weight disorders, EWD, *22*(2), 277–284. https://doi.org/10.1007/s40519-017-0364-2

van der Kolk, B. A. (2014). *The body keeps the score: Brain, mind, and body in the healing of Trauma*. Viking.

Vannucci, A. Flannery, K. M., & Ohannessian, C. M. (2017). Social media use and anxiety in emerging adults. *Journal of Affective Disorders, 207*(1), 163–166.

Wachtel, P. L. (2010). Beyond "ESTs" problematic assumptions in the pursuit of evidence-based practice. *Psychoanalytic Psychology, 27*(3), 251–272.

Weingarten, K. (1999). Stretching to meet what is given. In F. Walsh (Ed.), *Spiritual Resources in Family Therapy*, 1st ed. 340–358. Guilford Press.

Westen, D., Morrison, K., & Thompson-Brenner, H. (2004). The empirical status of empirically supported psychotherapies: Assumptions, findings, and reporting in controlled clinical trials. *Psychological Bulletin, 130*, 631–663.

Widiger, R. A. (2012). Classification and diagnosis: Historical development and contemporary issues. In J. Maddux & B. Winstead (Eds.), *Psychopathology: Foundations for a Contemporary Understanding* (2nd ed., pp.101–120). Erlbaum.

Winerman, L. (2013). NIMH funding to shift away from DSM categories. *Upfront* American Psychological Association. Retrieved from http://www.apa.org/monitor/2013/07-08/nimh.aspx on 11/21/2016

Woods, H. C., & Scott, H. (2016) #Sleepyteens: Social media use in adolescence is associated with poor sleep quality, anxiety, depression, and low self-esteem. *Journal of Adolescence, 51*, 41–49. https://doi.org/10.1016/j.adolescence.2016.05.008

Wright, J. H., Basco, M. R., & Thase, M. E. (2006). *Learning cognitive-behavior therapy: An illustrated guide.* American Psychiatric Publishing.

Yeyati, E. L., & Filippini, F. (2021). Social and economic impact of COVID-19. *Brookings Global Working Paper #158, Global Economy and Development program at Brookings.* https://www.brookings.edu/wp-content/uploads/2021/06/Social-and-economic-impact-COVID.pdf

2

Reconceptualizing "cure"

As a novice clinician, soon after my MSW work, I (TBN) had the privilege and pleasure of working in a rural county mental health center that served both the wealthiest and the poorest families in the state. We "treated" folks who could not afford care and those who wanted privacy from recognition commonly experienced in the neighboring urban city. The range of problems was extensive and provided excellent learning opportunities. One of the dilemmas that occurred often was the struggle over determining what could and could not be accomplished in therapy. Being new to the field of clinical work, I thought the best treatment possible would of course mean that clients would be relieved of their symptoms. Perhaps more important to me was the belief that the issues that caused those symptoms to develop could or should be resolved as well. I firmly believed that there was meaning behind the problems being presented, whether they needed problem solving, interpersonal understanding, or some form of medication. Fortunately, I had excellent supervision and astute and compassionate colleagues who taught me slowly but surely that "cure" was a misnomer for the work we did. At the minimum, we provided a relationship that offered, perhaps for the first time, a person who would sit with clients' pain and not require that they get over it, resolve it, or just thank God for the "growth" opportunity. I heard stories of inexplicable sadness and trauma that often was the result of being born in a tragic environment. However, I also heard stories of amazing resilience and humor which showed me that people in therapy often are the healthiest members in their family and communal systems. I was struck by the differences between my connection with certain clients and other clients. What was it that made the difference on how connected I felt and how effective I could be? My limited experience and knowledge pushed me to look for the tangible and perhaps nontangible elements of the work I was doing. I learned I had to rethink the purpose of my work with clients. If part of my job was supplying a relationship in addition to or in service of reducing symptoms, what did I need to know about that relationship and the factors that facilitated and impacted the relationship? How would that relationship

Psychodynamic and Cognitive Behavioral Theory and Practice. Terry B. Northcut and Shveta Kumaria, Oxford University Press. © Oxford University Press (2025). DOI: 10.1093/9780197508404.003.0002

be impacted or changed by the techniques or theories I utilized? What was the client's experience of that relationship and any techniques I used?

This community mental health center where I worked fortunately had the economic resources at that point in time, which allowed me to continue my training and education so that I could learn the types of treatments available. Because I was new and inexperienced, I tended to be assigned cases that had been proven to be troublesome or plagued by continuing crises. Directive techniques as well as strictly behavioral interventions tended to be met by clients with skepticism and/or "voting with their feet" in terms of not returning for further sessions. I gradually learned to listen to multiple levels of meaning that clients were trying to tell me. What was startling and gratifying to me was the relief and ease with which clients responded when I was able to put into words something which they had only felt and not yet articulated. I also learned that this ease in affective turmoil was not always the result. At times I was too zealous to demonstrate that I knew something "brilliant" which left clients cold or angry. Other times I could be too passive in confronting clients about addictions or illegal behavior. One of the hardest things to learn in supervision was to have a clear understanding of what theories helped me understand presenting problems but not let those theories cloud my vision to the point that I could not see or hear the client. It helped enormously to be able to discuss at length with a supervisor how theory can fit with practice and how theory can show the way for a broader conceptual understanding of what we (and our clients) feel in day-to-day interactions. That understanding could then be communicated with clients in the most attuned way. Theoretical knowledge laid a foundation which informed how I collaborated with clients in developing our therapeutic relationships. I was learning the art and science of psychotherapy—that there are times when there may be a technically "correct" or "best" way to intervene but knowing when and how to do so involved attunement, intuition, and at times creativity. As a result, I loved my work despite frustrations, disappointments, and some vicarious traumatization, but realized I had so much to learn about integrating theory and practice and understanding what works in treatment. During subsequent years in professional practice, doctoral study, teaching, and in personal therapy, I have often revisited this concept of "cure" to negotiate the winds of health care funding and research as well as client needs and values.

It is difficult to pin down what is meant by cure and even the idea of "treatment" but if we want to make decisions about how to work with someone experiencing mental health problems, we should have clarity about what we are trying to accomplish. Treatment goes beyond an absence of symptoms and can sometimes facilitate adaptation and/or adjustment with the environment as well as internal growth. Likewise, "treatment" may mean advocating for and with clients to change the oppressive systems impacting their environments. At the very least, there are several aspects to understanding cure within a given society besides those factors described in Chapter 1. Our concept of "cure" also shapes and is shaped by the terminology we use. For the purposes of this text, the terms treatment, psychotherapy, clinical work, and interventions will all be utilized knowing that there are indeed differences in meaning depending on your position in society and in your training. Each professional discipline has a unique perspective and a value base on which terms are used in mental health care and why. In general terms, counseling professions have developed by trying to understand symptomatology or problems, as well as the effects of war, poverty, and violence albeit with a particular specialized focus. Social work emphasizes the "regenerative potential" (Weick, 1992) of the clients we serve with the belief that this potential is most active when the biopsychosocial context of persons is honored and understood (Ornstein & Ganzer, 2005). As our society has changed over time, we have revised that focus to be a biopsychosocial-spiritual ecological perspective reflecting a broader understanding of familial and cultural diversity and the impact of global warming. Consequently, social workers are more likely to use the label of "clients" to minimize the effects of labels and reduce the impact of the power of our position. The profession emphasizes that language matters—how we label the people we work with reflects a power dynamic that must be considered and deconstructed.

Psychiatry, on the other hand, has been based on the medical model of solving psychological problems which were thought to have a root in biology. Clients were viewed as patients based on the Latin translation of the word as "one who suffers." The biopsychosocial model was not introduced into psychiatry until 1980 (Cabaniss et al., 2015; Engel, 1980) and has been slow to change the medical terminology. The emphasis is still on "healing" the patient of their suffering, albeit with evolving understanding of neurobiology, the impact of trauma, and rapidly changing pharmaceuticals.

Psychology on the other hand was heavily influenced by the "Boulder Model" (Baker & Benjamin, 2000; Frank, 1984), which emphasized graduate student training focused on the need for skills in scientific methodology (clients became "subjects") and in clinical field work (clients were "patients" and seen individually). A professional emphasis on contextual factors came later after years of clinical research, rather than from a fundamental value such as with the social work profession. One of the best examples of how psychology has changed over the years is Wampold & Imel's "contextual model" (2015), which will be discussed in subsequent chapters. This research has utilized results from empirical studies on therapeutic effects and common factors present in "successful" psychotherapy" as the medium for healing or cure while at the same time recognizing that healing and cure might be different for different clients coming from different contexts. There is also a branch in the profession of liberation psychology (Burton & Guzzo, 2020) stemming from, but not limited to, the Latin American movement which places emphasis on social justice. While this branch has remained on the margins so far, the emphasis on reworking psychological concepts and methods from the perspective of the oppressed populations has gained steady growth with global challenges of ecological and climate crises, continued human rights violations, population displacements and massive refugee movements, and medical and economic challenges resulting from the recent international pandemic. Social work could benefit greatly from collaborating with liberation psychology.

Psychiatry, psychology, and social work have made strides in broadening the view of what is "treated" and offer different but essential perspectives in determining the focus of clinical care. Broadening the focus of what is meant by cure, and even eliminating the use of the term cure, makes room for those in therapeutic relationships to actively engage in the world as well as understand the impact of oppressive social forces. In this text, we favor the use of the term "client" as a reflection of our professional social work bias. The root of the term patient is also accurate given that we meet our clients at the point of "dis-ease" of some kind (whether subjective or objectively defined) that is causing the client suffering. Clients suffer also from societal problems that must be considered and addressed. As with my questioning early in my career, the challenge is negotiating where and how to intervene and at what level. While the use of the term "clinical" implies an individual focus for some professionals, our work is more accurately conceptualized as occurring at the interface between clients and systems whether on a micro-, mezzo-, or macrolevel (Austin et al., 2016). Clients do "suffer" as the term "patient" suggests, however, they are also active agents in their worlds and therefore are collaborators in their own healing. Within the clinical milieu in which client and clinician collaborate, there are decisions to be made that involve making choices about what must take precedence in the focus. Clinical work is not "one size fits all" that must be accomplished in a singular treatment that cures everything or with the same method throughout the life stages of our clients. Understanding the context of the many layers of presenting problems is the essential first step. "Cure" and our treatments methods must be reconceptualized to reflect the need for contextual focus.

Focus on the context and process of a problem has been especially difficult within Western cultures, which has had a complicated relationship with the intersection of the internal world and the external worlds. We have great difficulty allowing for the fact that internal and external worlds are not so distinctly separate. Bueskens (2014) argues that "good psychotherapy is sociological."

> [I]f we want to understand human action, agency and meaning, both perspectives are required *(sociology and psychotherapy)*—we need both structure and agency ... to do justice to the human experience. We need an understanding of society and the individual and a recognition that the relations between the two are mutually constitutive not unidirectional. Importantly, one does not trump the other and if it does, we end up with a truncated understanding of the human experience. (p. 438)

Likewise, in the West, we have slipped around the ideas of what phenomenon should be included in the terms mind and body. When the scientific medical model holds center stage, mind and body are viewed as separate and the *body* is treated as something to be treated and cured of any symptom or biological manifestation of illness (e.g., often involving medication). The concept of *mind* is ambiguous and difficult to define. Sometimes the term is generalized to mean simply "thinking," leading to the implication if we can fix our thinking, we will get better. It is easier to isolate the two variables rather than trying to find a way to describe and study the interaction. However, as naturalist John Muir (2011) observed, when we try to observe one thing in nature, we cannot help but pull on the connecting strings with everything else.

As discussed in Chapter 1, research has shown how tightly woven mind and body are (Harrington, 2008) leading us to move beyond strictly observable, well-controlled experiments that confirm cause and effect suppositions. For the purposes of our work in considering effective ways to intervene with individuals seeking assistance to alleviate suffering whatever the contributing contextual factors, we will begin with current research on the physical body, which paves the way to greater contextual understanding of problems and the subjective experiences of those problems. Studies in neurobiology play an important role as *a* beginning place, but not *the* final answer to understanding and responding therapeutically to disease.

Neurobiological contributions

One of the most promising avenues of exploration in the area of mental health services is in the remarkable results of studies of the brain. Technological advances in brain scanning have revealed several important findings critical in our current understanding of the interaction of mind and body and subsequently how that interaction will shape or form a symptom and/or its relief. Interpersonal neurobiology is an interdisciplinary framework developed in the late 1900s. One of the architects of this movement is Daniel J. Siegel, who brought together a wide range of scientific disciplines, such as anthropology, neuroscience, sociology, linguistics, psychiatry, and so on, to conceptualize how the mind and brain are based in relationships which dynamically interact. This newer discipline emphasizes our neurocircuitry which regulates the flow of energy and information through our neural pathways. The "hardwiring" regulates and determines intrapersonal and interpersonal relationships that are often the first arena in which "dis-ease" shows itself in clinical work. There are numerous resources that provide excellent explanations of how the brain operates and is organized (Beck, 2017; Cozolino, 2017; Levine, 2010; Ogden & Fisher, 2015; Schore, 1994; Shapiro & Applegate, 2018; Siegel, 1999; van der Kolk, 2014). A brief summary is included here, just to familiarize or remind the reader of the relevant terms that will be referred to throughout the book.

As with any organ in the body, the brain is comprised of cell activity that has a way of communicating cell to cell. The cells in the brain (neurons) have three components: the body of the cell (containing DNA), the dendrites (or branches that receive signals from other cells), and the axons that send signals to other cells. The dendrites communicate to the axons of neighboring cells by releasing or firing neurotransmitters or chemicals that are "taken up" or absorbed by the other cell. When these cells continually "fire" to predictable other cells, a neural circuit is established, so the brain "wires in" a particular pattern. The dendrites and the axons do not physically connect—there is a minute gap, called a synapse, over which the neurotransmitters travel. Medications commonly used to cope with affective disorders do so by altering the rate at which certain neurotransmitters are reabsorbed back into axons instead of being processed via the dendrites in the neighboring cell. Neurons get triggered to release a neurotransmitter through patterns in neurocircuitry, such as when confronting some form of danger.

We know when faced with physical pain, or other daily biological needs, that the brain stem (the bottom or reptilian part of the brain) is activated. The hypothalamus-pituitary-adrenal (HPA) axis is the pathway that triggers a response to stress, trauma, or injury. The hypothalamus reacts first by emitting a corticotropin-releasing hormone into the bloodstream, which then activates the pituitary gland to release adrenocorticotropic (ACTH), a hormone that triggers the adrenal gland to in turn release the stress hormones adrenalin (also known as the "fight-or-flight hormone") and cortisol (which increases glucose and reduces inflammation) into the bloodstream (Knudsen, 2021).

If danger is detected, chemicals are released that activate the limbic system, another part of the brain that is the seat of our emotions. The brain stem and the limbic system comprise the emotional part of the brain which has been shaped by genetics, temperament, and experience. Environmental factors, not just internal biological processes, can impact whether gene characteristics are "turned on or turned off." In the past, one description of this dynamic process is the diathesis-stress model, which describes the ongoing interaction of the environment and an individual's biology that can produce mental dysfunction in some way (e.g., Kendler et al., 1995; McKeever & Huff, 2003; Monroe & Simons, 1991; Robins & Block, 1989). A particular stressor can activate a genetic predisposition, which in turn creates a neural pattern that can be rigidly adhered to. If there is repeated trauma, for example, the stress response system is continually activated, leading to a state of hyperarousal, even when not being threatened in some way. However, this wear and tear on the body from being in constant alert sets up neural patterns that are difficult to change despite the brain's proven plasticity.

> The way our neurons connect up with each other depends on what *happens* to us ... The fine organization of the brain is literally *sculpted* by the environment in which it finds itself.
>
> (Solms & Turnbull, 2002, 11, italics in the original, as cited in Shapiro & Applegate, 2018, 11).

When considering how the brain operates when it is involved in the "healing process," we have to first remind ourselves that the "brain" is really a system that is constantly adapting and readapting to an almost infinite number of stimuli. Shapiro & Applegate (2018) emphasize the brain as a nonlinear dynamic system. Nonlinear dynamics assumes that development is complex, dynamic, and constantly moving toward increased complexity. With such complexity it is clear that change is not linear, despite our longing for discrete stages with a clear trajectory. As a system, the brain is continually influenced by the internal environment of the body and from the external environment in which it resides—which also further impacts other systems in the body. The implication is that our understanding of "mind" is beyond the physical brain; it includes all of the processes that "regulate the flow of energy and information within our bodies and within relationships" (Siegel, 2012). Consequently—a "cure" for mental health problems must address an ongoing dynamic interaction that is occurring in our physical bodies. In essence, we need our brains to be capable of processing limitless stimuli in a manner that supports optimal functioning.

To give an example of this nonlinear functioning, we know the interaction of child and caregivers shapes the neural networks in the brain, which then must change again to process the ever-evolving physical and emotional functioning of both individuals. In other words, parents/caregivers do not continue to provide the exact same kind of interaction across different stages in development and competencies of the child. Each relational partner, child and caregiver, changes and adapts to each other and to ongoing environmental stimuli and effects. A parent praising a child for picking up his toys helps a child feel a sense of mastery and competency. However, that same message to an adult child would feel patronizing and insulting. Schore (1994; 2000; 2001; 2008) emphasizes that you cannot isolate the self from the environmental context of which it is a part because that self is constructed within a relationship matrix that is continually changing. Consequently, a parent is a different parent with each child they have (e.g., one disciplinary technique may work with one child but not with his or her siblings).

Once we attained the technical capability to study brain organization and the dynamic changes, researchers were then able to examine how variations in brain organization and functioning impacted the emergence of mental health problems (Shapiro & Applegate, 2018). A common concern of clinicians and interpersonal neurologists is how to help clients gain greater affective regulation given the over- or under-regulation common in forms of depression, anxiety, and behavioral difficulties. While this regulatory function does not represent the totality of mental illness, it is a common denominator in many disorders. Responding to findings in research about common domains in diagnostic categories, the DSM-5 manual incorporated dimensional measures to try and account for the fact that lines between different disorders are often blurry in real clinical life and over the course of one's lifespan (Mullins-Sweatt et al., 2016). We all demonstrate characteristics of a variety of disorders not necessarily because of the severity of dysfunction, but because many diagnostic categories encompass problems in the same dimension. Advances in neurobiological research have provided clinicians with confirmation that difficulties in regulation of affect are a common manifestation of many diagnostic symptom constellations. Consequently, one goal of clinical work is to understand how therapy can impact and/or improve affect regulation.

In addition to affect regulation, interpersonal strategies or patterns also are a necessary focus of clinical work. Evolution has taught us that we have developed from the lower more primitive parts of the brain (brain stem) to the higher more advanced functioning. The "higher" parts of the brain embodied in the cerebral cortex are responsible for forming ideas and the mental representations or schemas of self, others, and the environment (Shapiro & Applegate, 2018) to use the terminology common in psychodynamic theory and CBT. The cerebral cortex is comprised of two hemispheres, popularly known as the right hemisphere and the left hemisphere. Simply put, the right hemisphere has been linked to creative thinking, processing of nonverbal communication, and somatic sensations. The left hemisphere is more analytical, able to process language, connect different phenomena, and coordinate fine motor movements. Each hemisphere contains four lobes: the occipital, temporal, parietal, and frontal. The frontal lobe is what has been more commonly talked about in clinical and educational circles as it is considered the seat of executive functioning so necessary to succeed in most educational systems and in many jobs, such as abstract reasoning, judgment, and attention. Between the cerebral cortex and the brain stem is the limbic system (orbitofrontal cortex, anterior cingulate, amygdala, and hippocampus). "These regions perform the function of integrating and regulating a wide variety of mental and emotional processes, including attachment, and are believed to potentiate the human capacity for assigning meaning to internal and external stimuli" (Shapiro & Applegate,

2018, p. 14). It is the orbitofrontal cortex that is critical in terms of controlling mood and adjusting and tweaking social interactions.

This is a very brief, oversimplified description of the parts of the brain/mind involved in the *experience and regulation of affect* and *interpersonal interactions and relationships.* Each of the lobes and systems within the brain communicate with each other in styles that are shaped by experience and continue to shape those experiences. As the brain processes information, it strengthens certain neural connections and drops off those connections that do not get reinforced. Likewise, if a part of the brain has not yet developed, it is not possible to process experiences in ways that require advanced capacities. For example, we have learned that adolescents utilize different parts of the brain when evaluating facial expressions of others. Without the benefit of a fully developed frontal cortex at this age, adolescents rely more on the amygdala, rendering their processing of others' emotions as often an overreaction or overemotional (Spinks, 2002). This knowledge helps clinicians and parents understand and interact more effectively with what may seem to be an unreasonable teenager. Another example of the necessity of understanding brain development is Bruce Perry's work with the Neurosequential Model of Therapeutics (NMT). His model provides an integrated understanding of the sequencing of neurodevelopment embedded in the experiences of the child in order that "treatment" is based on sound assessment of the brain's development. For example, the results of trauma and/or insufficient attachments may mean the child cannot process a particular form of therapy before necessary neurological development can occur (Perry, 2019; Perry & Szalavitz, 2006) Knowledge of neurodevelopment is critical to design and support clinical practices, programs, and policies for children and their families.

The more specific neurological patterns get reproduced, verified, and/or strengthened the more likely those integrative capacities can be utilized to process new information and stimuli. This rudimentary information reconceptualizes one aspect of cure or treatment as helping to increase the flexibility and facility in brain functioning to allow individuals to mobilize their own neuroplasticity in the service of greater range of functioning and feeling. "Cure" then becomes an enhancement of a process rather than an end state. So how does one "increase the flexibility and facility of brain functioning"?

The first step in this process is understanding the brain's circuitry when confronted with threats of any kind. There is extensive literature on the physiology of responding to trauma (see Bessel van der Kolk's 2014 text for one such resource). However, we also need to be aware of our client's interpersonal sense of safety when interacting with us. When feeling frightened or alarmed, consciously or unconsciously, we cannot learn or adapt. Clinical wisdom also asserts that "feeling safe" translates into a more productive therapeutic environment. Geller and Porges (2014) studied what they have termed the polyvagal method, which is a way to conceptualize how the autonomic system evaluates the level of safety or danger. This evaluation process, neuroception, is how our brain processes whether we feel safe with another, albeit outside of our own awareness (Porges, 2001). In clinical work, that sense of safety is communicated via what has been termed *therapeutic presence* in psychotherapy research. This presence requires the therapist to be present on several dimensions simultaneously; physically, cognitively, emotionally, and relationally (a challenge when factoring in technologically assisted treatment). Numerous research studies have found this presence as connected to positive outcome in treatment (Geller, 2013a and 2013b). If a therapist is "present" with a client, the client's sense of safety is enhanced. Now obviously our ability to perceive another is influenced by the prior neural circuits established in conjunction with the current experience. The work of therapy may be to expand the client's neural networks and increase their "window of tolerance" in experiencing difficult emotions and accommodate and integrate different stimuli (Ogden & Fisher, 2015; Siegel, 1999). An attuned, "present" therapist can monitor with the client how and when their window of tolerance is too narrow for current circumstances. As this neuroception process occurs in the presence of a "present" therapist (also tuned into their own neuroceptive process), the current context can be experienced and consolidated into new memories and scaffold integration across neural networks. With the advances in neurobiology and clinical research we have been able to more specifically describe the traditional concept of a "corrective emotional experience" (Alexander & French, 1946). Chapter 5 and 6 will delve deeper into research that has explored how "safe relationships" can change the course of our interpersonal development and lead to curative relational experiences which also act to stabilize affective dysregulation. Chapters 7 and 8 will provide case illustrations of this process.

Fortunately, the brain's neuroplasticity has been confirmed over and over in research, which confirms what clinicians have long known; clients benefit and change as a result of therapeutic relationships. *Specifically, we now understand that clinical work is to scaffold the development of more integrative neural connections, which means increasing the facility of the brain in managing affect and negotiating interpersonal contexts.* As we focus on more accurate understanding of how and where there is difficulty in these two domains, we (the client and clinician together) are cognitively and affectively drawing attention to this process, which expands the *window of tolerance.*

Monitoring contextual factors

What makes this process of expanding clients' neurobiological flexibility and facility through safety and presence so complicated is understanding and managing the many contextual factors as discussed earlier in. Hammond (2015) posits that culture is "software for the brain's hardware" (22).

Part of the difficulty in understanding the brain's role in negotiating and influencing our interpersonal world and any form of mental health interventions is that as we look more at context, we see how contexts differ widely within the same society and between societies. Our brains make sense of the world we are in, within the contexts of our relationships, which are also embedded within a cultural context. The more our population has diversified, and our technology has familiarized us with these variations, we are able to see that cultures differ in how the mind and the body and affective experiences and expressions are understood (Geertz, 1973; Kirmayer, 2007; Markus & Kitayama, 1991; Saari, 2002).

Obviously, cultural differences can be as specific as what foods you eat, but on an even broader level they can shape how we conceptualize "self," our identity, and what is defined as a problem. If we think the mind and the body are separate entities, and don't understand how our brain processes interpersonal experiences, we are more likely to focus on individual treatment in isolation of the culture. For example, in Western cultures, the emphasis is still on helping an individual self to be more autonomous and fulfill personal goals, hence an egocentric model or one that prioritizes psychotherapy as a valued form of healing (Kirmayer, 2004). Alternatively, a cosmocentric perspective proposes that a self is defined by one's ancestors and therefore values connecting the individual to spirits and ancestors for balance in health, which leads to the use of rituals or ceremonies to engage the spirits that have gone before us (e.g., Africentric, Bojuwoye, 2005). An ecocentric value and worldview purports that the self cannot be viewed as separate from nature and the natural world in which we live, resulting in healing traditions that celebrate the natural and physical environment (e.g., Native American, Kimmerer, 2013). Consequently, "treatment" is reconnecting the individual to land and wildlife. A socio-centric perspective focuses on a "self" defined by relationships to others and consequently advocates completing rituals that "engage the whole family, clan, or community" (e.g., Kirmayer, 2004, p. 244; Mageo, 2011). Of course, these are generalizations, as most societies vary on a continuum regarding the perspective of a self in relation to others, but in the context of migration and generational shifts, clinicians must take into account the complexity of what is valued for healing. The role of spirituality for individuals and families is also critical. Certainly, a spiritual perspective would involve "cure" as tending to the soul or the spirit and cannot be divorced from tending to the mind and the body.

Each perspective shapes the goal of any form of intervention, and subsequent evaluation of successful treatment must reflect the culture in which it is embedded. This cultural context will have reinforced the neural patterns of its members to help shape what behavior induces a more nuanced sense of safety. A client's window of tolerance may likewise appear very narrow to a clinician from a different culture. Any mental health treatment evaluating individual functioning in the areas of affective regulation and interpersonal dynamics must take into account the need to make accurate appraisals of the economic, political, sociological, and cultural environment. A client of color who does not experience a sense of safety in everyday life, especially around law enforcement because of the history of racism and violence, will necessarily respond to the visual stimuli of an oncoming police car with a fight or flight physiological reaction. This reaction to a white social worker who has more of a benevolent experience of the law enforcement system may seem extreme and unwarranted. The responsibility is on the clinician to understand those contextual factors from a macro and mezzo level before interacting on a micro level with clients. Yes, clients bring a subjective experience that is vital and most important to understand, but negotiating and understanding the blatant and subtle racism and marginalization inherent in American culture and in social systems that are supposed to provide care must take precedence before clinical work with an individual can begin. It is good judgment on the part of some clients in certain cultural groups to be skeptical of whether clinicians from other cultures or races can form an effective therapeutic alliance. However, knowledge of power differentials and racism does not mean that all clients and clinicians automatically share the same subjective experience of these conditions. Our approach to mental health care has to make room for the intersubjective and interpersonal impacts of the structural fabric that has woven a historical racism into how we conceptualize mental health and deliver services. Understanding these ongoing dynamics as experienced by clients and clinicians will continue to be discussed in subsequent chapters and in case illustrations.

We also cannot overlook the impact of the COVID-19 pandemic and its lingering impact. The concept of depression and accompanying loneliness has changed drastically within the context of a global pandemic. Clients' functioning and symptomatology and the functioning of clinicians has shifted to the essential focus on adjusting to isolation, quarantine, and grieving in absentia when loved ones die in isolation. In addition, many white-collar jobs adapted to quarantine by shifting to work from home—a change in the work environment that cannot be undone. When economically feasible, employees want to maintain the flexibility of not commuting to work further than their living room. The increased flexibility of work environments still perpetuates a sense of isolation that has to be consciously responded to and rectified. Our best means to cope with the loneliness in our current context requires a familiarity with technological tools and an ability to afford these tools, which continues to highlight the health care and economic disparities. Psychotherapy has to maintain an awareness of and understanding of the impact of increased reliance on treatment that, for many, cannot be in-person.

The concept of cure from a medical standpoint also has to include an understanding of psychiatric medications and the individual and public perceptions of these "symptom relievers." To some degree social and individual problems have been medicalized with accompanying positive and negative impacts. As we gained knowledge about how the brain functions in varying mental health states, psychiatric medication and pharmaceutical companies grew rapidly and capitalized on the commodification of dis-ease. While media campaigns and tell-all narratives of public figures led to some change in attitudes toward mental illness and the use of medication (Mojtabai, 2009), clients and clinicians must continue to advocate for a more nuanced and contextualized understanding of cure.

Cognitive behavioral therapy has blossomed, rightfully so, with empirical evidence of the many different iterations of treatment that can have an impact on individual functioning. Psychodynamic psychotherapy will continue to struggle with the need to be scientific and quantifiable versus valuing the more qualitative narratives if economics continues to make the final decisions as to who receives treatment and what kind of treatment that will be. What is "provable" and verifiable in a visible change in behavior with the lowest cost to health care providers is still a preferred form of treatment regardless of the meaning that type of service holds for patients. Psychoanalysis still tends to be very costly for patients and reserved for the middle and upper classes because of the preferred frequency of sessions and the emphasis on a subjective conceptualization of treatment or "cure." Research in psychodynamic psychotherapy is trying to catch up with the more prolific cognitive behavioral methods and the rapidly changing theories that take into account neurobiological findings which will be discussed in subsequent chapters (Yakeley, 2018). Early researchers, Greenberg & Watson (2005), Leichsenring et al. (2004), Leichsenring et al. (2008), Luborsky (1984), Strupp & Binder (1984), Wampold & Imel (2015), and Weiss (1993), all utilized psychodynamic understanding to build or study psychotherapy models that allow for the integration and testing of psychotherapy while trying to factor in other theoretical frameworks when appropriate. In the current psychodynamic research, our challenge is to bridge both perspectives (CBT and Psychodynamic) to find a more nuanced and reconsideration of cure.

Conclusion

Results of interpersonal neurobiological and psychopharmacology research demonstrate that the integration within the brain circuitry and what qualities represent greater indications of health provide an important component in mental health treatment models. Currently, we know that flexibility and facility in integrative capacities in the brain improve the likelihood of viable and effective responses in our worlds. We also know a sense of biological *safety allows the brain to function more effectively and with a greater window of tolerance for affect.* The *cultural context* continues to remind us that physical, psychological, and sociological ideas about safety and health for all individuals and in what environment differ in significant ways. As a result, the concept of cure is recontextualized from a static result, but a "stepping into" the therapeutic process in a manner that enhances facility and flexibility in functioning and quality of life. This facility and flexibility necessarily also means advocacy work (on the part of clients and clinicians) to change the circumstances that create dis-ease.

Implicit in this understanding is an appreciation that both client and therapist are ongoing, active, participants in the therapeutic process, each integrating ongoing information and experiences in ways that enhance, reinforce, and/or create new connections. Neither client nor clinician is blank slate when engaging in a therapeutic relationship. Likewise, symptom reduction cannot be the only factor in consideration; the process through which those symptoms may occur rises in importance. A new, safe, clinical relationship fosters further integration and strengthening of neural circuits that assist clients in moving in their desired directions (Bohart, 2007). The elements that are critical to the process of greater neural integration and increased sense of safety will be considered in subsequent chapters through examining psychodynamic theory, CBT, and common factors that help scaffold successful therapeutic interpersonal interventions.

References

Alexander, F. G., & French, T. M. (1946). Psychoanalytic therapy: Principles and applications. Ronald.

Austin, M. J., Anthony, E. K., Knee, R. T., & Mathias, J. (2016). Revisiting the relationship between micro and macro social work practice. *Families in Society, 97*(4), 270–277. https://doi.org/10.1606/1044-3894.2016.97.33

Baker, David B., & Benjamin Jr., L. T. (2000). The Affirmation of the Scientists-Practitioner: A look back at Boulder. *American Psychologist,* **55**(2), 241–247. https://doi.org/10.1037/0003-066X.55.2.241. PMID 10717972.

Beck, N. (2017). Beginning with the body: The neurobiology of mindfulness. In T. B. Northcut (Ed.), *Cultivating mindfulness in clinical social work,* (pp. 43–62). Springer.

Benjamin, L. S. (1979). Use of structural analysis of social behavior (SASB) and Markov chains to study dyadic interactions. *Journal of Abnormal Psychology, 88*(3), 303–319.

Bohart, A. C. (2007). An alternative view of concrete operating procedures from the perspective of the client as active self-healer. *Journal of Psychotherapy Integration, 17*(1), 125–137.

Bojuwoye, O. (2005). Traditional healing practices in southern Africa: Ancestral spirits, ritual ceremonies, and holistic healing. In R. Moodley & W. West (Eds.), *Integrating traditional healing Practices into counseling and psychotherapy* (pp. 61–72). SAGE Publications, Inc., https://www.doi.org/10.4135/9781452231648.n6

Bueskens, P. (2014). Beyond the paradigm war: Good psychotherapy is sociological. In P. Bueskens (Ed.), *Mothering and psychoanalysis: Clinical, sociological and feminist perspectives* (pp. 433–444). Demeter Press.

Burton, M., & Guzzo, R. (2020). Liberation psychology. In L. Comas-Diaz & E. Torres Rivera (Eds.), *Liberation psychology: Theory, method, practice, and social justice* (17 10). American Psychological Association.

Cabaniss, D. L., Moga, D. E., & Oquendo, M. A. (2015). Rethinking the biopsychosocial formulation. *Lancet Psychiatry, 2*(7), 579–581.

Cozolino, L. (2017). *Why treatment works: Using our minds to change our brains.* W. W. Norton.

Crits-Christoph, P., Gibbons, M. B. C., & Mukherjee, D. (2013). Psychotherapy process-outcome research. In M. J. Lambert (Ed.), *Bergin and Garfield's handbook of psychotherapy and behavior change* (pp. 298–340). Retrieved from https://ebookcentral.proquest.com

Engel, G. L. (1980). The clinical application of the biopsychosocial model. *American Journal of Psychiatry, 137,* 535–544.

Frank, G. (1984). The boulder model: History, rationale, and critique. *Professional Psychology: Research and Practice, 15*(3), 417–435. https://doi.org/10.1037/0735-7028.15.3.417

Geertz, C. (1973). *The interpretation of cultures: Selected essays.* Basic Books.

Geller, S. M. (2013a). Therapeutic presence as a foundation for relational depth. In R. Knox, D. Murphy, S. Wiggins, & M. Cooper (Eds.), *Relational depth: Contemporary perspectives* (pp. 175–184). Palgrave.

Geller, S. M. (2013b). Therapeutic presence: An essential way of being. In M. Cooper, P. F. Schmid, M. O'Hara, & A. C. Bohart (Eds.), *The Handbook of Person-Centered Psychotherapy and Counselling* (2nd ed., pp. 209–222). Palgrave.

Geller, S. M., & Porges, S. W. (2014). Therapeutic presence: Neurophysiological mechanisms mediating feeling safe in therapeutic relationships. *Journal of Psychotherapy Integration, 24*(3), 178–192.

Greenberg, L. S., & Watson, J. C. (2005). *Emotion focused therapy for depression.* APA

Hammond, Z. (2015). *Culturally responsive teaching and the brain: Promoting authentic engagement and rigor among culturally and linguistically diverse students.* Corwin/Sage.

Harrington, A. (2008). *The cure within: A history of mind-body medicine.* W. W. Norton.

Kendler, K. S., Kessler, R. C., Walters, E. E., MacLean, C., Neale, M. C., Heath, A. C., & Eaves, L. J. (1995). Stressful life events, genetic liability, and onset of an episode of major depression in women. *The American Journal of Psychiatry, 152*(6), 833–842. https://doi.org/10.1176/ajp.152.6.833.

Kimmerer, R. W. (2013). *Braiding Sweetgrass: Indigenous Wisdom, Scientific Knowledge and the Teachings of Plants.* Milkweed Editions.

Kirmayer, L. J. (2004). The cultural diversity of healing: Meaning, metaphor and mechanism. *British Medical Bulletin., 69,* 33–48. https://doi.org/10.1093/bmb/ldh006. PMID: 15226195.

Kirmayer, L. J. (2007). Psychotherapy and the cultural concept of the person. *Transcultural Psychiatry, 44*(2), 232–257.

Knudsen, D. (2021). The neurobiology of trauma: Impact on physical health and affect regulation. *Certificate in Advanced Psychotherapy, Loyola University.* Nov. 5. Unpublished.

Leichsenring, F., & Rabung, S. (2008). Effectiveness of long-term psychodynamic psychotherapy: A meta-analysis. JAMA. *300*(13), 1551–1565. https://doi.org/10.1001/jama.300.13.1551. PMID: 18827212.

Leichsenring, F., Rabung, S., & Leibing, E. (2004). The efficacy of short-term psychodynamic psychotherapy in specific psychiatric disorders: A meta-analysis. *Archives of General Psychiatry., 61*(12), 1208–1216. https://doi.org/10.1001/archpsyc.61.12.1208. PMID: 15583112.

Levine, P. (2010). *In an unspoken voice: How the body releases trauma and restores goodness.* North Atlantic Books.

Luborsky, L. (1984). *Principles of psychoanalytic psychotherapy: A manual for supportive-expressive treatment.* Basic Books

Mageo, J. (2011). Empathy and attachment in Samoa. In D. Hollan & J. Throop (Eds.), *The anthropology of empathy: Experiencing the lives of others* (pp. 69–93). Berghahn.

Markus, H. R., & Kitayama, S. (1991). Culture and the self: Implications for cognition, emotion, and motivation. *Psychological Review, 98*(2), 224–253.

McKeever, V. M., & Huff, M. E. (2003). A diathesis-stress model of posttraumatic stress disorder: Ecological, biological, and residual stress pathways. *Review of General Psychology, 7,* 237–250.

Mojtabai, R. (2009). Americans' attitudes towards psychiatric medications: 1998-2006. *Psychiatric Services, 60*(8), 1015–1023.

Monroe, S. M., & Simons, A. D. (1991). Diathesis-stress theories in the context of life stress research: Implications for the depressive disorders. *Psychological Bulletin, 110*(3), 406–425. https://doi.org/10.1037/0033-2909.110.3.406.

Muir, J. (2011). *My first summer in the Sierra*, p.110. Houghton Mifflin Company

Mullins-Sweatt, S. N., Lengel, G. J., & DeShong, H. L. (2016). The importance of considering clinical utility in the construction of a diagnostic manual. *Annual Review of Clinical Psychology, 12,* 133–155.

Ogden, P., & Fisher, J. (2015). *Sensorimotor psychotherapy: Interventions for attachment and trauma.* W. W. Norton & Company.

Ornstein, E. D., & Ganzer, C. (2005). Relational social work: A model for the future. *Families in Society: The Journal of Contemporary Social Services, 86,* 565–572.

Perry, B. D. (2019) The neurosequential model: A developmentally-sensitive, neuroscience-informed approach to clinical problem solving. In J. Mitchell, J. Tucci & E. Tronick (Eds.), *The handbook of therapeutic child care: Evidence-informed approaches to working with traumatized children in foster, relative and adoptive care* (137–158). Jessica Kingsley Publishers. London

Perry, B. D., & Szalavitz, M. (2006). The boy who was raised as a dog: And other stories from a child psychiatrist's notebook—what traumatized children can teach us about loss, love, and healing. Basic Books.

Porges, S. W. (2001). The Polyvagal theory: Phylogenetic substrates of a social nervous system. *International Journal of Psychophysiology, 42,* 123–146.

Robins C. J., & Block P. (1989). Cognitive theories of depression viewed from a diathesis-stress perspective: Evaluations of the models of Beck and of Abramson, Seligman, and Teasdale. *Cognitive Therapy and Research, 13,* 297–313.

Saari, C. (2002). *The environment: Its role in psychosocial functioning and psychotherapy.* Columbia University Press.

Schore, A. N. (1994). *Affect regulation and the origin of the self: The neurobiology of emotional development.* Erlbaum.

Schore, A. N. (2000). Attachment and the regulation of the right brain. *Attachment and Human Development, 2,* 23–47.

Schore, A. N. (2001). Effects of a secure attachment relationship on right brain development, affect regulation, and infant mental health. *Infant Mental Health Journal, 22,* 7–66.

Schore, A. N. (2008). Modern attachment theory: The central role of affect regulation in development and treatment. *Clinical Social Work Journal, 36,* 9–20.

Shapiro, J. R., & Applegate, J. S. (2018). *Neurobiology for clinical social work: Theory and practice.* W. W. Norton.

Siegel, D. (1999). *The developing mind.* Guilford Press.

Siegel, D. (2012). *Pocket guide to interpersonal neurobiology: An integrative handbook of the mind.* Norton.

Solms, M., & Turnbull, O. (2002). *The brain and the inner world: An introduction to the neuroscience of subjective experience.* Other Press.

Spinks, S. (2002). One reason teens respond differently to the world: Immature brain circuitry. https://www.pbs.org/wgbh/pages/frontline/shows/teenbrain/work/onereason.html

Strupp, H. H., & Binder, J. L. (1984). Psychotherapy in a new key: A guide to time-limited dynamic psychotherapy. Basic Books.

van der Kolk, B. (2014). *The body keeps the score: Brain, mind, and body in the healing of trauma.* Viking.

Wampold, B. E., & Imel, Z, E. (2015). *The great psychotherapy debate: The evidence for what makes psychotherapy work* (2nd ed.). Routledge.
Weick, A. (1992). Building a strengths perspective for social work. In D. Saleeby (Ed.), *The strengths perspective in social work practice* (pp. 18–26). Longman.
Weiss, J. (1993). *How psychotherapy works: Process and technique.* Guilford Press.
Yakeley, J. (2018). Psychoanalysis in modern mental health practice. *The Lancet Psychiatry, 5,* 443–450.

3

Historical and current innovations in psychodynamic theory and practice

Introduction

The umbrella term of "psychodynamic" includes a great number of theoretical perspectives ranging from classical psychoanalysis (rarely practiced today in its purest form), ego psychology, object relations, self-psychology to intersubjectivity and relational models. What these perspectives share is the understanding that there is an unconscious, albeit an internal world, that shapes individuals' experiences interpersonally and with wider social systems. In addition, different cultures and different social groups may experience a cohort or larger pattern of interacting that is unique to that group. For example, Western societies that are focused more on the individual are more prone to promote a perspective on the individual that begins internally and moves outward. Consequently, theories of human behavior in the social environment start by examining individual functioning. For more collectivist cultures, a focus on the individual is less syntonic; the community identity is more the focus, which leads to macro and mezzo interventions. It is perhaps more helpful to talk about an issue of balance—which is given primacy in a specific unique context: the individual and/or the group (family, society, culture, country, etc.). We live in a transitory time where there is mobility, particularly in developed countries, in which fewer individuals remain in their city or country of origin their entire lives. Many individuals move or attempt to "transcontext," as Saari (2002) proposed—shifting identity and shared meanings based on environmental context. Likewise, the theoretical frameworks labeled as psychodynamic were needed to adapt to changing cultural and societal contexts. These theories continue to require an ability to transcontext to differing practice environments in order to retain value in understanding individual subjective experiences.

As psychodynamic clinicians, we are focused on forming therapeutic relationships that allow us to empathize with the individual, understand

Psychodynamic and Cognitive Behavioral Theory and Practice. Terry B. Northcut and Shveta Kumaria, Oxford University Press. © Oxford University Press (2025). DOI: 10.1093/9780197508404.003.0003

developmental influences, and consider our impact on the therapeutic relationship, all while also considering the broader social context influencing the individual. These theories get shaped and tested based on the types of questions asked within that point in time, reflecting societal values and the theorists' internal world. For example, Freud personally and professionally experienced anti-Semitism, which raised the question for him—why some people are malevolent—leading him to develop a theory of understanding influenced by the Darwinian idea of evolution and those aspects of what he thought were the negative aspects of human nature. Ego psychology was shaped by theorists living in a more comfortable social and economic position leading them to question where and how resiliency develops. Object relations theorists were influenced by World War II and large-scale separations of families and children which led to focus on how we achieve a unique, separate intrapsychic identity from our caregivers. The British School of Object Relations theorists, Winnicott (1971) in particular, emphasized what types of relationships are "good enough" to nourish development. Self-psychology with its emphasis on the narcissistic needs of a cohesive self, flourished in the United States following the 1960s rebellion against impinging social and political environments. Intersubjectivity models developed in a time of rebellion against the restrained and cautious style of post–World War II and analytic schools that excluded many different voices (Seligman, 2019). The focus was then on the need for authenticity, dialogue, and mutuality for healthy development of the self.

Fred Pine (1988) discussed the four psychologies—drive, ego, object, and self—as four conceptually separable perspectives on the functioning of the human mind. The usage of "four psychologies" provides a helpful framework for our discussion of the historical theories that have attempted to characterize the intrapsychic world.

Drive theory

Historical overview

While Sigmund Freud is credited with the founding of psychoanalysis during his lifetime (1856–1939), other theorists and clinicians have expanded his views, at times hesitating to challenge the validity of the concept of drives as sole determinants of development. Just as the understanding of Freud and his interpreters or revisionists is necessary for determining applicability in today's practice world, so is understanding the philosophical context with which Freud was operating. As early as the 1600s Descartes struggled with how to explain the connection between an immaterial mind and a physical body, following the Greek idea of a separation between the mind and the body, or Brainard's (2017) idea of first and third person views, respectively. Freud supported the idea that the mind and the body were separate and used his theory to help explain the process by which the two entities connect (Gabbard, 2005). As a result, psychoanalytic theory can be said to be a metaphorical tool for examining the "psychological space" that connects the mind and the body. Drive theory then attempts to explain how the mind and the body affect the functioning of each other in this dynamic "space."

Charles Brenner (1955) often considered the "dean of psychoanalysis" (Carey, 2008), and the "intransigent purist of American psychoanalysis" (Malcolm, 1981) stated that traditional psychoanalysis rests on two primary hypotheses. The first principle of psychic determinism proposes that nothing happens by chance in our psychic world: All actions or behaviors, feelings, and thoughts are related in some way. The second assumption is that consciousness is the exception, rather than the rule of everyday life, which explains why we don't always know or understand the connection between two "events" (i.e., actions, feelings, thoughts). An "event" may be hidden or unconscious, which obscures our understanding of the connection. These two assumptions are critical for understanding how psychoanalysis functions as a theory of human behavior and as a model for practice.

Metapsychological assumptions

According to Strachey's translation of Freud's ideas in the twenty-four-volume *The Standard Edition of the Complete Psychological Works of Sigmund Freud* (Freud, 1923), psychoanalysis rests on five core ideas about how the psyche or mind operates. These core ideas are considered Freud's metapsychological assumptions. There are numerous texts that describe the context and conflicts in which Freud developed his ideas (Berzoff, 2012; Berzoff et al., 2011; Borden, 2009; Brenner, 1955; Eagle, 1987; Gay, 1988; Goldstein, 1994; Greenberg & Mitchell, 1983; Mitchell & Black, 1995;

Palombo et al., 2009). This context includes his personal history, the medical community at the time of his writing, and the political, social, and economic environments in which he was living. Relevant for our understanding here is that he was trying to answer the question of what causes physical dysfunctions when there is no readily apparent medical cause. Freud, the self-proclaimed "Godless Jew," was living in the time of World War I, and the postwar period with Hitler's growing power. He was very conscious of the need for legitimacy via a scientific rationale for explaining how our minds can contribute to pathology. Each metapsychological assumption was developed by Freud to serve as a building block for a comprehensive theory of the mind and reinforce the theory's internal consistency and coherency. The goal was to develop a scientifically valid psychological theory that would stand up to the scrutiny of the medical community.

The first metapsychological assumption was *topographical*, as Brenner (1955) described in his landmark text. The topographic assumption proposes that there are layers of consciousness: the unconscious, the preconscious, and the conscious—hence, the metaphor of our minds as icebergs with the largest portion underground and not visible. A very popular illustration of this process is the "Freudian slip," where a person says one thing but means another. The true meaning of what was trying to be stated has been partially disguised or repressed but has broken through the barriers of unconsciousness to emerge in the preconscious which has influenced the conscious use of language. For example, a woman may call a friend's new partner by the name of a previous one whom she liked better. What is covered is the aggression or dislike of the new person in favor of the prior partner.

A second metapsychological assumption was *dynamic*, a system of energy that identified drives as the mechanism by which the mind operates. Freud believed there were two drives fueling our human agency: aggressive and sexual. In the broadest interpretation, the aggressive drive has been considered the drive to "push apart" or propel psychic separation from other components, thoughts, or actions in the mind. Likewise, the sexual drive, our libido, was believed to be the pull for connection or attachment between components of the mind. Freud's use of aggression and sexual terminology was meant to be rooted in the biology of the body with strict interpretations of these terms. At that time, it was considered revolutionary to assume that babies were born with these two drives in constant operation, struggling for gratification in an era that barely considered sexuality as part of normal male and female functioning. Binary classifications were also considered the only possible designation during this early understanding of gender. While aggression didn't have the same negative connotation to the professional as sexuality, there was still very little acceptance that the gratification of anger and aggression was in some way essential for normal development (Berzoff et al., 2011).

The third metapsychological assumption, *structural*, helped clarify how the drives are contained and are gratified by identifying the components of the mind as the id, ego, and superego. The id was the repository of the drives containing the unconscious mental processes, which were operated by primary processes, that is, not bound by rational thought and the reality principle (e.g., as in our dreams or in psychotic thought). Drives sought gratification according to the pleasure principle by emerging into the conscious world. The ego served as the mediator between the drives and the external world in order to secure as much gratification as possible while negotiating what was acceptable or feasible to the outside world. The superego contained the ideals of the ego and the standards for behavior that got established out of conflict or fear, that is, the moral precepts of the mind. The conflict between drive gratification and the moral guidelines of the superego resulted in the ego trying to find the most workable solution that appeased both. That "solution" or compromise by the ego often entailed behavior, thoughts, or feelings that would be considered symptomatic of the conflict and not necessarily "normal" functioning. These solutions involved defenses which allowed the conflict to remain unconscious even if it impaired the ego's full energy to adapt. (Defenses became more of a focus in ego psychology, discussed later in this chapter.)

The key to resolving symptoms was to uncover the unconscious drive that was seeking gratification to free up the energy needed for the ego to continue to try to manage the drives which resulted in symptomatic behavior. For example, in the classic case of hysteria illustrated in the case of Dora, it was hypothesized that a physiological symptom, coughing and difficulty in breathing, stood in place of the drive that was being thwarted—her supposed attraction to her father's friend and jealousy of the father's relationship with a woman other than her mother. Setting aside the many appropriate critiques of this interpretation, the idea is that the ego employs a defense to protect against the realization of the impulses of the drives, in this case, the defense of somatization.

A fourth metapsychological assumption was *economic*, which described where and how the energy of the drives was functioning. For example, pleasure, or gratification of the sexual drive, was believed to be the result of the cathexis of the energy, or the attachment of that energy to the mental representation of the biological part of the body experiencing pleasure at that point in time. In infancy, we derive our greatest satisfaction and growth enhancement by being fed orally, which means the sexual drive (pleasure) is being gratified through the mouth. If for some reason there is overgratification through the oral cavity or undergratification, a fixation may occur resulting in development being "stuck" at the oral gratification level. The drive energy then is hampered from being able to move freely and seek out other modes of gratification. Development then becomes halted or at least impaired as the ego struggles to reconcile the lack of gratification for the sexual drive and the simultaneous energy from the aggressive drive seeking release. A symptom such as excessive biting may result. If development proceeds in a relatively balanced way with both drives adequately gratified via the oral zone, the ego can facilitate a cathexis of the drives to another biologically gratifying zone; for example, the anal area, in which the physically developing child is newly focused. If all goes well, then development can proceed to another erogenous zone as warranted by physical development. However, when trauma or some non-gratifying experience halts the drive energy and disrupts the process, the individual may regress to a prior level of functioning that was more gratifying, for example return to the predominance of oral pleasure. A common example is of a child having advanced in development to focus on potty training, regressing to wanting to bottle or breast feed when a younger sibling is born and receives much attention and focus. These ideas of how the child negotiates different sources of drive gratification led to the development of the fifth metapsychological assumption.

The fifth assumption was considered *genetic* or *developmental*. Growth, biological and emotional, proceeds along developmental lines based on where the psychic energy is receiving gratification: oral, anal, phallic, latency, and genital. When development is housed in different biological areas, certain tasks must also occur that are unique to that developmental phase. For example, during the anal phase, a child is learning about controlling his/her bodily functions, particularly functions of elimination, how and when to "hold on" and when to "let go." These behavioral representations manifest themselves in personality characteristics that are said to represent the level of gratification received during that phase of development. For example, symptoms may develop that demonstrate an individual is too tightly controlled, whether in the bodily functions of elimination or perhaps more removed into a personality characteristic that is dominated by "holding too tightly" to certain items, ideas, or issues. The regulation of money may be another area that provides a window into what development in the anal phase was like. An adult may have great difficulty hanging onto money or may hold too tightly to any money earned and consequently may be considered "anal-retentive." The phallic phase of development is said to be dominated by the need to resolve the oedipal conflict. Children are aware of their genitalia at this stage of development and are hypothesized to receive erotic pleasure from attaching to the representation of the parental figure of the opposite sex. Heterosexuality is assumed to be the norm in traditional psychoanalytic theory, most easily seen in the description of what normal behavior supposedly looks like during this stage. Boys want their mothers as a sexual object yet fear their fathers will be jealous and consequently aggressive and castrate them for their desire for their mother. The boys must gradually relinquish their wish for the mother out of fear of retaliation by their father, and later in the genital phase of development redirect that energy toward cathecting the mental representation of a member of the opposite sex outside the parental unit. Girls, in a similar fashion in this heterosexual model, desire their father and realize they have already been castrated (here again, male development is considered the norm). Girls must likewise give up the attachment to the paternal figure and reinvest during the genital phase to the mental representation of another male non-family figure.

Therapeutic action

Returning to Freud's question of what causes and brings relief to the physical and mental suffering of patients, we consider now the impact of his theory on clinical work. Using the technique of free association or "chimney sweeping," as his patient Anna O. appropriately called it, allows for the client's unconscious conflicts to emerge in the dynamic of the treatment relationship, resulting in transference. If analysts remain "blank slates" and don't inject themselves into treatment relationships, any variation in the process and resulting content of the clients' disclosures was assumed to be coming from their unconscious. This was a somewhat noble attempt to be able to control what variables had an impact on the individual and isolate "cause and effect" of symptoms. While minimizing the action of the analyst in order to be as "scientific" as possible, personal characteristics, patterns, and the environment still played a role, albeit an overlooked one, in the treatment. Freud hypothesized that the unconscious thoughts, feelings, dreams, and so on would be stimulated by the clients' personal issues and not by the analyst's, which would then be unconsciously projected onto the analyst or the analytic relationship and then get reenacted as if these conflicts were occurring in the relationship with the analyst. This process, called transference, then could be contained in the therapeutic relationship, forming a "transference neurosis" (Gabbard et al., 2012). The analyst would interpret the patient's unconscious conflicts, as "a surgeon inserts a knife" (Stepansky, 1999), retrieving the memory and conflict allowing for the process of "working through," which would then allow a reintegration of the events with their associated affects. Freud's paper "Remembering, Repeating, and Working Through" (1914) described the process of treatment, further discussed by Strachey (1934) in the paper "The nature of the therapeutic action of psychoanalysis." Classical psychoanalysis assumes that all behavior evolves out of some conflict of the drives striving for gratification and the egos attempts to "rein them in" as in Freud's metaphor of the horse, rider, and the crop, being the id, ego, and the superego, respectively. In order for the patient to "remember and repeat" the original trauma or memory in therapy, they must have sufficient ego strength to tolerate the regression that would inevitably occur in freely associating on the analytic couch several times per week and still be able to function effectively outside the therapy. While Freud continued to focus on the mental apparatus responsible for psychic development, he opened the door to understanding the role of the analyst–patient relationship as a facilitator of the therapeutic process.

The therapeutic task was to observe the reenactments of the clients to ultimately connect the current projected experience with the prior unconscious experience which had occurred in early development. Mental health was viewed as the ability to achieve as much gratification of the drives as possible in order to fuel the ego's ability "to love and to work" (Elms, 2001; Erikson, 1963, p. 265; Freud, 1961). In practice, this would be observed by the analyst as the patient's attempt to work through the conflict by repeating it with the therapist, a representation of a conflict that must be freed up to allow development to continue. Psychopathology or symptoms meant that there was a conflict between impulses and the ego or superego which resulted in fixations or regressions which stymied psychosexual development. For purposes of understanding the differences between the emphases of each of these psychodynamic models, a case history will be examined from each lens.

Let's take the case of Dora referred to earlier and reframe it in a contemporary context (Debbie) to compare and critique a classical interpretation with the other four psychologies.

Debbie is an eighteen-year-old, White cisgender female student at a local university. She presents as a bright, engaging young woman. She was referred to as the therapist for symptoms of depression, a history of suicidal thoughts (no attempts), and poor health. Specifically, she has had a history of migraines and difficulties with coughing and breathing. The shortness of breath began when she was approximately eight years old. A family doctor at the time related it to stress. At age twelve her migraines and coughing episodes began. The migraines ceased at age sixteen but the coughing attacks continued, albeit sporadically. At times, coughing affects her voice so much that she can barely speak. Debbie was reluctant to see a therapist, just as she had been reluctant to see physicians about her symptoms, feeling that they did not listen to or believe her.

Debbie's father, in his late forties, has been ill since she was six. He has chronic lung disease. When Debbie was ten, her father also suffered some visual damage and slight paralysis. His illness is cyclical, necessitating the family to relocate according to doctors, treatment, and so on. Debbie's mother is described as an "obsessive cleaner." According to Debbie, the cleaning behavior is quite compulsive, involving ritualistic cleaning that consumes all her time. Debbie is quite critical of her mother. She does report on a close relationship with her brother, who is eighteen years old. However, their relationship has been strained recently as the brother tends to side with the mother in family arguments. Debbie describes her feeling closer to her father and his side of the family. That closeness has also been strained, due to increasing family arguments.

Increased family conflicts appear to relate to Debbie's increasing depression, and "unfriendliness." Debbie describes some of these conflicts as due to problems with friends of her father. She believes her father is having an affair with the wife of his friend, a woman she has been close to in the past. Debbie also reports that the husband of this woman has made advances to her that she has rebuffed. She feels her family does not believe her reports as they continue to plan dinners with this couple and expect Debbie to care for their children—which places her in regular contact with both the husband and the wife. Debbie's leaving home to attend college was her attempt to alleviate her problems; however, her symptoms have increased rather than decreased since moving to this city.

Example with Debbie

According to psychoanalytic theory, conflicts within the ego trying to gratify id impulses of sex and aggression are contributing to Debbie's symptoms of depression, breathing problems, and migraines. An assumption might be made that Debbie is suffering from an oedipal conflict that has been reexperienced in the relationship with the adult male who is a friend of the family. Her father's illness during the oedipal phase of development interfered with the successful resolution of the conflict. In addition, Debbie's psyche unconsciously converted her sexual desires for her father into psychosomatic symptoms. Her anger at her mother for her rival status for the father's love was also transferred to the wife of the family friend who allegedly was having an affair with the father. The treatment goals for Debbie would be insight into her repressed conflict and the resulting symptoms and a reexperiencing of the oedipal conflict with the therapist which would free up drive energy to allow development to move forward and symptoms to be alleviated. As part of the treatment course, regression would occur, which would allow for a reworking of the earlier conflicts. "Removing the symptoms" without alleviating the fixation at the oedipal phase would create other symptomatic behaviors. This of course is an oversimplification of Debbie's symptomatology and does not consider her current life situation as a college student away from home and the intervening variables of her brother's perceived abandonment or rejection. Likewise, I have condensed Debbie's symptoms and experiences to reflect the application of a classical interpretation.

Critique

Reviewing the metapsychological assumptions allows us to see the areas in which psychoanalytic theory has been most criticized, as well as its greatest strengths. Freud's bias that male heterosexuality was the norm meant that women and anyone with any variation of sexual orientation or gender identity were deficient and therefore not "normal." While acknowledging that female development was a "dark continent," Freud still moved forward with his theory pathologizing the process by which women develop their sense of morality (acceptance of their castrated state) and the focus of their identity and intellect (identification with mother as inferior object, and desire for pregnancy via father as a substitute for having a penis). This heteronormative theory resulted in women, nonbinary, and non-heterosexual individuals to be considered pathological. There is evidence Freud found this view limiting in his letter to a mother of a homosexual son in which he counseled her that there was nothing to be ashamed of in homosexuality, it was a variation in sexual functioning (Freud, 1951). However, by assuming homosexuality was a form of arrest in sexual development, Freud fostered the destructive societal and psychological impact of using male heterosexuality as a standard for "health" and normalcy.

Another critique of psychoanalysis relates to Freud's reliance on self-analysis and extrapolating psychological history from the free associations of adults. Certainly, his perception was biased even in trying to interpret his own dreams and experiences, especially when you compare that to a scientist "objectively" examining data obtained from another scientist. Freud was also guilty of adultomorphization or extrapolating symptoms from adults and assuming they demonstrated behavior, thoughts, or feelings that were part of normal development of children (Eagle, 1987). In addition, the assumption that the sexual and aggressive drives were universal and the emphasis on the resolution of the oedipal conflict as essential for growth also reflected a bias of Freud's geographical limitations, cultural background, and perhaps his own individual development. While he was fascinated and knowledgeable about other societies across time and place, he was limited to current knowledge at that time in history. The strengths of psychoanalytic theory visible in the metapsychological assumptions are the necessary emphasis on sexuality and aggression (albeit we now think it is reductionistic to assume only those two qualities are most important) that we have an unconscious "world" that can influence our thoughts, feelings, and behavior, and the understanding that development builds on experiences that happen in prior stages (the epigenetic principle).

Ego psychology

Theorists growing up in different social, political, and economic environments questioned Freud's idea that all human development evolves from conflict. Heinz Hartmann, having been raised in a more economically secure family environment which revolved around a diverse group of colleagues and friends, questioned why some people are able to grow and develop without apparent conflict (Mitchell & Black, 1995). Hartmann paved the way for understanding resiliency and the human capacity to adapt. Instead of viewing Freud's id as being the only element of our psyche present from birth, and therefore influencing all development, physical, emotional, behavioral, and so on, Hartmann proposed that we are all born with an "undifferentiated matrix" that includes innate qualities that can develop without influence of the drives and their push for gratification. According to Hartmann and ego psychology, individuals are born with an ability to adapt to the world around them, provided there is an "average expectable environment." Certain ego functions have a primary autonomy from the drives and are conflict-free, meaning that they do not develop in response to frustration and conflict. Instead, they have their own energy source apart from the drives and develop and mature given the average expectable environment. However, if there is conflict or the environment is "below average," these functions can lose their autonomy and become associated with conflict in development. The ego functions considered as having a primary autonomy from the id include attention, memory, concentration, learning, perception, motor functions, biological functions, and so on. A striking example of how these functions can be impaired is the "failure to thrive" babies not raised in an "average expectable environment" who are not able to physically grow and meet normal maturational benchmarks.

With the shift in emphasis from all development arising because of id energy, Hartmann moved psychoanalytic theory forward to allow for an individual to be able to use innate talents or strengths to extract sufficient energy from the average environment to allow development to proceed without grappling with conflict between the pleasure-seeking drives and the constraints of reality. The analytic focus could be on the ego and its functioning as opposed to only interpreting underlying forbidden wishes (Columbo, 2012). This shift in technique allows the therapist to draw on the clients "innate givens" or strengths in order to enlist their help in negotiating through areas that are caught up in conflict. For example, if someone is born with intellectual strengths, in times of stress when defenses are activated, the person may be able to use their cognitive capacities to employ the defense of intellectualization and efforts at mastery to give the ego more energy to fight other battles. Consequently, treatment can be more ego-supportive and rely less on the need to resolve conflicts to access drive energy because there is innate energy still available via the energized intellect. It is not a coincidence that the language describing this process portrays a battle of opposing forces with defensive maneuvers required to protect the psyche. Referring to Freud's structural metapsychological assumption, the three components of the psyche—the id, ego, and superego—are working at cross purposes given their different objectives and functions (i.e., gratification versus appeasing the social environment as manifest in the superego). Freud's concept of the psyche as dominated by a metaphor of energy relies on having enough energy to channel the forces of the drives when the occasion requires a delay in gratification. A "healthy" psyche has enough energy to gratify as much as possible of the drives yet maintain the important negotiation with the external world to facilitate future gratifications.

Hartmann (1934) brought more focus to the ego with specifics about how it functions. By assuming that there are parts of an ego that are not fueled by drive energy, he turned his focus to the "apparatus of secondary autonomy," the ego functions influenced by both innate strengths or deficits and neutralized energy from the drives. The activity of neutralizing the drive energy would reduce the amount of available energy for developing healthy ego functions included in the apparatus of secondary autonomy such as reality testing, judgment, defenses, and so on. Object relations was also considered an ego function with secondary autonomy representing our internalized schemas of self and other and their interactions.

Anna Freud (1966) invested her efforts in exploring and elaborating on the functions present in secondary functions of the ego, particularly the defenses. Many of the defenses have been integrated into the everyday English language today. For example, we talk about the *denial* of reality, the *regression* in the service of ego in acts of creativity or expressions of sexuality, the *displacement and/or sublimation* of aggression in sports or war, the *projection* of our thoughts and feelings onto others, rather than recognizing them as our own, and so on. Likewise, we can use the defense of intellectualization, fueled by intellectual capabilities and neutralized drive energy, to cope when overwhelmed or anxious. Another example is a person anxious about an impending serious medical procedure might read all about the procedure, watch videos of the process, and explore the extensive research that has been conducted on this procedure. Alternatively, a defense of denial and repression might mean an individual "forgets" that the process will be occurring within the next month and misses all preparatory doctor's appointments.

Introjection and identification are two other defensive processes that also help protect the ego as it negotiates internal conflicts when confronted with difficulties in the environment. A child may internalize the ideas or actions of parents or adults (e.g., that a child shouldn't cry when hurt) that provides an illusion of a connection with the significant other, even if it requires the negation of self-esteem or self-identity. If the introjected thoughts or beliefs become integrated into the personality as a consistent mode of interaction in the environment (e.g., the repression of emotions occur in most relationships), identification has occurred. This process described first by Ferenczi and subsequently by Anna Freud was a critical contribution to explaining the process of "identification with the aggressor" often seen in traumatized children. Theory was inching toward shining light on the influence of the environment.

A significant omission in Hartmann's work was clarification of what constitutes an "average expectable environment" that provides the pool of resources fueling independent ego development. Erikson (1950) provided more focus on the environment by examining the social world during development, having witnessed different cultures and his experiences with diverse populations. He broadened the concept of the psychosexual stages to become psychosocial phases of development. In studying the Oglala Sioux and the Yurok Native Americans, Erikson realized that the emotional problems they were having had less to do with difficulties with drive gratification, and everything to do with an inability to live with the values of their ancestors, in a world dominated by White people and their drastically different values. Erikson also proposed that development continues throughout life and is not limited to the phases of birth through adolescence. These psychosocial stages have a positive and negative component, according to Erikson, that requires the ego to adjust to better negotiate the disequilibrium that comes with movement into a new developmental phase. According to the epigenetic principle, in order for healthy growth to occur, the psychosocial tasks associated with each stage must be renegotiated in order to move forward. Each phase then subsequently integrates the experiences of previous phases and results in a new level of organization. If there is fixation at one level of development, all subsequent phases will be affected (Gedo & Goldberg, 1973). Erikson shifted the focus from the biological source of gratification to the resolution of the psychosocial stages: trust versus mistrust (oral), autonomy versus shame and doubt (anal), initiative versus guilt (phallic), industry versus inferiority (latency), identity versus role confusion (genital), intimacy versus self-absorption (young adulthood), generativity versus stagnation (middle adulthood), and integrity versus despair (older adulthood). For example, an infant whose biological and emotional needs are not met is not able to trust that the environment will be responsive to his/her/their needs. Consequently, the child will be mistrustful of others, and unable to progress smoothly, achieving healthy autonomy and initiative.

Therapeutic action

With new emphasis on innate ego strengths and the role of the environment, psychoanalytic treatment could focus on facilitating the ego's capacity to adapt. Strict classical theory required a "neurotic" level of development in the patient (i.e., normal development had progressed at least to the oedipal stage so that reliable reality testing was achieved) to tolerate the inevitable regressions necessary for the unfolding of the transference neurosis. Ego psychology, however, allows for focus on the full spectrum of developmental disruptions. Depending on the context in which a patient is seen, the negative transference can be the focal point, since it interferes with the progression of treatment. However, the ego can also be supported without challenging or confronting intrapsychic conflicts in order that functioning outside the treatment relationship can continue.

The presence of rigid defenses indicates the ego is overwhelmed and treatment should focus on making sure other functioning parts of the ego are supported before trying to uncover the sources of the defenses. In essence, the goal in ego-supportive work is to understand what is driving the defense before confronting or trying to take away that defense. Ego-supportive work provides scaffolding to make sure the ego is sufficiently strong enough to manage the unpacking of defenses. For example, a client with a traumatic background of abuse at the hands of family members denies having any animosity toward those abusers. An ego-supportive therapist would not necessarily focus on challenging that potential defense against anger and aggression as being necessary to ensure the ego is not overwhelmed trying to manage the conflicts. Rather the focus can begin with current functioning, and potential difficulties expressing anger in current relationships. Likewise, any possible negative transference that could interfere with the therapeutic relationship would be critical to prioritize as long as sufficient defenses could maintain current levels of functioning.

The therapeutic action of ego psychology is to support the ego's highest level of development unless the defenses get in the way of flexibility and other ego functions. A "healthy" ego has the capacity to minimize anxiety and allow for optimal satisfaction between the drive gratification and the demands of the environment, in essence to be freed up to "love and to work," as Freud described it. Impaired ego functioning due to conflicts between structures (id, ego, and superego) creates depression, anxiety, and/or other physical manifestations. Ego functions are then more rigidly structured and/or limited, which interferes with functioning adequately within the surrounding environment.

Example with Debbie

Clinical work with Debbie would focus on her ego functioning to assess what is working well with current life and what functions show evidence of rigidity or insufficient energy interfering with her ability to function well. Debbie's current ego functions in impulse control, judgment, and reality testing appear to be intact given the limited information we have. However, it is possible that she is demonstrating the defense of repression of anger at father for his illness and his lack of availability to be the gratifier of her impulses, potentially the conflicts around her sexuality related to the family friend (although there is strong evidence that this was an actual event rather than a fantasy as Freud interpreted it), and anger at the woman who "won" the affections of the father. Introjection of this anger has resulted in numerous somatizations which also allowed her to identify with the father's symptoms related to problems in breathing. Apparently, Debbie has been successful in applying for and getting accepted at college, indicating some evidence of intellectual strengths as being a possible "innate given" that has continued developing in the apparatus of primary autonomy. Treatment could involve supporting Debbie's use of intellect to become aware and identify her anger to increasingly manage her own anger as it gradually surfaces in her current relationships and in the treatment relationship. This focus would free up some of the introjection of her aggression, which would alleviate some of her depression—leaving her with more energy to tackle current developmental tasks. Certainly, conflicts with sexuality and the expression of those impulses would need "remembering, repeating, and working through"; however, the timing of those interpretations can be managed by continuing to support the ego's highest level of development so that college work can continue. Today, we would want to understand possible and/or probably trauma in her development, which highlights one of the limitations of ego psychology.

Critique

The emphasis on adaptation given an "average expectable environment" was a noteworthy shift in perspective; however, it did little to explicate the qualities essential in that environment for healthy growth. The assumption was that health is the ability to adapt to the external world without understanding the role of the impingements and/or traumas from the outer world. Ego psychology also does not expand our understanding of the subjective internal experience of the client and therapist except to relegate it to the result of conflict or a deficit in adaptation. Culture, class, race, and economic conditions were not the focus. With Erikson, this perspective was expanded to allow for strengths in the external environment, but he still emphasized a very gendered view of development that rated males as having superior or the norm of desired identity development. A focus on separation from nuclear families and subsequently having children was also considered the norm as a life cycle accomplishment which minimized feelings and behaviors that may have been attempts to preserve relationships that form the foundation for other functioning.

Object relations

The work of Hartmann and Erikson demonstrated the progression of psychoanalysis by clarifying and expanding theoretical concepts. With more emphasis on the ego and the environment, attention turned to object relations and the process by which the mental representation of others (objects) is internalized. At this point in time (1940 and 1950s), there was a clear presence of psychoanalysis in America as well as Europe, although across both continents the focus was on understanding the process of interaction between individuals in the environment. Both countries were experiencing the aftermath of World War II, including social and economic upheaval. "More than six million people were evacuated from England's cities and relocated in the countryside following the Blitz in 1940" (Borden, 2009). Theorists and practitioners such as Donald Winnicott focused on the impact on children of separation from parents and helped establish youth hostels for homeless children. Disruptive behavior in children and youth began to be connected to early disruptions of attachment relationships along with deprivation and loss. Psychodynamic theory expanded to allow greater scrutiny about the impact of early parental child relationships on our internal subjective experiences.

The "British School" (Anna Freud, Melanie Klein, Donald Fairbairn, Donald Winnicott, John Bowlby, Harry Guntrip, etc.) had its own divisions and foci separate from the American School. For example, Anna Freud focused on developmental lines and ego functions. Melanie Klein emphasized the internal world of the preverbal world of children through her work with child therapy. Fairbairn proposed that the ego was object seeking from birth on, and consequently object relations were a critical component that influenced the development of the ego. Winnicott focused on the environment of the therapeutic relationship and the functions of transitional objects in facilitating the development of object relations. John Bowlby and subsequent followers studied the relationships between a child and his primary caregiver (usually the mother in that era) that yielded a particular attachment style. Harry Guntrip focused on the process of withdrawal from primary object relations leading to what he termed the schizoid position. Each of these theorists had their own unique histories and traumas that influenced their theoretical contributions and the aspect of development. Focus shifted away from the need to gratify impulses to discharge tension heightened the importance of forming bonds and maintaining connections with primary objects as the main purpose of the psyche. Reworking those attachments freed up the ego to negotiate current relationships rather than relying on transferred patterns of prior failures.

From the American school, Margaret Mahler (1972) focused on the question of how self-representations and object representations form and differentiate within the psyche. Specifically, she wanted to understand why some patients were psychotic, in which self and object representations were blurred, and other patients demonstrated what she viewed as normal development where there is a healthy differentiation between the self and object representation. Mahler focused on the period of development between birth and four years of age, using direct observations of mother–child pairs to understand this process of separation–individuation. She built on the concepts of Freud's psychosexual stages and Erikson's psychosocial stages by elaborating on early childhood development as progressing through the stages of autism, symbiosis, practicing, differentiation, rapprochement, and object constancy (Mahler et al.,1973). Mahler assumed that at birth infants were not cathected to the environment but moved into a state of symbiosis with the object representation of the mother. Subsequently, the child's mental psyche progressed through a process of differentiation until they could reach a state where the self and object representations could be held stable or constant despite the inevitable frustration in everyday life. As part of this process children went through a phase of rapprochement during which they struggled to manage their need to utilize their capabilities and yet recognized that they couldn't do everything. Returning to "home base" was not a satisfactory solution because it ignored their accelerating competencies. Successful rapprochement meant a child could achieve object constancy and reconcile both their need for others and also their own evolving identity.

Clinical implications meant an attempt to explain why some children had difficulty separating from the primary caregiver. For example, a child not supported in differentiating from mother would have difficulty taking initiative and consequently experience depression when confronted with opportunities to separate from the maternal figure (e.g., play groups and school). If children were not able to achieve object constancy, they would be vulnerable to splitting (another form of ego defense) that considers all "objects" (persons in their representational world) as either "all good" or "all bad." Splitting indicates a difficulty in maintaining representations of the self and the other as integrated, including both good and bad.

Therapeutic action

Therapy from a Western object relations perspective builds on ego strengths to enable work on the further development or improvement of self and object representations and supporting achieving object constancy shifting the focus from presumed conflicts between the ego and id. What this means is that in therapy the relationship between the client and therapist is primary. The work is around the client's ability to establish and negotiate a secure attachment with the therapist and therefore extend that "template" with external relationships. Prior relational problems will manifest themselves in the transference and therefore be reenacted necessitating the therapist making themselves available as a "good object" that can be gradually reconciled with more realistic representations. Object relations extended the focus on deficits in development that interfere with "normal" development. Therapeutic work required supplying or filling in the deficits so that interpersonal relationships could progress.

Example with Debbie

Debbie is coming into treatment soon after her recent physical separation from family as she attended college. (Some theorists have identified adolescence as a "second separation-individuation.) Her internal representations of others appear to be coalesced around the all-good father representation with whom she identifies and idealizes, and the all-bad mother which she rejects as she does parts of herself, a form of splitting. These internal object relationships were disappointing, which led to Debbie's unreliable self-representation, which subsequently was challenged when she experienced frustration or a disconnection from others as evident by their lack of understanding of her needs. Moving away to school involved a separation that manifested the internal difficulties with separation and individuation and resulted in a lack of confidence about her own ability to negotiate physical separation and competency in school. Because her self-representation was weak, early identification with father and his illness resulted in an exacerbation of physical symptoms. Successful working through her internal object relationships in the establishment of a new attachment with a therapist would allow her to "free up" the energy fixated during early childhood and provide energy for her to negotiate a rapprochement between an idealized or devalued other and an insecure self.

Critique

As with ego psychology's emphasis on the nuclear family for development, object relations extended the emphasis on a maternal primary caregiver. With such a focus, although consistent with the era and European and

American culture at the time, it did not consider cultural differences in family configuration, different caregiving roles, and tended to blame any dysfunction on faulty mothering. The model emphasizes deficits in the development of a separate autonomous identity as often the result of an intrusive or neglectful mother, ignoring systemic contextual factors such as poverty, oppression, and inadequate medical care. The emphasis on attachment and the quality of the parent–child relationship was an important shift but perpetuated a myth that the all-powerful mother could "cause" everything from depression to psychosis.

Another important critique of the American school of object relations was its emphasis on separation and individuation as a goal for healthy development. Western cultures tend to emphasize the importance of autonomy from the parents, both interpersonally and intrapsychically. Many non-Western cultures (e.g., Asian, Native American, and African) place more emphasis on interdependence and maintaining a connection to family and community before there can be a focus on the self, if ever (Berzoff et al., 2011). Infant researchers since Mahler, such as Beebe and Lachmann (1994), Emde (1981 & 1988), and Stern (1995), have used advanced technology to observe infants and their caregivers to show that infants are relational from birth and do not pass through a phase of autism. Likewise, advances in interpersonal neurobiology have demonstrated that human growth and functioning are heavily influenced through the development of relationships that rely on interpersonal interactions between infants and human caregivers (Siegel, 2010, 2012). These interactions become generalized and get replayed in subsequent relationships (Stern, 1995). Object Relations theorists moved the focus from the development of the ego to highlighting development as occurring primarily in the context of the primary attachment relationship. At that time, the capacity to observe the neuroplasticity of our brains across lifespans and the multiple contexts in which relationships are formed and negotiated was not yet available. In addition, there was no consideration of the impact of oppression and racism on the development of identity (Tummala-Narra, 2016).

Self-psychology

By the end of the 1950s, classical psychoanalysis had moved from a focus primarily on drive gratification to ego functioning and to the importance of early object relations for development. Self-psychology offered yet another expansion of Freud's theory. Up to this point in theory development, psychoanalytic therapy was considered a "one-person psychology" in which the therapist analyzes the other person: the patient. The focus is on the individual of the patient. Kohut (1959) began the process of movement from a one-person psychology to a two-person psychology by turning attention to the necessity of empathic immersion on the part of the therapist during the process of treatment, beyond intrapsychic countertransference. For example, he noticed his patients did not seem to respond well or show improvement from strictly analytic interpretations that addressed oedipal conflicts. These patients seemed to need certain other functions from the therapist, not just a surgeon's precision with interpretation. Rather, the patient needed the therapist to immerse him/herself into the subjective world of the patient via empathy, or what Kohut (1959) also called "vicarious introspection" (p.459). When the therapist was effectively attuned to the patient's internal world, a different form of transference could occur, rather than one that relied on an interpretation of conflicts of a neurotic nature (Elson, 1986).

While initially conserving Freud's concept of the two intrapsychic drives—sex and aggression—by the time of Kohut's (1984) posthumous publication, *How Does Analysis Cure?*, he had moved beyond utilizing the drives as the force behind development. In Kohut's vision, development occurred via a triple helix with three components of the self: the grandiose self, the idealized imago, and the alter ego or twinship pole intertwined over the course of the lifespan. Consequently, the therapist (a selfobject) would need to mirror, tolerate idealization, and allow himself/herself to be viewed as like the client based on which type of transference was needed, to allow the client to grow in each of these dimensions. When these three components of the self were able to internalize the functions provided by the therapist via a process identified as transmuting internalization, they coalesce to form a cohesive, nuclear self that could be maintained during minor disruptions of connections. Aggression was the consequence of an empathic failure in the environment in one of these three areas (mirroring, idealization, and twinship) and resulted in "narcissistic rage" and/or dysregulation of one's core identity (a concept currently discussed often in interpersonal neurobiology, for example, Siegel, Perry, Tronnick, and Schore). Kohut believed that everyone has "normal" narcissistic needs that must be supported and gratified in order that a cohesive self can develop, one that is able to withstand the routine empathic failures present in ordinary life.

The core of Kohut's theory involves the experiential relationship between the self and the empathic "selfobject." Selfobject is the child's internal perception of people in his environment who serve essential psychological functions. If development proceeds normally, these selfobject functions will be integrated and allow the development of healthy, age-appropriate selfobject relationships in the future. Kohut believed that a normal child ideally grows up in an empathic-responsive environment, peopled by others who are in tune with his or her psychological needs and wishes. As a result, the child experiences a merger with the all-powerful selfobject. When the selfobject is calm and collected, the child's needs, anxieties, and rage are calmed, such that he or she begins to experience the rudiments of a stable, cohesive self. Over the course of time, the child will experience disappointment and frustration or "empathic failure." To the extent that this failure does not exceed the child's capacity to manage it, maturation continues. But if the empathic failure occurs too early or too violently, the stability of the self is compromised, leading to loss of self-esteem and diminished capacity to consistently function in the world. Kohut postulated that self-disorders, particularly the borderline and narcissistic personality disorders, result from early empathic failure on the part of the parents, particularly the mother. Repeated empathic failures result in a lack of cohesion in the child's sense of self leading to physical and emotional symptoms interfering with healthy functioning.

Therapeutic action

The task of treatment from a self-psychological theoretical view is for the client to be able to ultimately form healthy selfobject relationships outside the therapeutic relationship as they age and develop through internalizing those functions initially met in therapy. This does not mean, however, that the therapist can concretely meet needs unmet in childhood. The therapeutic "glue" to solidify a fragile sense of self is the therapist's empathic understanding and immersion into what the client's subjective experience of their past and present. For example, a client may be frustrated that you cannot be available every hour of every day. Therapists cannot meet that idealized expectation; however, we can empathize with the client's experience of living in a world that is not geared to their expressed needs. In this sense, self-psychology is also a deficit model which emphasizes failures of the caregivers to supply the needs of the child that must be subjectively experienced by the therapist attuned to the subjective needs of the client in the present. It is out of that empathic immersion of the therapist into the client's internal world that a connection can be made and ultimately internalized within the client. Likewise, when failures in empathy inevitably occur, the attuned therapist can acknowledge the failure and reconnect with the internal experience of the client.

Kohut's emphasis on the importance of the therapeutic relationship, and not just on the actions of making interpretations, built on prior work by Sandor Ferenczi and Franz Alexander. Ferenczi insisted that "when you cannot break out of a psychic prison alone, we'll have to do it together," and emphasized the critical role affective states of both client and therapist as they related to each other in order to reduce the suffering of the client in the present (Gabbard et al., 2012). The "corrective emotional experience" is most associated with Alexander, who focused on the "working through process" originally proposed by Freud but altered the concept to view the therapeutic relationship as the curative element in analytic work (discussed further in Chapter 5) and not relying on interpretations alone (Christian et al., 2012).

Example with Debbie

With self-psychology's emphasis on the necessity of attuned selfobject functioning for the development of cohesive nuclear self, the presence of symptoms indicates fragmentation from empathic failures in the client's world. In the case of Debbie, her selfobjects failed to provide the opportunity for mirroring, idealization, and twinship. Further difficulty was experienced because they could not hear her experience of the father's friend's aggressive and offensive sexual overtures to her. The father's ongoing illness, frailty, and affair were experienced as ineffective, and inattentive mirroring and ultimately disappointment. The mother's not listening well or believing Debbie's experience likewise failed to mirror her needs. The excessive cleaning also resulted in inattentive mirroring as the mother was preoccupied with her own needs and issues. The brother's switch in allegiance also minimized Debbie's much needed twinship experience.

Therapeutic progress for Debbie would result with the empathic immersion by the therapist into Debbie's subjective experience providing a new experience in the present. "Contrary to (her) experience in childhood, *the sustaining echo of empathic resonance* is available in this world" (Kohut, 1984, p. 78 as quoted in Christian et al., 2012). Consequently, Debbie would be able to experience a sense of aliveness or zest, as Kohut described it, that would allow her to mourn what she didn't experience in childhood and seek out current relationships that support her coalescing self.

Critique

Understanding the subjective experience of clients in their life in the world was a huge contribution, including room for the internalized experience of oppression, culture, and class. "Mental health is defined by the subjective experience of well-being, cohesion and vigor within the individual self" (Flanagan in Berzoff et al., 2011, p. 181). However, the emphasis is still on an individualistic idea of health and not the primary focus on communal or familial identity valued in non-White cultures. There was also greater freedom to acknowledge the failures in empathy on the part of the therapist. While Kohut made progress in moving us toward a two-person psychology by considering the empathic milieu of the therapy, and the role of the therapist in maintaining that environment, there still existed a focus on deficits in parenting and the need of the therapist to provide the corrective emotional experience without focusing as much on the person of the therapist in the relationship. That focus would emerge in the intersubjective and relational schools developing concurrently with Kohut.

Intersubjective and relational schools

Kohut's self-psychology brought necessary focus to the process of what is occurring between client and therapist and shifted the emphasis from separation individuation to a life-long need for relationships. While the theory still focused on what the patient needed from the therapist, it moved away from the rule of abstinence at all costs so that the therapist could respond in the manner most compatible with selfobject needs. Successive schools of psychodynamic theory, such as the intersubjective and relational models, would turn the focus to "two-person" psychologies and concentrate on what both the patient and the therapist bring and experience in the therapeutic work (Endnotes 39 & 40; Safran & Muran, 2000; Segal, 2013). As can be expected from the name of the approach, intersubjectivity is not a monolithic concept that can be studied as a defined objective phenomenon (Lichtenstein, 2020). The inherent subjectivity makes scientific study (i.e., psychotherapy process and outcome studies) difficult to say the least. To further muddy the waters, there are at least two separate but parallel streams: the more psychoanalytic tributary and the relational, feminist approach, fed by, but not limited to, work at the Stone Center at Wellesley, currently labeled Cultural Relational Therapy.

The intersubjectivity movement occurred out of the rebellion in the 1960s and 1970s in the context of Civil Rights, feminist advances, and an ecological orientation which valued "authenticity and recognition; the critique of power and arbitrary authority; spontaneity, experimentation, uncertainty and improvisation; and social and cultural awareness" (Seligman, 2019, p. 146). Theorist practitioners such as Mitchell (1988, 1993), Ogden (1994), Stolorow and Atwood, (1992), and Wallerstein (2015) pushed against the boundaries of existing theories to bring back into the therapy room the voices silenced by society and the rigid models of psychotherapy, especially in the area of race, gender, creativity, and sexuality. Likewise, Belenky, Clinchy, Goldberger, and Tarule (1986), Carol Gilligan (1984), and Jean Baker Miller (1976) focused on finding their own voices and the voices of women in treatment by recognizing that women find their identity through mutuality in empathic relationships. These women recognized that the Eriksonian psychosocial stage model focused solely on male development, that is, identity must be formed before intimacy can occur. Both streams of intersubjective thought recognized "another person is needed to experience our own self" (Bohleber, 2013, p. 800). Instead of subject–object relationships typical of previous psychoanalytic models, now the focus would be on subject–subject as the essential therapeutic milieu.

Relational/intersubjective therapy in general posits that change occurs as a result of experiencing and participating in "mutually-reciprocal meaning-making" (Buirski et al., 2020; Segal, 2013, p. 377). The process and experience of generating meaning within the therapeutic dyad is the critical change agent as opposed to insight, or selfobject experience; "intrapsychic determinism gives way to an unremitting intersubjective contextualizing" (Bohleber, 2013, p. 803; Stolorow & Atwood, 1992, p. 330). The client and therapist create together an "analytic third" that is always present, forcing them to bump up against and continually readjust their interactions (Ogden,

2004). What is critical about that constructed emotional experience is that the two worlds of the therapist and patient join together to understand their joint context. As a phenomenological process, an intersubjective process captures the essential emotional complexity and connections that had been missing in previous psychoanalytic theories.

Relational and intersubjective theory is consistent with advances in neurobiology, as mentioned earlier, which emphasizes the plasticity of the brain through adulthood, allowing for and facilitating new patterns of interaction through the development of new neuronal connections. Likewise, the "mutual regulation" (Tronick, 2007) that occurs during the process of exploring the relational matrix of therapy enhances and broadens the level of complexity of responses in social interactions. Certainly, the patient is still the focus, but it is recognized that both patient and therapist evolve in the process and the therapist is more able to reflect on his or her own experience to determine how and when to intervene with the client to negotiate their ongoing dynamic relationship.

One area of development withing relational approaches impacted by what we have learned from neurobiology, the neurobiology of trauma, and even the earlier work by Ferenczi is the idea of embodiment or the role biology plays in this realm of intersubjectivity. Our connections with others are "embodied" as well as taking place in the mind in the here and now. Psychological and sociological theories have struggled with the concept of the relationship of the body and the mind, as we talked about in Chapter 2. How do we understand mental anguish? A product of the mind or the body when the origin stems from sociologically defined social problems. Obviously, it is both. For our purposes here, we can rely on clinical researchers such as Bessel van der Kolk (2014) to remind us that the physical body reacts continually (even if invisibly) to a perceived threat to safety whether real or imagined. We all carry "pockets of embodied distress" (Rumble, 2010, p. 133) that influence how we experience ourselves and the selves of others. These distress pockets disrupt the unity of the mind, the body, and the world and make it difficult to understand our own reactions and those of others in our environment. Affective communication consequently receives heightened priority as an essential part of this decoding process. Rumble (2010) suggests "affective communication among the two (infant and caregiver), the rhythm and success of the call, and the response determine the emotional relationship between the two parties and also the quality of their attachment" (Kiss, 2021, p. 147). The caregiver's job is to hear, experience, and interpret that call to keep it within the child's tolerable limits and aid in self-regulation. Likewise, affective decoding must be a continual process between client and clinician as well to assist in developing and maintaining the analytic third. Intersubjectivity relies on a call and response that can be understood, particularly when there are disruptions that must be mended.

Therapeutic action

The goal of intersubjective therapy is to facilitate within the relationship an ability to integrate past traumatic experiences, including shame that resulted from the devaluing, critical, and humiliating experiences of living in an environment that is unreceptive to one's emotional experience (Kenny, 2013, p. 190). The goal is not to "recover" these traumas, as Freud believed, but rather integrate them so that they are not stuck in flashbacks or what Stolorow calls "portkey" experiences (like Harry Potter) which keep the trauma dissociated (Kenny, 2013). Generally, when the trauma is re-integrated in the mind and the body, there is a shift away from shame to open up more feeling states such as sadness, grief, joy, and so on. The concepts of transference and resistance become recontextualized. Transference then is the new experience of the therapeutic relationship as shaped by the therapist's and patient's "intersubjectively derived organizing principles" (Kenny, 2013, p. 194). Consequently, "resistance" is not something defensively existing in the isolated mind of the client or any of us—it results from when this new intersubjective system (between client and therapist) becomes dangerous or triggering shame, which then triggers patterns of interactions that while protective disconnect relationally from others. Here we can see the influence of Harry Stack Sullivan's (1968) work on interpersonal psychoanalysis and "activating systems." Clinical pairs no longer focus on remembering repeating and working through. Instead, empathy, recognition, and responsiveness provide the framework for treatment. What makes this a particularly difficult theory, perspective, or framework is that this is not a *content* theory as was Freud's, Hartman's, Mahler's, or Kohut's. This is a *process* theory that relies on first experiencing each other and ultimately investigating the unique themes and meaning structures that take shape in a person's unique developmental history which get experienced within the realm of the new relational context.

Example with Debbie

Clinical work with Debbie no longer focuses on her internal conflicts, ego functioning, impaired object relations, or selfobject failures. An intersubjective therapy would call on the therapist and client to focus on their relationship in the present, not a new concept of course, but focused on understanding Debbie's experiences in the here and now with the therapist paying close attention to her mind and body experiences. It shifts Debbie's treatment to focusing on the impact of her father's poor health, her not being believed about Herr's sexual assaults and insults, the trauma of her experience with Herr, her family code of secrecy, and the destabilizing impact of her move and college responsibilities, and the impact of the therapist and therapy on her "security systems" that warn when her window of tolerance has been maxed out. Zooming into her experience of her body in the moment slows down the therapeutic transactions so she and the therapist both can modulate what is happening currently between them (Danielian & Gianotti, 2012; Gianotti, 2022) and how triggers were responded to in the past and get activated in the present experience. The therapeutic process is ongoing, cycling in and out of mutual enactments and disembedding themselves from their enactments (Christian et al., 2012).

Critique

An obvious critique is the ambiguity inherent in an intersubjective perspective. How do you teach or explain how to practice intersubjective therapy? As Danielian and Gianotti (2012) say, "words fail experience," which makes it even more important to stay in the present. The intersubjective process itself defies easy explanation or even familiar language (p. 11). While trying to bring back the voices often marginalized in our society, the approach still doesn't provide answers or solutions to living in an environment that actively demonstrates that you really have no physical safety or security, let alone empathy for one's suffering, which reminds us again that the work of psychotherapy is not correcting mezzo or macro social problems. What is the focus is the clients' subjective experience of that social dis-ease and how it gets perpetuated in treatment while offering a "sustaining echo of empathic resonance." Intersubjective theory and practice do allow for bringing trauma of all kinds and the ongoing and lingering effects into the therapeutic space as the practice itself is a form of ongoing exposure therapy allowing for successful mastery.

Another advancement in developmental research adding to an understanding of the intersubjective worlds of mother and child and interpersonal is the work of Fonagy et al. (1991). As mentioned, Bowlby's work on attachment theory from the British School of Object Relations added the concept of a relational template of sorts that framed subsequent relationships. Peter Fonagy and others at the Anna Freud Centre (Fonagy et al., 2012) originated the concept of mentalization, the ability to imagine and interpret the mental states of self and others (e.g., desires, feelings, needs, etc.). They found that not only is the security of an infant's attachment predicted by the parent's security of attachment during their pregnancy, but more importantly by the parent's ability to mentalize or think about their own childhood relationship to their parents. Fonagy's work speaks to the process of attachment and the accompanying ability to understand interpersonal behavior. By extending the concept of attachment to more specifically examine the cognitive processes involved in that process, Fonagy et al. (1991) has provided an entry point we will discuss further in Chapter 5 and the case illustrative chapters to focus on ways in which CBT can offer a means to enhance the capacities within the construct of a safe therapeutic relationship.

Conclusion

Psychoanalysis has come a long way since Freud's original ideas attempted to bridge the mind and the body through the psyche. The focus has moved over time in its emphasis on uncovering and resolving conflicts in the intrapsychic world, to clients' strengths and resources, to understanding the role of the environment, and the role of the therapist and client relationship. Theoretical pluralism has resulted in there not being one unified theory that is preserved by "Freudians" resisting all change. Instead, there have been important shifts in understanding client narratives and in empirical research supporting those theories (Leichsenring & Rabung, 2008; Leichsenring et al., 2004).

Theorists and clinicians try to distinguish between what has been found empirically to be helpful for different client symptoms and the need to understand the meanings of different times and different circumstances in the lives of clients. Any effort to consider strengths and weaknesses of any theoretical framework requires recognition not only past historical contexts but also ongoing important sociological and cultural changes occurring in our world. Integration is best served by building on the vitality of current theories that attempt to rectify the failings of past work. Freud's dreams of developing a theory to unite mind and body is progressing through the continued focus on the evolving client and therapist relationship, and a changing understanding of what constitutes the mind and the body. As Cozolino observes (2018), "health, both mental and physical, is inextricably tied up in the quality of our relationships with each other and the broader culture ... each generation has to learn that the everyday assumptions of individualism are in many ways an illusion" (Cozolino, xi). Treatment must likewise be predicated on the relationship between client and clinician.

References

Beebe, B., & Lachmann, F. M. (1994). Representation and internalization in infancy: Three principles of salience. *Psychoanalytic Psychology, 11*(2), 127–165. https://doi.org/10.1037/h0079530

Belenky, M. F., Clinchy, B. M., Goldberger, N. R., & Tarule, J. M. (1986). *Women's ways of knowing: The development of self, voice, and mind.* Basic Books.

Berzoff, J. (Ed.). (2012). *Falling through the cracks: Psychodynamic practice with vulnerable and oppressed populations.* Columbia Press.

Berzoff, J., Flanagan, L. M., & Hertz, P. (2011). *Inside out and outside in: Psychodynamic clinical theory and practice in contemporary multicultural contexts*, 3rd ed. Jason Aronson.

Bohleber, W. (2013). The concept of intersubjectivity in psychoanalysis: Taking critical stock. *International Journal of Psychoanalysis, 94*, 799–823.

Borden, W. (2009). *Contemporary psychodynamic theory and practice.* Lyceum.

Brainard, F. S. (2017). *Reality's fugue: Reconciling worldviews in philosophy, religion, and science.* Pennsylvania State University Press.

Brenner, C. (1955). *An elementary textbook of psychoanalysis.* International University Press.

Buirski, P., Haglund, P., & Markley, E. (2020). *Making sense together: The intersubjective approach to psychotherapy.* Rowman & Littlefield Publishers.

Carey, B. (2008, May 22). Charles Brenner, psychoanalyst, dies at 94. *New York Times*, retrieved 8/30/12 https://www.nytimes.com/2008/05/22/nyregion/22brenner.html

Christian, C., Safran, J., & Muran, J. C. (2012). The corrective emotional experience: A relational perspective and critique. In L. G. Castonguay & C. E. Hill (Ed s.), *Transformation in psychotherapy: Corrective experiences across cognitive behavioral, humanistic and psychodynamic approaches* (pp. 51–67). American Psychological Association. https://doi.org/10.1037/13747-000

Columbo, D. (2012). Freud and his circle. In G. O. Gabbard, B. E. Litowitz, & P. Williams (Eds.), *Textbook of psychoanalysis* (2nd ed., pp. 3–17). American Psychiatric Publishing Inc.

Cozolino, L. (2018). Foreword. In J. R. Shapiro & J. S. Applegate (Eds.), *Neurobiology for clinical social work* (pp. xi-xii). W.W. Norton & Company.

Danielian, J., & Gianotti, P. (2012). *Listening with purpose: Entry points into shame and narcissistic vulnerability.* Aronson.

Eagle, M. N. (1987). *Recent developments in psychoanalysis: A critical review*. Harvard University Press.

Elms, A. C. (2001). Apocryphal Freud: Sigmund Freud's most famous "quotations" and their actual sources. *Annual of Psychoanalysis*, *29*, 83–104.

Elson, M. (1986). *Self-psychology in clinical social work*. W. W. Norton & Co.

Emde, R. N. (1981). Changing models of infancy and the nature of early development: Remodeling the foundation. *Journal of the American Psychoanalytic Association, 1*, 179–219.

Emde, R. N. (1988). Development terminable and interminable: I. Innate and motivational factors from infancy. *International Journal of Psycho-Analysis, 69*, 23–42.

Erikson, E. H. (1950). *Childhood and society*. W. W. Norton.

Erikson, E. H. (1963). *Childhood and society*. 2nd ed. NY: Norton.

Fonagy, P., Steele, M., Steele, H., Moran, G. S., & Higgitt, A. C. (1991). The capacity for understanding mental states: The reflective self in parent and child and its significance for security of attachment. *Infant Mental Health Journal, 12*(3), 201–218. https://doi.org/10.1002/1097-0355(199123)12:3≤201::AID-IMHJ2280120307≥3.0.CO;2-7Routledge/Taylor & Francis Group.

Freud, A. (1966). *The ego and the mechanisms of defense* (Revised ed.). International Universities Press. (original edition published in 1936)

Freud, S. (1914). Remembering, repeating, and working through. In J. Strachey (Eds.), *The standard edition of the complete psychological works of Sigmund Freud* (Vol. 12, pp. 145–156) Hogarth Press, 1962.

Freud, S. (1923). The ego and the id. In J. Strachey (Eds.), *The standard edition of the complete psychological works of Sigmund Freud* (Vol. 19, pp. 3–66). Hogarth Press, 1962.

Freud, S. (1961). Civilization and its discontents. In J. Strachey (Eds.), *The standard edition of the complete psychological works of Sigmund Freud* (Vol. 21, pp. 64–145). Hogarth Press.

Freud. S. (1951). *Historical notes: A letter from Freud. The American Journal of Psychiatry, 107*(10), 786 - 787.

Gabbard, G. (2005). *Psychodynamic psychiatry in clinical practice* (4th ed.). American Psychiatric Publishing.

Gabbard, G., Litowitz, B. E., & Williams, P. (2012). *Textbook of psychoanalysis* (2nd ed.). APA Publishing.

Gay, P. (1988). *Freud: A life for our time*. W. W. Norton.

Gedo, J., & Goldberg, A. (1973). *Models of the mind: A psychoanalytic theory*. University of Chicago Press.

Gianotti, P. (2022). *Embracing therapeutic complexity: A guidebook to integrating the essentials of psychodynamic principles across therapeutic disciplines*. Routledge.

Gilligan, C. (1984). *In a different voice*. Harvard University Press.

Goldstein, E. (1994). *Ego psychology and social work practice* (2nd ed.). W. W. Norton.

Greenberg, J. A., & Mitchell, S. A. (1983). *Object relations in psychoanalytic theory*. Harvard University Press.

Hartmann, H. (1934). *Ego psychology and the problem of adaptation*. International University Press.

Kenny, D. T. (2013). *From id to intersubjectivity: Talking about the talking cure with master clinicians*. Karnac Books.

Kiss, K. D. (2021). Intersubjectivity and embodiment in the field of psychotherapy. *Studia Ubb. Philosophia, 66*(2), 141–152.

Kohut, H. (1959). Introspection, empathy and psychoanalysis: An examination of the relationship between mode of observation and theory. *Journal of the American Psychoanalytic Association, 7*(3), 459–483.

Kohut, H. (1984). *How does analysis cure?* University of Chicago.

Leichsenring, F., & Rabung, S. (2008). Effectiveness of long-term psychodynamic psychotherapy. *Journal of the American Medical Association, 300*(13), 1551–1565.

Leichsenring, F., Rabung, S., & Leibing, E. (2004). The efficacy of short-term psychodynamic psychotherapy in specific psychiatric disorders. *Archives General Psychiatry, 61*(12), 1208–1216.

Lichtenstein, D. (2020). Review essay: *Intersubjectivity in psychoanalysis: A model for theory and practice* by Lewis Kirshner. Routledge, 2017 (Paperback) 168 pages. *American Imago, 77*(2), 337–343.

Mahler, M. (1972). On the first three sub phases of the separation-individuation process. *International Journal of Psychoanalysis, 53*, 333–338.

Mahler, S. M., Pine, F., & Bergman, A. (1973). *The psychological birth of the human infant.* Basic Books.

Malcolm, J. (1981). *Psychoanalysis: The impossible profession.* Knopf.

Miller, J. B. (1976). *Toward a new psychology of women.* Beacon Press.

Mitchell, S. A. (1993). *Hope and dread in psychoanalysis.* Basic Books.

Mitchell, S. A. (1988). *Relational concepts in psychoanalysis: An integration.* Harvard University Press.

Mitchell, S. A., & Black, M. J. (1995). *Freud and beyond: A history of modern psychoanalytic thought.* Basic Books.

Ogden, T. H. (1994). The analytic third: Implications for psychoanalytic theory and technique. *The Psychoanalytic Quarterly, 73*(1), 167–195. https://doi.org/10.1002/j.2167-4086.2004.tb00156.x

Ogden, T. H. (2004). The Analytic Third: Implications for Psychoanalytic Theory and Technique. *The Psychoanalytic Quarterly, 73*(1), 167–195. https://doi.org/10.1002/j.2167-4086.2004.tb00156.x

Palombo, J., Bendicson, H. K., & Koch, B. J. (2009). *Guide to psychoanalytic developmental theories.* Springer.

Pine, F. (1988). The four psychologies of psychoanalysis and their place in clinical work. *Journal of the American Psychoanalytic Association, 36*(3), 571–596. https://doi.org/10.1177/000306518803600301

Rumble, B. (2010). The body as hypothesis and as question: Towards a concept of therapist embodiment. *Body, Movement and Dance in Psychotherapy, 5*(2), 129–140. https://doi.org/10.1080/17432979.2010.494852

Saari, C. (2002). *The environment: Its role in psychosocial functioning and psychotherapy.* Columbia University Press.

Safran, J. D., & Muran, J. C. (2000). *Negotiating the therapeutic alliance: A relational treatment guide.* Guilford.

Segal, E. (2013). Beyond the pale of psychoanalysis: Relational theory and generalist social work practice. *Clinical Social Work Journal, 41*, 376–386.

Seligman, S. (2019). Relational psychoanalysis as a "child of the sixties": Politics, innovation, and the transition from adolescence. *Psychoanalytic Inquiry, 39*(2), 146–155.

Siegel, D. (2012). *The developing mind: How relationships and the brain interact to shape who we are* (2nd ed.). Guilford.

Siegel, D. J. (2010). *The mindful therapist: A clinician's guide to mindsight and neural integration.* Norton Series on interpersonal neurobiology. W. W. Norton.

Stepansky, P. (1999). *Freud, surgery, and the surgeons.* Routledge.

Stern, D. (1995). *The interpersonal world of the infant.* Basic Books.

Stolorow, R. D., & Atwood, G. E. (1992). *Contexts of being: The intersubjective foundations of psychological life.* Analytic Press, Inc.

Sullivan, H. S. (1968). *The interpersonal theory of psychiatry.* W.W. Norton.

Tronick, E. (2007). *The neurobehavioral and social-emotional development of infants and children.* W. W. Norton & Co.

Tummala-Narra, P. (2016). *Psychoanalytic theory and cultural competence in psychotherapy.* APA.
van der Kolk, B. (2014). *The body keeps the score: Brain, mind, and body in the healing of trauma.* Viking.
Wallerstein, R. S. (2015). Psychoanalysis as I have known it: 1949–2013. *Psychoanalytic Dialogues, 25*(5), 536–556. https://doi.org/10.1080/10481885.2015.1077037
Winnicott, D. W. (1971). *Playing and reality.* Tavistock Publication.

4

Historical and current innovations in cognitive behavioral theory and practice

Introduction

In this chapter, we hope to show readers the historical development of CBT and demonstrate how it has been open to feedback and aspires to be responsive and integrative (Beck, 2020). Just as we emphasized in our chapter on psychodynamic theories and therapies, we provide here some general information about CBT and its subsidiaries, recognizing that we cannot fully capture the depth and breadth of CBT therapies. We also wish to help the reader critically examine the evidence base of CBT. Lastly, we utilize this information to present in the next chapter our ideas about how to bridge CBT and Psychodynamic Therapy (PDT).

The term cognitive behavior therapy (CBT) encompasses many therapeutic approaches under its umbrella, often serving as a short-term moniker for any therapies that are *not* psychodynamic. These approaches include behavior therapy, cognitive therapy, cognitive processing therapy, mindfulness-based cognitive therapy (MBCT), acceptance and commitment therapy (ACT), and dialectical behavior therapy (DBT). Typically, CBT therapies focus on the here and now and are experiential, directive, and pragmatic. The therapist takes on a more active role, and at times, a didactic one, in addition to collaborating with the client to focus on events that are relatively easily observable and accessible. Observable behaviors and accessible cognitions stand in stark contrast to the inferred unconscious motivation in PDT. CBT focuses more on what is maintaining the symptoms, rather than attending to or deciphering the developmental origins of the symptoms (Newman et al., 2022). However, as Wachtel (2011) points out, both PDT and CBT have evolved to the point of some synergy. "Both (*PDT and CBT*) aim to *enter* the patient's experience rather than critiquing it, and both root the therapeutic effort in the dialectic between *accepting* the patient's experience

Psychodynamic and Cognitive Behavioral Theory and Practice. Terry B. Northcut and Shveta Kumaria, Oxford University Press. © Oxford University Press (2025). DOI: 10.1093/9780197508404.003.0004

of the world and helping him to *change* those features of his assumptive world that are contributing to his pain" (Wachtel, p. 16).

First, it is important to set the sociological context in which CBT developed and flourished. CBT theories arose in response to the zeitgeist of the times: a move to industrialization and automation, with a focus on cost saving and skill building so that people could be kept in the labor force. If symptoms could be eliminated quickly, employees could return to work quickly. Just as PD was trying to be considered credible to the medical profession, so too was CBT. Neoliberal policies that focused on economic rationalization and individual responsibility set the stage for CBT to gain prominence, and some might even say to push it to dominance (Rasmussen, 2018).

Behavior therapy

Historical overview

Behavior therapy, a precursor to CBT, originated in the twentieth century, in the era of the scientific revolution, with a determined focus on working with behavior that was observable. It is often mistakenly believed that behaviorists denied the existence of internal mental phenomena, where in fact, they believed the mind was a "black box" full of unknowable and nonessential contents, making it useless to focus on (Dowd, 2004). Early behaviorists such as Pavlov, Skinner, Watson, and Jones instead examined antecedents and consequences of behaviors; that is, what happened before and what happens after a focused behavior that causes it to either be repeated, maintained, or extinguished. Watson's work on Little Albert (Watson & Rayner, 1920) showed how a seemingly benign object could be conditioned to evoke a fear response. In this case, a white rat was paired with a loud sound that scared an infant (called Little Albert) and after a few pairings, the presentation of the white rat was enough to make the child cry. In addition, when a fear-producing object was consistently paired with another benign object or stimulus, the fear response was generalized: In Albert's case, the fear-producing white rat was paired with other stimuli such as Santa Claus masks and dogs, which evoked the same crying response. In the clinical setting, for example, a veteran returning from war in the Middle East might be triggered by the smell of incense, a person wearing a hijab, or the sound of loud thunder, and consequently try to escape the situation. In this case, trauma from the war is associated with previously benign objects, sights, and smells, and causes the body to have the same fear response that was developed in the war zone. These kinds of generalizations most likely had an evolutionary basis, for example, a movement in the grass could be a predator, and hence all movement in the grass was suspect. While humans have evolved since the time we lived and roamed in the wild, there are parts of the brain that regulate fear and emotions that still respond in a more primitive fashion to feared objects and the appearance of threats (e.g., fear of the dark, fear of heights). To better understand how behavior is reproduced, generated, altered, or extinguished, behaviorists identified a number of *processes* that they believed caused change.

Operant conditioning: B.F. Skinner's work (1957) focused on reinforcers and punishers: Reinforcers increase the likelihood of a behavior increasing in frequency, and punishers decrease the chance of a behavior recurring. For example, every time a person with social anxiety cancels a social engagement, the relief that follows reinforces the likelihood that this behavior (avoidance of social interaction) will be repeated. Likewise, every time a child throws a temper tantrum in a restaurant and receives ice cream as an enticement to be quiet, the child learns that crying leads to a reward (ice cream and parental attention), which increases the chance of tantrums being repeated.

Systematic desensitization: Wolpe (1968) wrote that the bond between a feared object and anxiety can be lessened or weakened if a person engages in behaviors that reduce anxiety such as deep breathing, muscle relaxation, and eating while imagining these fearful situations. The process of reciprocal inhibition weakens the association between the object and the fear response, for example, inhibiting one behavior by eliciting another behavior. Behaviorists designed systematic desensitization as a technique that utilizes reciprocal inhibition to introduce a contrasting calming behavior that offsets the onset of anxiety. For example, if a person is afraid of spiders, every time one appears, the person is encouraged to start deep breathing and sip a glass of ice-cold soda. The response of deep breathing and drinking signals to the brain that there is nothing to be feared, and the conditioned response between fear and the spider is weakened. Behaviorists determined that one cannot have an anxious mind in a calm body.

Exposure: Exposure therapy, as the word implies, means exposing oneself to a feared object within a safe and controlled environment. Rather than reducing the anxiety, avoiding the feared object maintains it. Consequently, then, the opposite of this avoidance (i.e., facing the feared object) should bring the anxiety down. This mechanism is called habituation, as one is "habituated" to the object through repeated exposure. For example, through slow, repeated, gradual exposures to a spider—which may be feared for a variety of reasons—and the option to leave a room if the fear becomes overwhelming, a person will move closer and closer to the spider. In the process, the individual realizes that the expected outcome of being so close to the spider (e.g., being bit or poisoned) does not always take place. As a result, the belief that a spider is dangerous is disconfirmed as the fear is reduced. Later theorists (Craske et al., 2014) have suggested that the association between the object and fear does not weaken with exposure but rather is replaced by new learning between the object and emotion. This new learning (spider = neutral emotion) competes with the previously learned association (spider = fear) and eventually replaces that belief.

Exposure can be carried out in slow, incremental steps beginning with a nonanxious object or event and leading up to the most feared one. A "hierarchy of fears" is constructed where a client starts at point zero with respect to a stimulus with no fear associated with it, then builds up to what causes the most fear in a rating from 0 to 100 on the fear ladder. To continue with the spider example, zero on the fear hierarchy might be reading a children's book about a spider, and an extreme fear (100) might be holding a spider in one's hand. The exposure process would occur over a number of sessions, beginning with the client holding the children's book, then moving to looking at a picture of a spider in the book, looking at a live spider across the room, looking at a spider in a glass jar, and finally ending with the client being able to hold a spider in hand with minimal anxiety or fear. Prolonged exposure can also be applied to trauma work, where an individual is exposed to the highest level of the feared stimuli (i.e., flooding) or exposed to the feared stimuli for lengthy periods of time (in a safe environment). This process can be carried out in a real setting (in vivo), using the client's imagination, or even through virtual reality or simulations.

Exposure in conjunction with response prevention has been shown to be useful in treating obsessive compulsive disorder (OCD), PTSD, phobias, social anxiety, and agoraphobia (Foa & McLean et al., 2016; Rothbaum & Schwartz, 2002). An important component of all exposure-based therapies is the therapeutic relationship, albeit one in which the clinician educates the client about the rationale for the treatment, the cycle of avoidance, and the process of fear generalization. The normalization of avoidance is helpful to the client as well, since it shows how avoidance might work in the short term but actually interferes with the client's quality of life and desired goals. It is critical to help the client see the larger benefits of exposure therapy in terms of quality of life, rather than just focusing on symptom reduction.

Bridging behavior therapies to cognitive therapies

The history of behaviorism demonstrates its mechanistic qualities and emphasis, with little focus on what happens inside a person's mind apart from the triggers of certain behaviors. However, two behaviorists, Bandura (1969) and Meichenbaum (1977), bridged strict behaviorism with cognitive science by bringing attention to vicarious learning (through observation or modeling), intrinsic motivation, and the reproduction of learning via language and images. In his now-famous experiment with inflatable Bobo dolls, Bandura showed evidence of vicarious learning in adolescents through imitation and observation (Bandura et al., 1961). In the Bobo doll study, adolescents observed adults striking dolls and subsequently being praised for their aggressive behavior. The observation of this behavior, without receiving any overt reinforcement, increased the likelihood of adolescents striking the dolls. Bandura termed this social learning theory, reflecting that we can alter our behavior based on what we observe in a person we admire, or even a powerful character in a movie or a book. People can hear descriptions or explicit instructions (e.g., watching videos on YouTube) and learn new behavior, and that new behavior does not need to be explicitly rewarded or punished for a person to acquire it. For example, when working with parents of a child who is swearing, bullying others, and expressing negative biases toward a certain ethnic or racial group, a clinical social worker can use social learning theory to explain how children learn by observation, which can occur through television, social media, and observing others such as family members. Social learning theory also emphasizes "intrinsic motivation" that influences learning, contrasting it to older behavioral theories that focused on tangible reinforcements, including feelings of pride, accomplishment, and satisfaction that can motivate one to learn new behaviors and skills.

Bandura also explained why mastery of a task and pleasure in a task act as reinforcers as well, leading to an improved sense of self-efficacy. He used the term *triadic reciprocity* to describe the role of mood in how we interpret experiences and influence how we learn. This focus on the interpersonal and social was an important step in moving behavioral theories to the cognitive era.

Meichenbaum (1977) used his observation that children speak to themselves when performing a difficult task to show that changing one's "private speech" can lead to changes in external behavior. He developed stress inoculation training (SIT), where clients are taught to rehearse adaptive internal dialogue to perform new behaviors, thus increasing their self-efficacy in performing those behaviors. In addition to Bandura and Meichenbaum, thinkers of this era, such as Piaget, Chomsky, and their contemporaries, set the stage for a cognitive revolution in the field of psychotherapy. The expansion in the understanding of language structures, social learning, and findings supports the view that people can and want to change and that change is not always reactive. This was a stark contrast to the early deterministic psychoanalytic theories, and it enabled a newer understanding of psychological distress with models to address that distress.

Let us reexamine the case of Debbie, whom we discussed using psychodynamic therapies in Chapter 3. Here we have summarized Debbie's case again to demonstrate how a behavioral therapist might work with her:

> Debbie is an 18-year-old White cisgender female student at a local university who presents as a bright, engaging young woman. She was referred for symptoms of depression, a history of suicidal thoughts (no attempts), and poor health. Specifically, she has had a history of migraines and difficulties with coughing and breathing. The shortness of breath began when she was approximately 8 years old; at the time, the family doctor related it to stress. At age 12 her migraines and coughing episodes began, and though her migraines ceased at age 16, the coughing attacks continued, albeit sporadically. At times, the coughing affects her voice so that she can barely speak. Debbie was reluctant to see a therapist, just as she had been reluctant to see physicians about her symptoms, feeling that they do not listen to or believe her.

Debbie's father, who is in his late forties, has been ill since she was six with a chronic lung disease. When Debbie was ten, her father also suffered some visual damage and slight paralysis. His illness is cyclical and requires the family to relocate closer to doctors, treatment, and so on. Debbie described her mother as an "obsessive cleaner" and noted that her cleaning behavior is quite compulsive, involving ritualistic cleaning that consumes all of her time. Debbie is quite critical of her mother, and does report a close relationship with her brother, who is eighteen months her senior. However, their relationship has been strained recently, as the brother tends to side with the mother in family arguments. Debbie describes feeling closer to her father and his side of the family, though that closeness has also been strained due to increasing family arguments.

Increased family conflicts appear to relate to Debbie's increasing depression and "unfriendliness." Debbie describes some of these conflicts as due to problems with friends of her father. She believes her father is having an affair with the wife of one of these friends, a woman Debbie has been close to in the past. Debbie also reports that this woman's husband has made sexual advances to her that she has rebuffed. She feels her family does not believe her reports, as they continue to plan dinners with this couple and expect Debbie to care for their children—which places her in regular contact with both the husband and the wife. Debbie's leaving home to attend college was her attempt to alleviate her problems; however, her symptoms have increased rather than decreased since moving to this city.

A behavior therapist would assess Debbie's level of depression, suicidal ideation, and reportedly poor health and take a case history. Here, the therapist is looking for triggers for behaviors, the actual behaviors, what follows the behaviors, whether there are any behavioral skill deficits, and whether there are any negative consequences of the behaviors (in this case, avoidance of social contact and her "unfriendliness"). The behavior therapist would then ask Debbie to explain which of the issues she is presently experiencing that she would like to address first. Hypothetically, if Debbie chooses her depression, the therapist will share with her a conceptualization of why Debbie might be experiencing depression. This conceptualization is based on identifying the behaviors that precede her low mood and the reinforcers that follow this low mood.

If Debbie agrees that she can understand and work with this conceptualization, the work will start. The behavior therapist would ask some questions to gather information: When does Debbie feel more depressed? When does she feel less depressed? What is she doing at the time of her low mood? What are the behaviors of others around her at those times? Debbie would then identify positive reinforcers that may occur when she withdraws and avoids others (e.g., relief from anxiety, improved mood, or perhaps getting attention from her parents). Debbie and the therapist could also identify the negative reinforcers when she withdraws, such as increased conflict within the family. The maintenance factors for her depression could be the lack of exposure to situations that could provide her with a sense of accomplishment, mastery, or pleasure. The work would involve helping Debbie see the connection between behavior and mood states, including helping her schedule activities that give her pleasure and a sense of mastery each day.

Debbie and her therapist would then draw up reinforcement schedules to keep Debbie motivated to engage in these activities. So, if Debbie attends one lecture a day (something she finds unpleasurable), she can then browse Instagram for thirty minutes; if she has lunch at the cafeteria for the entire week (something she has been avoiding), she can then go to the movies (if this is something that she likes) or not go home that weekend (if this is something she has been dreading). The therapist would also work on Debbie's assertiveness skills around saying "no" to her parents when they force her to be with their friends. The therapist would practice this in the sessions with her, give her homework tasks such as practicing her assertiveness skills at school or with friends, and work on feedback she receives from the environment (and the therapist) until she feels more confident saying no to her parents when they invite her to visit their friends. This self-efficacy, behavior skills training, exposure, and opportunities to experience mastery and pleasure should help Debbie slowly overcome her depression.

Critique

The problem with a strictly behavioral approach is that it ignores the role of affect, as well as systemic factors. For example, a behavior therapist would not address the issue that Debbie's father's friend is making unwanted advances towards her and all the people and situations that work to ignore or repress that reality. In addition, a strictly behavioral approach would not address the impact of growing up in a household where Debbie's mother had mental health issues, and her father was chronically ill. Debbie undoubtedly experienced helplessness around her inability to impact the family system and be valued other than through the attention of somatic distress. She was continually placed in the position of being associated with the person who was making unwanted advances toward her, which would increase her sense of isolation and loss of control. Behavior therapy does not consider Debbie's world where she has escaped an impoverished environment by going to college but has not yet learned how to thrive (rather than merely survive) and found what makes her happy.

Cognitive therapies

Historical overview

Currently, cognitive therapy is usually combined with behavior therapy, hence the label of CBT. However, historically, before the two were combined, theorists such as Albert Ellis (1962) and Aaron Beck (1979) began focusing primarily on cognitions. Their approach is sometimes referred to as second-wave CBT. Ellis and Beck had some similarities and a few key differences: They were both trained in humanistic and psychodynamic therapies but found themselves focusing more on the current aspects of a client's life, the concept of "self," and the belief that we are disturbed not so much by events but by how we view these events. They both believed that the therapist is not a passive participant in the therapeutic work, but a more active contributor, partner, and even a teacher. Although they did not discount developmental experiences in psychopathology, their work focused on cognitions and underlying beliefs and how they influenced emotions and behaviors. Both believed that a modification of these cognitive processes could lead to a more direct route to symptom alleviation and adaptive functioning.

Ellis (Ellis, 1989; Ellis & Dryden, 2007) in particular was impatient with the slow process of psychoanalysis and felt he could move things along more quickly by focusing on dysfunctional thoughts that seemed to lead to problematic behaviors. As a result, he developed Rational Emotive Therapy (RET), which was later changed to Rational Emotive Behavior Therapy (REBT). Rational Emotive Therapy emphasized a linear direction from thoughts to affect behavior, with thoughts requiring primary intervention. Ellis believed that humans have a predisposition to think irrationally, and in a way that contradicts good sense. These irrational thoughts arise from absolutist beliefs such as "I *must* always be loved," "I *should* be successful at everything I do," "My life *should* always be stress-free," "I *must* never fail," and so on. Ellis (2003) termed these *musts* and *shoulds* as the "tyranny of the shoulds," which set people up to fail. Because these absolute statements are impossible to achieve, this leads people to magnify their importance and "catastrophize" and "awfulize." When people catastrophize, they exaggerate the importance of an event and predict the worst possible outcome were the event to happen, leading to low mood, anxiety, and stress. Awfulizing refers to the tendency to focus on and amplify the negative aspects of a situation, so that things are just not bad but also horrible and the worst they could possibly be.

Ellis advocated for a forceful, vigorous disputing of a client's irrational beliefs by working with clients to show that when unpleasant incidents occur, clients have a *choice* to either sink into self-pity, self-blame, despair, or inaction (Ellis et al., 2010). He posited that were clients to think rationally, they would see that they have a choice to be more adaptive and self-serving. Ellis was deeply influenced by the Greek stoic philosopher Epictetus, who said that "it is not what happens to you, but how you react to things, that matters." He would show clients that they can react with calm rationality and action, changing their beliefs about situations and self, and this can make them feel better, giving their lives a different trajectory. Rational Emotive Behavior Therapy has at its base a model of disputing that Ellis termed *ABCDEF*, where A stands for *adversity/antecedent/activating event*, B stands for the irrational *belief* about the adversity, C is the emotional or behavioral *consequence*, D stands for *disputing the belief*, E is the *effective new belief*, and F is the new *feeling*. To disrupt the ABC sequence that leads to low mood states, interrupting the sequence with D and E could lead to new feeling states.

Aaron T. Beck (1979, 1993) was trained as a medical doctor and a psychoanalyst. In his project exploring the differences in the dreams of clients who were depressed and those that were not, he noticed that the dreams of his depressed clients were characterized by hopelessness, deprivation, and disappointment, as was their reality. This was different from a more psychoanalytic explanation of depression related to hostility and rage turned inward (directed at the person themselves). He noted that by not addressing cognitions actively (as contrasted with PDT) we are missing an opportunity to understand clients' ways of processing information that keep them depressed and thereby offering them ways to feel better and engage in more adaptive behaviors.

The core of Beck's CBT is that cognition (i.e., automatic thoughts and beliefs) mediates the relationship between situations and one's emotional/behavioral reactions. While his early focus was on the linear direction of thoughts leading to emotions and behaviors, his later work emphasized the bidirectional impact of affects, cognitions, and behavior. In clients who are depressed, these automatic cognitions are often pessimistic, and lead them to perceive themselves, the world, and the future to be negative (i.e., the negative triad). Negative automatic thoughts such as "I can't stand it!" or "It's awful that this happened" arise from rigid beliefs formed over a person's lifetime and give us information about how people think implicitly about themselves. People usually do not question these ideas about themselves and instead consider them real and valid. These beliefs, such as "I am bad and therefore unlovable," may have been developmentally formed, but they function in later life to filter out evidence that stands contrary to these beliefs while allowing in evidence that reinforces these beliefs, thereby strengthening them.

The work of the CBT therapist is to help shake these beliefs by helping clients attend to evidence that contradicts these beliefs that they have been filtering out, along with showing clients how dysfunctional these beliefs are and how they affect their moods and functioning. Once clients can see a shift in mood states following a shift in their beliefs, they are then taught to be experts in their own dysfunctional thoughts, and in correcting them (Beck & Dozois, 2011; Beck 2020).

For a more detailed historical evolution of cognitive therapy, we refer our readers to our chapter on utilizing CBT interventions in psychodynamic practice (Northcut et al., 2016) as well as numerous other resources (e.g., Beck, 2020; Dowd, 2004; Leahy, 2002; Tolin, 2024). The processes that underlie cognitive therapy are discussed next.

Cognitive distortions: While the term *cognitive distortion* is associated with Beck and his associates, we can also see this concept in Ellis's work, where he calls them *cognitive errors* or *erroneous thinking*. These are best described as thinking or information-processing errors that lead people to filter information in a way that negatively impacts their view of themselves, the world, or the future, ignoring any contradictory evidence or alternate explanations. Ellis helped clients rephrase these statements to remove the stress by using phrases such as "I will try to be successful" or "I would like to get the top grades in my class."

When clients experience depression, their negative filter is "tuned up" so that they see the world through this lens, leading them to behave in ways that reinforce these negative cognitions and keep the negative emotions in place. Beck identified some of these cognitive errors, including catastrophizing, all or none thinking, and personalization. For example, clients who are experiencing anxiety related to their bodies might hyperfocus on their bodily functions so that every little change is "catastrophized" as an oncoming heart attack or symptom of some serious illness, rather than thinking that the symptom might be indicative of anxiety rather than a serious illness. In this case, the client has a *confirmatory bias*. Clients who are experiencing depression might feel that they are unworthy or use all or none thinking, such as the belief that if they don't wake up at 8 a.m., then the whole day is wasted, or if they don't get a 4.0 GPA, then they are bad students (negative labeling). Some other cognitive distortions include *personalization* (assuming personal responsibility for events over which you have no control), *discounting the positive* (explaining away any positive event as unimportant or a coincidence), *mind-reading* (assuming you know what people are thinking about you), or *related predictive thinking* (where clients predict how things will go in the future, thus avoiding actions and behaviors that can cause a change in their behaviors and beliefs).

Schemas: The second-wave cognitive model rests on the premise that everyone has a set of beliefs or schemas that are developmental and cultural in their origins. These schemas become "the basic rules of life" through which individuals interpret events around them: that is, "stable organizational patterns of thought that form the basic framework for classifying and evaluating experience" (Freeman & Oster, 1998). However, these schemas can get activated and lead to the types of cognitive distortions we discussed in the previous section. For example, an adult client who experienced neglect and abandonment as a child may come to see himself as "unlovable" or "bad," which leads to behaviors that confirm this belief. All incoming stimuli are then "filtered" through this lens, and behaviors then follow that reinforce these schemas. Schemas are often cognitively coded as absolutes (e.g., "I am unlovable," "I do not deserve happiness," "People will always leave me") and are quite rigid and not easily amenable to change. Schemas influence what is paid attention to and, equally importantly, what is ignored or not paid attention to. Schemas also dictate what attributions or assumptions we make about events that happen to us and what meanings we assign to them (Dowd, 2004).

The concept of schemas developed from the work of psychologists Bartlett (1932) and Piaget (1976) represents a large epistemological shift in CBT. The field moved from merely assessing and focusing on irrational cognitions to examining the deep structures from which these cognitions develop. We see this shift as responsive to the need for a more complex understanding of the clients we serve. From a CBT perspective, the term *schema* is used to describe a relational blueprint through which we look at ourselves, the world, and the future, but it also has a broader connotation as it applies to various aspects of cognition. In more common use, schemas can refer to any cognitive framework, whereas CBT focuses specifically on early developed, core beliefs that shape psychological functioning.

From a broader social work perspective, schemas can also be seen as biases and assumptions inherent in people's minds that are culturally informed and reinforced by the dominant culture, or through prejudice. These include schemas related to gender, race, and communities that are marginalized due to rigid schemas that can reinforce systems of power and oppression. These schemas lead to Black and White thinking (such as that the concept of marriage exists only between two people of different sexes, that White people are genetically and inherently superior to folx of color, or that men are inherently valuable to women), and people with power often behave in ways that reinforce these schemas. Holding certain beliefs about a certain set of people prevents us from accommodating new information about them and leads us to selectively process information that reinforces the schema (also called *confirmation bias*). Prejudice also reinforces behaviors that uphold these schemas and maintain these stereotypes. As mentioned earlier, schemas are resistant to change. We want readers to reflect on the skills from behavioral therapy and cognitive work discussed above that could be useful to agitate racial or gender stereotypes and prejudices.

Young and colleagues (2003) identified five broad groups of early maladaptive schemas based on this emphasis and understanding of schemas. These schemas of *unmet needs* are related to (a) disconnection/rejection, (b) impaired autonomy or performance, (c) impaired limits, (d) other-directedness, and (e) over-vigilance/inhibition. Schemas are also associated with ways of coping and feeling (called *schema modes*) that may be temporary states of mind: for example, an "angry child" mode where one feels unsupported, bitter, and feels like screaming; or a "punitive parent" mode where one feels the need to be punished for every little mistake. In some clients, such as those with personality disorders, these modes might be rigid or split off from the self. The work of schema-focused therapy focuses on identifying the protective aspects of the schema and the unhealthy aspects, conducting a dialogue between these two sides to heighten emotions, and testing the validity of these schemas. Some of the techniques used in this process involve experiential and imagery work, including role-playing, modeling, testing new behaviors, and using flash cards or keeping a diary between sessions to track progress. Unlike other CBT work, schema-focused work emphasizes therapeutic relationship as healing. The therapeutic relationship is seen to provide clients with a safe environment in which clients can learn ways to get their needs fulfilled in the real world in an effective manner. This "limited reparenting" technique in schema-focused therapy, emphasizing utilizing the therapeutic relationship for corrective emotional experience, reminds us of object relations work and transference analysis from PDT.

To understand how the process of CBT might look, let us explore this with the previously discussed example of Debbie. If Debbie had presented to her school counseling center with symptoms of depression, a history of suicidal thoughts (no attempts), and poor health, a second-wave CBT therapist might proceed to assess her level of functioning using structured tools (e.g., using Beck's depression inventory, BDI) to establish a baseline of how depressed she is now. Then, in collaboration with Debbie, the therapist would clarify goals for treatment; this is where Debbie would choose whether she would like to work on her migraine management, her depression, or something else.

In a CBT formulation, therapists work to establish what cognitions and behaviors keep the symptoms in place (i.e., maintain the symptoms), what cognitions mediate the client's response to the environment, and what emotions follow. Classically, as noted earlier, this is referred to as ABC, where A is the *antecedent* (what happens), B is the behavior that follows, and C is the *consequence* (emotional or behavioral). Thus, when Debbie goes to the cafeteria to get lunch and sees a classmate who ignores her and does not greet her (the antecedent), Debbie leaves the cafeteria without eating (behavior) and feeling deep shame and sadness (the emotion), which triggers her core schemas around being unlovable, being a failure, or not being good enough (the consequence).

Another important factor in all CBT formulations is understanding what "maintains" the symptoms of depression (Moorey, 2010). This includes cognitive patterns (e.g., automatic negative thoughts, rumination, self-depreciatory talk), behavioral patterns (e.g., unhelpful behaviors such as withdrawal and avoidance), and physical states (e.g., feeling tired, drowsy, low energy) that contribute to the maintenance of symptoms. If Debbie chooses to work on her depression, the first step is *psychoeducation*: explaining to her the cognitive model of depression and especially the cycle that maintains it (Grills et al., 2023). This step helps to "demystify" the problem and give her hope and a sense of agency and control.

The next step would be to establish Debbie's daily routine while she is at college by creating a record of her activity during the day. Clients who are depressed are often not engaging in activities and experiences that can change/challenge their depressive cognitions and/or give them opportunities for positive experiences that can disrupt negative ruminations. *Behavioral activation* early in the treatment of depression has been shown to contribute greatly to the change process.

Based on the chart of her daily routine, Debbie and the therapist will then work to establish an *activity schedule.* This chart ensures that there are enough activities in her day that bring a sense of pleasure and the mastery/accomplishment that has been missing in her life due to the depression. The chart breaks up each day to avoid either a full day of overwhelming tasks or no plans at all and helps to remove the decision-making aspect of what to do next, which can be paralyzing. Looking at the daily chart can also help to reveal the cognitions that get in the way of achieving goals or becoming activated to accomplish tasks.

Another way the therapist can help Debbie uncover her self-defeating cognitions is to ask her to keep a *daily thought record.* This thought record is for Debbie to jot down her thoughts as soon as a negative event occurs, noting the antecedent of the incident, the emotions that follow the incident, and what thoughts were running through her mind at the time. The therapist can also ask Debbie to rate her belief in the thought from 1 to 100, and to rate the strength of the emotion from 1 to 100. For example, when Debbie went to the cafeteria to get lunch and saw her classmate there who ignored her and did not greet her, Debbie felt deep shame and sadness and left the cafeteria without eating. She went back to her room and lay down, then was hungry and unable to sleep but was too ashamed to go to the cafeteria to get anything. She lay alone in her room for five hours, tossing and turning, ruminating and hating herself for not having the energy or courage to go out. In this example, the therapist would ask Debbie to record the thoughts that come into her mind before the shame and after her friend ignored her, then rate her belief in these thoughts.

Once Debbie and the therapist have identified the ABC of the sequelae of events, the automatic thoughts associated with an unpleasant event, and a rating of Debbie's belief in the thoughts, they can begin the process of testing Debbie's belief in these thoughts through a process of *guided discovery.* The therapist would ask questions to test these beliefs and said questions would involve determining evidence for and against the belief, alternate explanations for the behavior, and what Debbie would tell a friend who was undergoing the same experience (double standards). Here, the therapist is trying to highlight the dysfunctional thought patterns. In Debbie's example, she is demonstrating Black-and-White thinking and overgeneralizing ("My friend ignored me, and I am not worthy of friendship or love from anyone") and personalization ("My friend ignored me because of who I am or something I have done"). The therapist would ask Debbie if there was evidence that the friend was avoiding her and if there could be an alternate explanation for her friend's behavior. If Debbie was talking to another friend who shared a similar incident, what would Debbie say to her friend?

Debbie's CBT therapist can also use the *downward arrow technique* to get to the core schemas by asking questions such as "[i]f that were true, what would that mean?," "[i]f that were true, what does it say about you?," or "[i]f that were true, what does it say about the future?" For example, the therapist could ask Debbie: "Your friend not acknowledging you means what?" Debbie would respond that the friend does not like her. The therapist would then ask: "If that were true, what does it mean?," to which Debbie would respond that she will never have any friends in her life (negative automatic thought). The therapist could then repeat the "If that was true, what does that mean?" question, again and again to get to an absolute statement from Debbie, such as "it would mean I am unlovable." Once the core schema has been identified in this manner and Debbie is able to identify the dysfunctional thought patterns, then the experiential part of the work will begin.

Debbie and the therapist would identify whether Debbie has a social skill deficit or whether she is avoiding social interactions that could give her positive experiences of acceptance and validation. If Debbie's actions result from a social skill deficit, then social *skills training* would be carried out in the session via *role-play* and *modeling*. The therapist would ask Debbie to gradually test these newly learned skills through *exposure* to lower-risk situations, then processing the feedback she receives from them, correcting errors, and finally moving to social situations that she considers higher risk. At set points, the BDI would be administered to show Debbie's improvement in her depression and reinforce the changes she is making in her life. Similarly, if social avoidance is the issue, then exposure to social situations in a graduated fashion would be carried out. The therapist should maintain a warm, open, collaborative relationship with Debbie throughout, remaining open to feedback and any changes in the therapeutic journey that might be needed. The therapist would continue to help Debbie consolidate what she has learned, test her understanding of the "why" of her symptoms, and most importantly, be prepared for setbacks and relapses. Informing clients about setbacks and relapses is an important part of all CBT therapies, where clients are taught to identify signs of old patterns of thinking and behavior that indicate the beginning of another depressive episode and create a clear plan for what to do in those situations.

Critique

Second-wave CBT was a step forward in addressing the internal world of the client but falls short in addressing the external context the client lives in. It disregards the effects of social-environmental factors such as poverty, ableism, homophobia, and racism on neurobiology and how these factors affect our internal working models and the schemas through which we view the world and ourselves. We will discuss this further in a later section.

The third wave of CBT

The third wave of CBT evolved as a response to criticism about CBT being too mechanistic and problem-focused. Addressing this criticism meant reimagining and elucidating CBT as a philosophical imagining of the human experience rather than a technical package of skills. In addition, a sharp critique of CBT was the assumption that the world exists independently of the individual, and aligning to this "reality" was healthy, and symptoms of distress were a "cognitive distortion." However, symptoms do not always arise out of cognitive distortions. Symptoms of depression can be an adaptive response to a reality of the world that is embroiled in wars, genocide, and on a path to climate disaster. They can also be related to medical issues, side effects of medications, chemical imbalances that could be traced to genetic factors, and so on. Similarly, a client's substance misuse could be a coping strategy to racism in the workplace, rather than a product of cognitive distortions.

Early work by Vittorio Guidano (1987) emphasized the developmental aspect of cognitions and the mind as not merely an information processing system, but as actively constructing reality. Michael Mahoney further added to the understanding of schemas by classifying them into categories of core schemas and a defensive system of secondary schemas whose purpose is to defend the core schemas against rapid change that would threaten a person's sense of self and identity (Mahoney & Granvold, 2005). Mahoney was influenced by constructivists and integrated the idea of reality being a construction of the mind rather than an objective reality to be apprehended. He echoed the sentiments of the early PDT founders such as Pierre Janet in stating that there is a difference between narrative memory and the memory itself, and that people tell themselves stories that may not be true to their implicit memories (van der Kolk, 2003).

This new thinking emphasized that all of us construct our world through language, both internal and external, which shapes the idiosyncratic meaning we make of our interpersonal interactions and the world around us. This shift was monumental for the field of cognitive behavioral therapies, as it implied movement away from conscious cognitions and recognizing them as insufficient for change, along with examining core ways of knowing that are often implicit, nonverbal, and critical for change to a person's self-concept.

Acceptance and commitment therapy

One of the earliest therapies under third-wave CBT has been ACT developed by Stephen Hayes (Hayes et al., 1994, 1999, 2006). Acceptance and commitment therapy is based on relational frame theory (RFT) (Hayes et al., 2001), which rests on Skinner's work, along with that of Piaget, Chomsky, and other linguists. Relational frame theory posits that mental distress occurs as humans try to avoid negative thoughts and feelings, and that language helps us in this avoidance, which leads to maintenance of symptoms—for example, depression. One of the core outcomes expected from ACT is the development of psychological flexibility, which is the ability to be responsive to life's demands in creative and adaptive ways (Levin et al., 2012). It means not using avoidance to your detriment and being able to commit to moving in a goal-directed manner. Acceptance and commitment therapy uses six techniques or interventions to help people: *cognitive defusion*, which means noticing thoughts rather than being caught up in them (i.e., similar to the technique of mindfulness); *acceptance* of what is under your control and what is not and not being defensive; *self-as-context*, which is a process of pure awareness similar to the observing self; *being present in the moment* to perceive what is going on related to psychological flexibility; *orienting to values* to find direction and meaning in life; and *committing to actions* that are mindful and in the service of the values (Harris, 2019; Levin et al., 2012).

Acceptance and commitment therapy differs from second-wave CBT in not trying to change thoughts or emotions, but simply seeing them as they are, without assigning judgment (e.g., good, bad, ugly) to them. It does not attempt to alleviate symptoms and sees it as problematic that negative feelings and thoughts are labeled as symptoms (Jones-Smith, 2019). It emphasizes giving up avoidance and moving toward the values that are most important to the client, with the phrase "moving toward" implying action. In this way, ACT can also be seen as a form of (radical) behaviorism.

The core mantra of ACT involves taking a step toward one's values, observing the self-defeating talk, connecting to the transcendental self that is not fused with one's emotions and thoughts, and committing to action based on one's values to live a more vital and meaningful life. Avoidance in ACT is called *experiential avoidance*, as it stops clients from engaging in experiences that can change the story they tell themselves and keeps them from doing the things they want to live a fuller life. Cognitive fusion refers to believing the stories we tell ourselves about our behavior, for example, "I don't exercise because I'm lazy." Cognitive defusion involves separating the reason, urges, explanation, and emotional reasoning from the behavior; the real from the "not real." Clients are urged that instead of trying to change their feelings, sensations, and thoughts, they need to take actions that are in line with their values.

Over the past thirty years, ACT has accumulated a large amount of evidence through research supporting its use in treating anger management, pain management, anxiety, depression, and substance use issues. However, studies that support the efficacy of ACT have also been criticized on grounds of poor quality (Linardon et al., 2019; Öst, 2014). The most recent meta-analysis by Gloster et al. (2020) shows that ACT is more efficacious compared with no treatment and other forms of treatment but shows comparable efficacy to CBT as a treatment option.

Mindfulness-based therapies

The next set of therapies that come under the broad umbrella of the third wave of CBT are ones that center mindfulness. Mindfulness-based therapies are some of the most researched and practiced therapies in the past few decades, forming a kind of quiet revolution in the field of psychotherapy that has seismic impacts (Claessens, 2010). This move to centering mindfulness is a big departure from second-wave therapies, as there is no attempt to change thoughts, but rather to change the client's relationship with thoughts and emotions to manage reactivity to experiences. Mindfulness originates from Eastern Buddhist philosophy, and its essence involves awareness to the present moment and whatever thoughts and feelings come up (internal and external) deliberately and nonjudgmentally (Kabat-Zinn, 2003). The skill involved in mindfulness is decentering, which means loosening the association between thoughts and the perception that these thoughts are real. The role of the mindfulness practitioner is meta-cognitive and involves observing one's thoughts for what they are: transient and fleeting, rather than an objective representation of reality (Safran & Segal, 1996). Furthermore, mindfulness teaches us that unpleasant or unwanted thoughts are part of life, and that we are disturbed not so much from the content of these thoughts as from our responses to these thoughts. Emotional distress, then, arises either from avoidance of these thoughts or from active engagement with these thoughts that is perceived as real or fact (Tolin, 2024).

Thus, while mindfulness is seen as a large departure from second-wave CBT therapies, some elements remain constant: that the mind needs training in a didactic and experiential manner, and that avoidance and resistance keep symptoms in place. The mindfulness revolution in the field of psychotherapy has been led by Marsha Linehan's DBT (1993), Segal et al.'s (2018) MBCT, and ACT (Hayes et al., 1999), as discussed in the section above.

Mindfulness-based cognitive therapy was developed by Teasdale et al., (2000) to assist with relapse prevention in depressive disorders. They noted that the chances of relapse in a person who had two or more episodes of depressive disorder were 70–80% and that most clients reverted to their old patterns of thinking, which can lead to depression. Mindfulness can help these individuals break the pattern of rumination (i.e., "autopilot") by observing their thoughts and seeing how they are not facts.

In MBCT, there are two typical modes for the mind: the *being* mode and the *doing* mode. The *doing* mode is focused on outcomes, evaluating events in the past or future, and judging emotions as good or bad; there is nothing inherently good or bad in each mode. The doing mode motivates people to reach their goals and evaluate and reduce discrepancies between where they are and where they want to be. *Being* mode, meanwhile, is one of awareness to the present moment and not being in the future (e.g., things to do) or the past (e.g., what went wrong, what did I not do). The being zone is not a zone of not doing or apathy; however, if, while in the doing mode, the person exhibits compulsivity, rumination, or evaluative judgment, then the mind is brought back into the present awareness of the moment or the being mode through mindfulness. Unfortunately, clients may feel they are "failing" at mindfulness because of the compulsivity of the doing mode, which prevents them from staying in the being mode.

For depressed people who already feel that they are failing in many, if not all, areas of their lives, this emphasis on being—which they have difficulty maintaining—can feel like another criticism and set them up for failure. As a result, they feel they do not have a choice in feeling differently or doing things differently. This leaves them in a state of frustration, which then exacerbates their low mood and feeling of being unable to make any changes.

Mindfulness is quite powerful because inherent in the pause of rumination is a choice: for clients to engage differently with their thoughts and feelings, leading to different choices they make in their lives. The therapist's job is to educate the client that mindfulness is not about "doing it right" but about developing the "muscle" or habit of bringing the mind back to the present. Engaging in the practice of repeatedly bringing the mind back to the present will then bring relief even when the person feels unable to do so in other areas of their life.

A typical MBCT training consists of eight sessions presented in a didactic-experiential manner. The first session centers on attention and awareness, while subsequent sessions attend to breathing and focusing on somatic sensations, the "wandering mind," the use of breath to stay in the present, the connection between thoughts and emotions, allowing all thoughts, learning ways to pause and react, and taking care of oneself (Lee & Cho, 2021). Outcome studies of MBCT have shown that it prevents relapses in cases of recurrent depression for up to sixty weeks (Kuyken et al., 2016). Long-term mindfulness practice has also been shown to create changes in brain chemistry and structure, leading to better emotional regulation and emotional processing (Davidson, 2003; Davidson & Begley, 2012; Desbordes et al., 2012; Hölzel et al., 2011; Tang et al., 2015).

Dialectical behavior therapy was initially developed by Marsha Linehan (1987) to help clients with Borderline Personality Disorder and those who were self-harming. In common with other third-wave CB therapies, DBT focuses on accepting what is addressing psychological inflexibility, and creating unique ways to relate to emotional experiences (Dobson & Kazantzis, 2024). Dialectical behavior therapy emphasizes the importance of meaning making and mindfulness, as well as accepting what is not under your control. Dialectical behavior therapy believes that clients' difficulties arise out of both their individual learning histories (which validate maladaptive responses) and biological tendencies. It rests on the basic premise of stability and change, confrontation versus support, and reflection versus action, and posits that these two opposing states (dialectic) can be true at the same time. Some practitioners refer to this basic ideology of acceptance and change existing together as a "yes and ...." For example, this might mean validating a client's low mood *and* asking them to engage in some physical activity, validating that social interactions can be fear-inducing for a client, *and* encouraging them to walk into a social situation to overcome this hurdle. This connects to the concept of psychological flexibility, which is seen as a central change process in all third-wave CBTs, where clients tolerate difficult emotions, adapt to difficult situations, and choose actions that align with their values.

Dialectical behavior therapy is a modular approach that, at the basic levels, teaches four modules: mindfulness (including acceptance and change), distress tolerance, emotional regulation, and interpersonal effectiveness. Each module includes handouts with engaging acronyms that teach easy heuristics to help clients remember the skills, modeling and in-session practice, and support during and outside of sessions. Support takes many forms in DBT, including groups to practice and learn skills, an individual therapist to support clients and teach them how to apply these skills, and telephone coaching from an individual therapist between sessions. The therapist's stance is said to be a benevolent, demanding stance; the therapist admits to mistakes, models flexibility and compassion, and has an irreverent yet warm style. This attitudinal difference in the therapist is relevant because, in second-wave CBT, the therapist's style was perceived by some clients as invalidating their experiences and not supportive enough when their distress was high (Leahy, 2008). Third-wave therapies, in contrast, shift to a more humanistic stance.

The efficacy of DBT has been shown across a wide range of disorders, both nationally and internationally, including borderline PD, complex PTSD, substance use, depression, and anxiety. It is widely used in schools as a prophylactic treatment and a wellness initiative. In addition, as a response to changes in the field of diagnosis (discussed later in this chapter) and recognition of the need to respond to clients presenting with overcontrolled emotionality (rather than emotional dysregulation), a more recent development in DBT has been radically open DBT (RODBT). Lynch (2018) has been credited with moving DBT in this direction, where clients present with problems such as social isolation, perfectionism, autism, OCD, and more generally problems with social functioning and forming warm interpersonal bonds. Radically open DBT rests on radical openness, that is, actively seeking and being open to the things one wants to avoid with the aim of learning by challenging one's beliefs. Its focus is on social connectedness and social skills. Radically open DBT has shown efficacy in anorexia and chronic depression, in adults as well as adolescents (Gilbert & Codd, 2022; Isaksson et al., 2021; Little & Codd, 2020).

An integrative example of third-wave CBT

Let us examine the case of Debbie, discussed earlier, from a third-wave CBT perspective. Earlier, we said that certain ideas cut across third-wave CBT approaches, such as living a life aligned with values, mindfulness, and psychological flexibility. In this example, we will try to approach Debbie's care from a generic third-wave perspective rather than using a specific third-wave CBT theory to show the overlap between the three approaches—ACT, MBCT, and DBT—discussed above.

After carrying out an initial assessment and case formulation, Debbie would be introduced to the concept of mindfulness. Debbie and her therapist will practice mindfulness in session and address Debbie's questions until she begins to learn the process of observing her own thoughts and feelings in the moment. The next step would be to help Debbie understand her values and what stands in the way of living her life led by these values. The therapist can also work with cognitive defusion strategies to help Debbie see that she has a choice in responding to thoughts and feelings, rather than every emotion needing to be followed by an action or response.

Debbie can then look objectively at how her avoidance of conflict and low moods take her away from living the life she wants. She would then be helped to see the cost of avoidance and her current ways of coping that interfere with living a life led by her values. The therapist can help her hold the dialectic of "my life is terrible and full of sorrow, *and* I can do something to change it." She would be encouraged to do experiential exercises and expose herself to new experiences that lead her closer to the life she wants to lead. She would also be taught emotional regulation skills that would allow her to distance herself from strong urges or behaviors, such as anger, hopelessness, and suicidal ideation, that she has experienced in the past. She and the therapist would then reflect on the success and challenges of these experiential exercises to build a broader and more flexible repertoire of skills to overcome cognitive fusion, avoidance, and inflexibility (Bloy et al., 2011).

Empirical evidence

A robust record of published data that supports CBT's efficacy across populations and disorders (Butler et al., 2006; Hoffman et al., 2024; Hollon & Beck, 2013) combined with its cost efficacy and extensive marketing have contributed to a boom in provider support. Some disorders for which CBT is understood to be superior to other treatments include anxiety disorders, depression, bulimia, OCD, and social functioning. Many of these studies are randomized controlled trials (RCTs), which are the gold standard in research, as well as meta-analysis and replication studies that show the efficacy of CBT. However, the problems with meta-analysis can be significant, such as the inclusion of poor-quality studies, inadequate control groups, estimation of strong effects due to publication bias, and small sample size when inclusion criteria are specific (Cuijpers et al., 2010). For example, in their meta-analysis of CBT for adult depression, Cuijpers et al. (2013) found no indication of CBT's superiority compared to other therapies (e.g., IPT, supportive, psychodynamic), including pharmacological treatments. What was clear, however, was that medication plus therapy is better than medication alone. CBT and other therapies, such as IPT, have been shown to have a preventive aspect as well, such as in improving social and work functioning and delaying the onset of initial cases of depression (van Zoonen et al., 2014).

Anxiety disorders—more specifically, Generalized Anxiety Disorder (GAD), OCD, and Acute Stress Disorders—respond well to CBT compared to treatment as usual (TAU) or other psychotherapeutic therapies, such as supportive and dynamic therapies (Carpenter et al., 2018). Remission rates were about 50%, and clients saw gains even after therapy was discontinued. What is important to mention is that most studies did not include dropouts in the analysis, and as noted earlier, there was a strong publication bias. For meta-analysis, this means that studies with more positive results could have been chosen for inclusion or that studies with negative or similar findings to TAU were not included. Bulimia Nervosa and binge eating disorder are also a subset of eating disorders that respond well to CBT (Fairburn et al., 2015). One of the reasons for this could be that CBT-enhanced, for eating disorders, focuses on distress tolerance and affect management, as well as management of interpersonal distress. Newman et al. (2022) have cautioned that when examining studies comparing different treatment methods, it is important to center on what the focus of treatment is; for example, when the focus is on only eating behavior (i.e., the symptom), then both CBT and PDT have the same remission rates.

The field of social work and other behavioral health professions have been greatly impacted by the movement toward empirically supported therapies (EST) and evidence-based practice (EBP) in the training of practitioners, as well as by the methods used in clinical practice. CBT is an intervention that is often suggested for clients, as the empirical evidence for CBT is understood to be evidence-based and, therefore, superior to other forms of therapy. Evidence-based practice and EST are sometimes used interchangeably, contributing to confusion in the selection and application of clinical models (Drisko & Friedman, 2019). This confusion limits attention to client choices and values and prevents attention to diversity factors in treatment planning since EST does not consider client values. In addition, this gives power to the treatment providers rather than the client in determining the best choice of treatment. Additionally, under the guise of EBP, ESTs are being pushed, limiting choice, self-determination, dignity, and client worth, and putting into question the provider's competence, thus going against the values of the National Association of Social Workers (NASW).

Critique of cognitive behavioral therapies

Research on CBTs for most mental health issues shows significant positive outcomes. What this research fails to report, however, is the large number of dropouts from prolonged exposure therapies and that many people with PTSD still report symptoms after treatment (Banducci et al., 2023).

The research has also still not been critically examined to highlight concerns such as lack of racial and ethnic diversity in the samples, narrow diagnostic criteria, publication bias, research bias, and marketing small effect sizes as indicative of superiority, which would not lead to reliable changes or remission of symptoms (Wampold et al., 2017). Furthermore, there is not enough talk in the field about the effect of reinforcement-based strategies such as applied behavior analysis (ABA) and the reinforcement strategies used in most—if not all—weight-loss programs and apps that cause more harm in the long term than the benefits promised (Eikey, 2021).

A question that often comes up in our teaching social work—a field that emphasizes looking at the person-in-their-environment—is that if behavior principles are so consistent, can they be applied to any person irrespective of "context" (say, the person's cultural or religious background), and do these variables have any impact on the delivery of behavioral interventions? Behavior therapy has recognized this inherent logical flaw in its philosophy and could resolve it by either classifying itself as a set of skills rather than a theory or finding a way to respond to context. This critique has given impetus for the field to grow and define itself in contextual terms, as explained in the previous section on third-wave CBT.

There is little CBT research literature on how cultural differences are handled in therapeutic relationships, and most of this research recommends altering the modules or including family members in the treatment. There is often an assumption that CBT is value-neutral, which can even be stretched to the idea that CBT is color-blind. Huey Jr. et al. (2023) pointed out that very few studies focus on training clinicians to provide culturally tailored CBT and that, in fact, no studies showed whether this training, when provided, would lead to better client engagement or outcomes. Thus, the assumptions of value neutrality combined with the lack of training for clinicians to recognize either their own racial and cultural biases or systemic racism has been an ongoing issue in the practice of CBT.

Unlike the field of social work, where the work and conversation have been aimed at those oppressed and discriminated against by society, the field of clinical psychology has more recently begun talking about interpersonal stigma and structural stigma (Dovidio et al., 2011; Hatzenbuehler, 2017; Hebl & Heatherton, 1998; Link & Phelan, 2013). In referring to oppressed populations, CBT does not have a good record with individuals who identify as sexual or gender minorities. Behavior therapy interventions such as "conversion therapy" remain in use in parts of America and the world, even though they are not endorsed by the Association for Behavioral and Cognitive therapies. The conversation around queer bullying and racism has often led to interventions at the individual level (e.g., coping skills, assertiveness skills, engaging in community-level work, and advocacy). Racism is often spoken about as "occurring outside the therapy room," but implicit racism can also show up in the therapy room, where racist trauma can be enacted in the therapist–client dyad. In the therapy room, if the solution for internalized racism or symptoms of racial trauma that a client is sharing is evidence-based therapy, then we are locating solutions to systemic issues in the client and missing essential contextual factors. There is work that therapists need to do outside the therapy room as well to advocate for anti-racism in the communities they work in. Similarly, if we consider the example of a victim of date rape, if the therapist is only conducting work on PTSD symptoms and not acknowledging a system where the perpetrator of the rape can still walk free without punishment, then that therapist is acting complicity with power structures that harm clients. CBT therapists need to reckon with themselves and their professional organizations about addressing systemic issues that affect their clients. Addressing schemas around worth and hopelessness may actually be cruel for clients who are unhoused and do not know where their next meal is coming from. It also seems ironic to ask clients to do the work to heal from the trauma that was "caused'" by systemic forces that they could not control, such as forced migration and war.

There has been a call for CBT practitioners to have more "structural competency" (Metzl & Hansen, 2014), and even encouraging practitioners toward advocacy, lobbying, giving public statements, and organizing against structural discrimination (Ahuvia & Schleider, 2023). While this broad information is helpful, it still does not inform therapists—whether they are practicing CBT or any other modality—how to deal with their own biases and those of their clients, and how these biases influence the work they do aside from discussing microaggressions and an increase in subsequent dropouts. The therapeutic alliance we speak of in many places in this book is a kind of dance—a dance of awareness, communication, avoidance and acknowledgment, and techniques. In sessions, if we don't acknowledge the recent rollback of laws and policies that protect the rights of oppressed populations such as anti-trans legislation or the Dobbs ruling allowing states to prohibit abortions, then the potential for causing harm increases.

CBT theories have more recently started recognizing how ableism is woven into the structure of these theories, leading to a deficit-based approach to working with people with disabilities (PWD). CBT theories have faced criticism of radical behaviorism, which is the basis of applied behavior analysis that ABA can be traumatic for individuals with autism (Anderson, 2023). The reasons for that are the use of punishment and the repetitive nature of the tasks children are given to conform to neurotypical standards. The concept of intersectionality, including with PWD who are also racial or gender minorities, has also been ignored by the field. Lastly, the disproportionate burden that PWDs have to face (e.g., financial or the effort needed) in navigating complex medical systems still remains largely unacknowledged by the field (Olkin, 2017). As briefly mentioned earlier, a related concept is that of CBT-powered apps and ideas that rule the field of "weight loss" and are based on the premise that weight loss and gain are based on an individual's mindset, and that changing this can lead to weight loss. However, what is talked about less often is that at the end of the day, any measuring and calorie counting is calorie restriction and intake limitation, while the program ignores the social determinants of weight gain and the individual's access to healthy foods. These programs further ignore weight stigma in society and encourage disordered eating, shame, guilt, low self-esteem, and an increase in mental health issues such as depression and anxiety (Levinson et al., 2023).

Current innovations

In this section, we will discuss newer directions in the field of CBT at both the theoretical and practice levels that address some of the criticisms of CBT shared in this chapter. Our hope is to pave the way for more inclusive, targeted, responsive, integrative approaches that have the potential to reimagine clinical practice, and to offer increased access to services by decreasing barriers of cost, reach, and stigma.

Transdiagnostic and transtheoretical approaches as a precursor and support for integration

One of the strengths of CBT has been that its efficacy has been shown for various disorders in RCTs. However, the problem with this claim is that in the real world, clients presenting with only one disorder are very rare.

This means that the population included in RCTs does not mimic the real world, leading to questions about the applicability and generalizability of the research and its claim to successful outcomes. As a response, CBT and the field of psychological sciences has been moving away from diagnosing specific interventions to a broader understanding of commonalities that cut across diagnoses. The understanding is that there are certain common mechanisms that either underpin, maintain, or are a risk factor for more than one disorder. These transdiagnostic mechanisms are found in the domain of emotions, behaviors, imagery, thinking, reasoning, and attention. For example, emotional dysregulation might underlie a Borderline Personality Disorder profile as well as a mood-related disorder; or, distorted cognitions might underlie social anxiety as well as perfectionism (Kennedy & Barlow, 2018). The transdiagnostic treatment principles are broadly focused enough to allow therapists to modify their styles to suit the needs of clients without giving up their theoretical allegiances to particular schools of therapy.

For clinicians, this means that they can learn interventions that address a range of conditions rather than a single diagnostic entity. For example, clinicians learn affective regulation techniques and cognitive restructuring to address dysregulation or maladaptive cognitions that are seen in both anxiety and depression. Each intervention has a number of psychoeducational modules from which therapists can choose therapeutic interventions that best suit individual clients and provide a framework for understanding emotions (Barlow et al., 2017). One example of transdiagnostic work is the unified protocol developed for emotional disorders. This protocol includes emotion-focused work and CBT interventions focused on temperament or personality dimension of neuroticism that underly both anxiety disorders and depression. The five core modules that clinicians receive training on are (1) mindful emotion awareness, (2) cognitive flexibility, (3) identifying and preventing patterns of emotional avoidance, (4) increasing awareness and tolerance of physical sensations related to emotions, and (5) emotion-focused exposures, both situational and interoceptive.

Research on transdiagnostic treatment for disorders is still new, promising, and evolving to be more integrative. A recent study shines light on hope as a transdiagnostic mechanism of change involving both the cognitive and the emotional mechanisms in the treatment of anxiety disorders. Hope mediates the pathway between treatment and changes in anxiety (Gallagher et al., 2020). Inclusion of hope, which is traditionally thought of as a common factor, is meaningful because it brings practitioner wisdom into research, offering legitimacy to what centuries of clinicians know as true: that hope is a powerful common variable that cuts across therapies and predicts success.

Digital mental health interventions (DMHI)

Digital mental health interventions include therapy delivered over online video and voice platforms such as Zoom, and app-based mental health care, which could take the form of modular skill-building programs or text/chat-based interventions. These technologies have emerged as useful tools to treat disorders such as anxiety and depression while overcoming barriers to care such as access, provider availability, language, cost, and stigma while enhancing inclusivity (Weaver et al., 2023). However, the challenges that someone needs to have access to technology (e.g., a computer, smartphone, Internet) and know how to use that technology remain. Another direction is figuring out how best to deliver exposure therapies via telehealth; for example, with regard to whether exposure therapies can be delivered in group settings, say, in the case of communal PTSD after natural and human disasters. A recent meta-analysis of technology-assisted CBT (T-CBT) found high dropout rates and lack of re-engagement with the program, with the reasons cited including the didactic, text-heavy nature of the program, as well as the inability to tailor it to specific requirements of clients; in our opinion, this is quite problematic, as we believe there is no one-size-fits-all therapy. In addition, attending to the structural and environmental issues involved in the maintenance of the depression is not addressed in T-CBT. However, there is the potential to make T-CBT more engaging and modifiable, and thus make them more accessible to people who could not otherwise access mental health services. Research has shown that T-CBT with some supplemental support from a provider is comparable to face-to-face therapy (Andrews et al., 2018), and we wonder whether the supplemental support from providers may be an important change that DMHI has attempted to sacrifice in their emphasis on access and cost reduction.

No theory in itself is good or bad, but the way it is put into practice tells us whether it is a tool of liberation or oppression (hooks, 2014). In the previous section on critiques of CBT, we discussed how, in its rise to popularity, CBT practice studies were published that were not inclusive of diversity and were certainly used as a tool for oppression (e.g., conversion therapy and weight management apps). What if, instead, we examined behavior therapy as a tool of liberation? Within the larger context of social work as an example, we know that segregation and limited exposure to images of BIPOC folks or even immigrants in academia, science, and engineering keep certain stereotypes and biases, both internal and external, in place. Similarly, with immigrants, the narrative of illiterate folks who disproportionately use state funds does not fit with the reality of younger families who are willing to work and fill in gaps in employment for an aging society. Often, Black folks are exposed to media where they see other Black folks being murdered, shot, or in the prison system. Instead, one wonders whether, if BIPOC children were exposed to images of professionally successful Black doctors and engineers, this would increase pride and decrease fear and depression. On a similar note, if LGBTQ+ children were exposed to images of thriving LGBTQ+ members of society, would this lead to less internalized homophobia and stigma? Research has shown that even single-session exposure effectively reduces internalized stigma, minority stress, and stereotypes (Schleider et al., 2020; Shen et al., 2023). In this way, we can use the tools of CBT to tell a full, truthful story about oppressed populations.

The therapeutic relationship in CBT

The therapeutic alliance is as critical in CBT as it is in psychotherapy in general, albeit the role of the therapist in that relationship differs. While the field of CBT has been slow to give the therapeutic alliance the due attention it deserves, it has been the subject of a renewed focus, with three special issues in *Psychotherapy Research* devoted to it since 2022. Generally speaking, CBT embraces the humanistic principles of warmth, positive regard, and a nonjudgmental attitude. In addition, CBT emphasizes collaborative empiricism and Socratic dialogue (Kazantzis & Dobson, 2022). Collaborative empiricism encompasses a modeling of joint goal setting, openness to feedback, responsiveness, and flexibility in therapeutic collaboration, while Socratic questioning is a collaborative journey of discovery of the client's world (Kazantzis et al., 2017; Kazantzis et al., 2018). In the second wave of CBT therapies, which essentially marketed themselves as non-relationship-focused interventions that could bring about change, the role of the therapist has been more collaborative, active, and even didactic (Castonguay et al., 2018). More recent research has shown that positive shifts in the patient-perceived alliance in clients with GAD are related to symptom reduction and acknowledges the corrective experience of a democratic, equal, and reciprocal relationship (Coyne et al., 2019). Third-wave CBT therapists also bring in qualities of compassion, empathy, acceptance, and an ability to withstand strong emotions from the client (Jones-Smith, 2019). These therapists also highlight a shared predicament with clients and are able to join with clients in humanizing how we all get attached to our thoughts and feelings . In DBT, the therapist is warm and accessible yet models appropriate boundaries and uses irreverence and humor to help clients get out of their strong emotional states.

To sum up the findings of the role of the therapeutic alliance in CBT, it would be fair to say that for a long time it was believed that CBT could be delivered as interventions with the basic humanistic qualities of warmth and positive regard in place. More recent research has highlighted that the quality of the therapeutic alliance in CBT is related to symptom reduction—which comes as no surprise—but makes a case for training CBT therapists in alliance-building skills such as monitoring ruptures and managing repairs. Lastly, what CBT has finally been able to bring into research and practice is the need to focus on training in both cultural and systemic competence, which requires building reflexivity in practitioners to attend to both their internal biases and the external/systemic issues contributing to clients' problems and distress.

Conclusion

While this chapter has not been exhaustive in its coverage of all aspects of CBT, it has covered what we consider important influences and takeaways from this approach. CBT has evolved from a focus on behavior to consideration of our thoughts and behaviors to a greater emphasis on the complexity of human behavior by considering clients' values. The techniques utilized in CBT have consequently moved from looking simply at positive and negative reinforcers to cognitive restructuring and the incorporation of mindfulness approaches. As a result, we saw what began as a mechanistic approach, then a didactic one, became more humane over time with a recognition of the critical value of the therapeutic relationship. While many techniques in the models we discussed may resemble one another, when we sift through the different approaches, the key theme involves the need for all of us to achieve greater psychological flexibility by changing the relationships between our thoughts, feelings, and behaviors in ways that allow for maximum satisfaction and utility. Greater work is needed in CBT to train therapists in reflexivity to understand their own issues/biases and the influence of societal pressures to prioritize getting clients "well" quicker. The third wave of CBT has moved the field in that direction, though there remains a large gap in the field of CBT with understanding how to factor in the role of the socioeconomic environment (e.g., private troubles, public issues).

Perhaps one of CBTs greatest contributions is its emphasis on integration and responding and adapting to changes in the field of mental health. Beck continually highlighted the integrative aspects of cognitive therapy—starting with his early articles (1991), his contribution to *The Integrative Power of Cognitive Therapy* (Alford et al., 1997), and his interviews before his death. In his 1997 book, he wrote that cognitive therapy could not exclude significant others from therapy sessions when interpersonal conflicts are the presenting issue and that standard cognitive therapy does, in fact, focus on unconscious issues when clinical assessment shows early relational trauma. While this language is different from what is currently used, Beck came close to highlighting the developmental influences of the family and environment on the information-processing blueprint (schema) of an individual. We mention this to show how CBT has evolved (and is evolving) as it moves away from rigid parameters of what it includes, integrating aspects of the biological basis of behavior and the social world in its understanding of the client.

References

Ahuvia, I., & Schleider, J. L. (2023). Potential harm from emphasizing individual factors over structural factors in cognitive behavioral therapy with stigmatized groups. *The Behavior Therapist, 46*(7), 248–254.

Alford, B. A., Beck, A. T., & Jones Jr, J. V. (1997). The integrative power of cognitive therapy. *Journal of Cognitive Psychotherapy, 11*, 309–312. https://doi.org/10.1891/0889-8391.11.4.309

Andrews G, Basu A, Cuijpers P, Craske MG, McEvoy P, English CL, Newby JM. Computer therapy for the anxiety and depression disorders is effective, acceptable and practical health care: An updated meta-analysis. J Anxiety Disord. 2018 Apr; 55: 70–78. doi: 10.1016/j.janxdis.2018.01.001. Epub 2018 Feb 1. PMID: 29422409.

Anderson, L. K. (2023). Autistic experiences of applied behavior analysis. *Autism, 27*(3), 737–750.

Banducci, A. N., Fondren, A., Bocanegra, A., Crespo, M., & Contractor, A. A. (2023). Processing of positive memories technique: Feedback from trauma-exposed clients on processing

of positive memories technique components, format, and feasibility. *The Journal of Nervous and Mental Disease, 211*(4), 289–297.
Bandura, A. (1969). Social-learning theory of identificatory processes. *Handbook of Socialization Theory and Research, 213*, 262.
Bandura, A., Ross, D., & Ross, S. A. (1961). Transmission of aggression through imitation of aggressive models. *The Journal of Abnormal and Social Psychology, 63*(3), 575.
Barlow, D. H., Farchione, T. J., Bullis, J. R., Gallagher, M. W., Murray-Latin, H., Sauer-Zavala, S., ... & Cassiello-Robbins, C. (2017). The unified protocol for transdiagnostic treatment of emotional disorders compared with diagnosis-specific protocols for anxiety disorders: A randomized clinical trial. *JAMA Psychiatry, 74*(9), 875–884.
Bartlett, E. C. (1932). *Remembering: A study in experimental and social psychology.* Cambridge University Press
Beck, A. T. (1991). Cognitive therapy as the integrative therapy. *Journal of Psychotherapy Integration, 1*(3), 191–198. https://doi.org/10.1037/h0101233
Beck, A. T. (1993). Cognitive therapy: Past, present, and future. *Journal of Consulting and Clinical Psychology, 61*(2), 194.
Beck, A. T. (Ed.). (1979). *Cognitive therapy of depression.* Guilford Press.
Beck, A. T., & Dozois, D. J. (2011). Cognitive therapy: Current status and future directions. *Annual Review of Medicine, 62*, 397–409.
Beck, J. S. (2020). *Cognitive behavior therapy: Basics and beyond.* Guilford Publications.
Bloy, S., Oliver, J. E., & Morris, E. (2011). Using acceptance and commitment therapy with people with psychosis: A case study. *Clinical Case Studies, 10*(5), 347–359. https://doi.org/10.1177/1534650111420863
Butler, A. C., Chapman, J. E., Forman, E. M., & Beck, A. T. (2006). The empirical status of cognitive-behavioral therapy: A review of meta-analyses. *Clinical Psychology Review, 26*(1), 17–31.
Carpenter, J. K., Andrews, L. A., Witcraft, S. M., Powers, M. B., Smits, J. A., & Hofmann, S. G. (2018). Cognitive behavioral therapy for anxiety and related disorders: A meta-analysis of randomized placebo-controlled trials. *Depression and Anxiety, 35*(6), 502–514.
Castonguay, L. G., Youn, S. J., Xiao, H., & McAleavey, A. A. (2018). The therapeutic relationship: A warm, important, and potentially mutative factor in cognitive-behavioral therapy. In O. Tishby & H. Wiseman (Eds.), *Developing the therapeutic relationship: Integrating case studies, research, and practice* (pp. 157–179). American Psychological Association.
Claessens, M. (2010). Mindfulness based-third wave CBT therapies and existential-phenomenology: Friends or foes? *Existential Analysis: Journal of the Society for Existential Analysis, 21*(2) 295–308.
Coyne, A. E., Constantino, M. J., Westra, H. A., & Antony, M. M. (2019). Interpersonal change as a mediator of the within-and between-patient alliance-outcome association in two treatments for generalized anxiety disorder. *Journal of Consulting and Clinical Psychology, 87*(5), 472.
Craske, M. G., Treanor, M., Conway, C. C., Zbozinek, T., & Vervliet, B. (2014). Maximizing exposure therapy: An inhibitory learning approach. *Behaviour Research and Therapy, 58*, 10–23.
Cuijpers, P., Berking, M., Andersson, G., Quigley, L., Kleiboer, A., & Dobson, K. S. (2013). A meta-analysis of cognitive-behavioural therapy for adult depression, alone and in comparison with other treatments. *The Canadian Journal of Psychiatry, 58*(7), 376–385.
Cuijpers, P., Smit, F., Bohlmeijer, E., Hollon, S. D., & Andersson, G. (2010). Efficacy of cognitive–behavioural therapy and other psychological treatments for adult depression: meta-analytic study of publication bias. *The British Journal of Psychiatry, 196*(3), 173–178.
Davidson, R. J. (2003). Affective neuroscience and psychophysiology: Toward a synthesis. *Psychophysiology, 40*(5), 655–665.

Davidson, R., & Begley, S. (2012). *The emotional life of your brain: How its unique patterns affect the way you think, feel, and live—and how you can change them.* Hachette UK.

Desbordes, G., Negi, L. T., Pace, T. W., Wallace, B. A., Raison, C. L., & Schwartz, E. L. (2012). Effects of mindful-attention and compassion meditation training on amygdala response to emotional stimuli in an ordinary, non-meditative state. *Frontiers in Human Neuroscience, 6*, 292.

Dobson, K. S., & Kazantzis, N. (2024). Cognitive theory in psychotherapy. In F. T. L. Leong, J. L. Callahan, J. Zimmerman, M. J. Constantino, & C. F. Eubanks (Eds.), *APA handbook of psychotherapy: Theory-driven practice and disorder-driven practice* (pp. 175–190). American Psychological Association. https://doi.org/10.1037/0000353-011

Dovidio, J. F., Pagotto, L., & Hebl, M. L. (2011). Implicit attitudes and discrimination against people with physical disabilities. In R. L. Wiener & S. L. Willborn (Eds.), *Disability and aging discrimination: Perspectives in law and psychology* (pp. 157–183). Springer.

Dowd, E. T. (2004). Depression: Theory, assessment, and new directions in practice. *International Journal of Clinical and Health Psychology, 4*(2), 413–423.

Drisko, J. W., & Friedman, A. (2019). Let's clearly distinguish evidence-based practice and empirically supported treatments. *Smith College Studies in Social Work, 89*(3–4), 264–281.

Eikey, E. V. (2021). Effects of diet and fitness apps on eating disorder behaviours: Qualitative study. *BJPsych Open, 7*(5), e176.

Ellis, A. (1962). Reason and emotion in psychotherapy.

Ellis, A. (1989). The history of cognition in psychotherapy. In A. Freeman, K. M. Simon, L. E. Beutler, & H. Arkowitz (Eds.), *Comprehensive handbook of cognitive therapy* (pp. 5–19). Springer.

Ellis, A. (2003). Differentiating preferential from exaggerated and musturbatory beliefs in rational emotive behavior therapy. In W. Dryden (Ed.), *Rational emotive behaviour therapy* (pp. 22–34). Routledge.

Ellis, A., & Dryden, W. (2007). *The practice of rational emotive behavior therapy.* Springer.

Ellis, A., David, D., & Lynn, S. J. (2010). Rational and irrational beliefs: A historical and conceptual perspective. In D. David, S. J. Lynn, & A. Ellis (Eds.), *Rational and irrational beliefs: Research, theory, and clinical practice* (pp. 3–22). Oxford University Press.

Fairburn, C. G., Bailey-Straebler, S., Basden, S., Doll, H. A., Jones, R., Murphy, R., & Cooper, Z. (2015). A transdiagnostic comparison of enhanced cognitive behaviour therapy (CBT-E) and interpersonal psychotherapy in the treatment of eating disorders. *Behaviour Research and Therapy, 70*, 64–71.

Foa, E. B., & McLean, C. P. (2016). The efficacy of exposure therapy for anxiety-related disorders and its underlying mechanisms: The case of OCD and PTSD. *Annual Review of Clinical Psychology, 12*, 1–28.

Freeman, A., & Oster, C. L. (1998). Cognitive therapy and depression. In V. E. Caballo (Ed.), International handbook of cognitive and behavioural treatments for psychological disorders (pp. 489–520). Elsevier Science Ltd. https://doi.org/10.1016/B978-008043433-9/50018-3

Gallagher, M. W., Long, L. J., Richardson, A., D'Souza, J., Boswell, J. F., Farchione, T. J., & Barlow, D. H. (2020). Examining hope as a transdiagnostic mechanism of change across anxiety disorders and CBT treatment protocols. *Behavior Therapy, 51*(1), 190–202.

Gilbert, K., & Codd III, R. T. (2022). Radically open dialectical behavior therapy: Theory, assessment and case conceptualization. In W. O'Donohue & A. Masuda (Eds.), *Behavior Therapy: First, second, and third waves* (pp. 195–215). Springer.

Gloster, A. T., Walder, N., Levin, M. E., Twohig, M. P., & Karekla, M. (2020). The empirical status of acceptance and commitment therapy: A review of meta-analyses. *Journal of Contextual Behavioral Science, 18*, 181–192.

Guidano, V. F. (1987). *Complexity of the self: A developmental approach to psychopathology and therapy.* Guilford Press.

Harris, R. (2019). *ACT made simple: An easy-to-read primer on acceptance and commitment therapy*. New Harbinger Publications.
Hatzenbuehler, M. L. (2017). Advancing research on structural stigma and sexual orientation disparities in mental health among youth. *Journal of Clinical Child & Adolescent Psychology, 46*(3), 463–475.
Hayes, S. C., Barnes-Holmes, D., & Roche, B. (2001). Relational frame theory: A précis. In S. C. Hayes, D. Barnes-Holmes, & B. Roche (Eds.), *Relational frame theory: A post-Skinnerian account of human language and cognition* (pp. 141–154). Springer.
Hayes, S. C., Jacobson, N. S., Follette, V. M., & Dougher, M. J. (Eds) (1994). *Acceptance and change: Content and context in psychotherapy*. Context Press.
Hayes, S. C., Luoma, J. B., Bond, F. W., Masuda, A., & Lillis, J. (2006). Acceptance and commitment therapy: Model, processes and outcomes. *Behaviour Research and Therapy, 44*(1), 1–25.
Hayes, S. C., Strosahl, K. D., & Wilson, K. G. (1999). Acceptance and commitment therapy: An experiential approach to behavior change. Guilford Press.
Hebl, M. R., & Heatherton, T. F. (1998). The stigma of obesity in women: The difference is Black and White. *Personality and Social Psychology Bulletin, 24*(4), 417–426. https://doi.org/10.1177/0146167298244008et
Hoffman, S. N., Rassaby, M. M., Stein, M. B., & Taylor, C. T. (2024). Positive and negative affect change following psychotherapeutic treatment for anxiety-related disorders: A systematic review and meta-analysis. *Journal of Affective Disorders*. March 15; 349: 358–369. doi: 10.1016/j.jad.2024.01.086. Epub 2024 Jan 10. PMID: 38211753.
Hollon, S. D., & Beck, A. T. (2013). Cognitive and cognitive-behavioral therapies. In W. Lutz, M. Barkham, & L. G. Castonguay (Eds.), *Bergin and Garfield's handbook of psychotherapy and behavior change* (6th ed., pp. 393–442). Wiley.
Hölzel, B. K., Lazar, S. W., Gard, T., Schuman-Olivier, Z., Vago, D. R., & Ott, U. (2011). How does mindfulness meditation work? Proposing mechanisms of action from a conceptual and neural perspective. *Perspectives on psychological science, 6*(6), 537–559.
Hooks, B. (2014). *Teaching to transgress*. Routledge.
Huey Jr, S. J., Park, A. L., Galán, C. A., & Wang, C. X. (2023). Culturally responsive cognitive behavioral therapy for ethnically diverse populations. *Annual Review of Clinical Psychology, 19*, 51–78.
Isaksson, M., Ghaderi, A., Wolf-Arehult, M., Öster, C., & Ramklint, M. (2021). Sharing and connecting with others–patient experiences of radically open dialectical behavior therapy for anorexia nervosa and overcontrol: a qualitative study. *Journal of Eating Disorders, 9*, 1–10.
Jones-Smith, E. (2019). *Theories of counseling and psychotherapy: An integrative approach*. Sage Publications.
Kabat-Zinn, J. (2003). Mindfulness-based stress reduction (MBSR). *Constructivism in the Human Sciences, 8*(2), 73.
Kazantzis, N., & Dobson, K. S. (2022). Therapeutic relationships in cognitive behavioral therapy: Theory and recent research. *Psychotherapy Research, 32*(8), 969–971.
Kazantzis, N., Beck, J. S., Clark, D. A., Dobson, K. S., Hofmann, S. G., Leahy, R. L., & Wing Wong, C. (2018). Socratic dialogue and guided discovery in cognitive behavioral therapy: A modified Delphi panel. *International Journal of Cognitive Therapy, 11*, 140–157.
Kazantzis, N., Dattilio, F. M., & Dobson, K. S. (2017). *The therapeutic relationship in cognitive-behavioral therapy: A clinician's guide*. Guilford Publications.
Kennedy, K. A., & Barlow, D. H. (2018). The Unified Protocol for Transdiagnostic Treatment of Emotional Disorders: An introduction. In D. H. Barlow & T. J. Farchione (Eds.), *Applications of the unified protocol for transdiagnostic treatment of emotional disorder* (pp. 1–16). Oxford University Press. https://doi.org/10.1093/med-psych/9780190255541.003.0001

Kuyken, W., Warren, F. C., Taylor, R. S., Whalley, B., Crane, C., Bondolfi, G., ... & Dalgleish, T. (2016). Efficacy of mindfulness-based cognitive therapy in prevention of depressive relapse: An individual patient data meta-analysis from randomized trials. *JAMA Psychiatry, 73*(6), 565–574.

Leahy, R. (2002). *Clinical advances in cognitive psychotherapy: Theory and application.* Springer.

Leahy, R. L. (2008). The therapeutic relationship in cognitive-behavioral therapy. *Behavioural and Cognitive Psychotherapy, 36*(6), 769–777.

Lee, S. H., & Cho, S. J. (2021). Cognitive behavioral therapy and mindfulness-based cognitive therapy for depressive disorders. *Major depressive disorder: Rethinking and understanding recent discoveries*, 1305: 295–310.

Levin, M. E., Hildebrandt, M. J., Lillis, J., & Hayes, S. C. (2012). The impact of treatment components suggested by the psychological flexibility model: A meta-analysis of laboratory-based component studies. *Behavior Therapy, 43*(4), 741–756.

Levinson, C. A., Fitterman-Harris, H. F., Patterson, S., Harrop, E., Turner, C., May, M., ... & Becker, C. B. (2023). The unintentional harms of weight management treatment: Time for a change. *The Behavior Therapist, 46*(7), 271–282

Linardon, J., Gleeson, J., Yap, K., Murphy, K., & Brennan, L. (2019). Meta-analysis of the effects of third-wave behavioural interventions on disordered eating and body image concerns: Implications for eating disorder prevention. *Cognitive Behaviour Therapy, 48*(1), 15–38.

Linehan, M. M. (1987). Dialectical behavior therapy for borderline personality disorder: Theory and method. *Bulletin of the Menninger Clinic, 51*(3), 261.

Linehan, M. M. (1993). Dialectical behavior therapy for treatment of borderline personality disorder: implications for the treatment of substance abuse. *NIDA Research Monograph, 137*, 201-216.

Link, B. G., & Phelan, J. C. (2013). Labeling and stigma. *Handbook of the Sociology of Mental Health*, 525–541.

Little, J. N., & Codd, R. T., 3rd, (2020). Radically Open Dialectical Behavior Therapy (RO DBT) in the treatment of perfectionism: A case study. *Journal of Clinical Psychology, 76*(11), 2097–2108. https://doi.org/10.1002/jclp.23062

Lynch, T. R. (2018). *Radically open dialectical behavior therapy: Theory and practice for treating disorders of overcontrol.* New Harbinger Publications.

Mahoney, M. J., & Granvold, D. K. (2005). Constructivism and psychotherapy. *World Psychiatry, 4*(2), 74.

Meichenbaum, D. (1977). Cognitive behaviour modification. *Cognitive Behaviour Therapy, 6*(4), 185–192.

Metzl, J. M., & Hansen, H. (2014). Structural competency: Theorizing a new medical engagement with stigma and inequality. *Social Science & Medicine, 103*, 126–133.

Moorey, S. (2010). The six cycles maintenance model: Growing a "vicious flower" for depression. *Behavioural and Cognitive Psychotherapy, 38*(2), 173–184.

Newman, M. G., Basterfield, C., Erickson, T. M., Caulley, E., Przeworski, A., & Llera, S. J. (2022). Psychotherapeutic treatments for generalized anxiety disorder: cognitive and behavioral therapies, enhancement strategies, and emerging efforts. *Expert Review of Neurotherapeutics, 22*(9), 751–770. https://doi.org/10.1080/14737175.2022.2125800

Northcut, T. B., Heller, N. R., & Kumaria, S. (2016). Utilizing cognitive-behavioral interventions in psychodynamic practice. In J. Berzoff, L. M. Flanagan, & P. Hertz (Eds.), *Inside out and outside in: Psychodynamic clinical theory and psychopathology in contemporary multicultural contexts*, (4th ed., pp. 220–248). Rowman & Littlefield.

Olkin, R. (2017). *Disability-affirmative therapy. A case formulation template for clients with disabilities.* Oxford University Press.

Öst, L. G. (2014). The efficacy of acceptance and commitment therapy: An updated systematic review and meta-analysis. *Behaviour Research and Therapy, 61*, 105–121.

Piaget, J. (1976). Piaget's theory. In B. Inhelder, H. H. Chipman, & C. Zwingmann (Eds.), *Piaget and his school* (pp. 11–23). Springer. https://doi.org/10.1007/978-3-642-46323-5_2

Rasmussen, B. (2018). A critical examination of CBT in clinical social work practice. *Clinical Social Work Journal, 46*(3), 165–173. https://doi.org/10.1007/s10615-017-0632-7

Rothbaum, B. O., & Schwartz, A. C. (2002). Exposure therapy for posttraumatic stress disorder. *American Journal of Psychotherapy, 56*(1), 59–75.

Safran, J., & Segal, Z. V. (1996). *Interpersonal process in cognitive therapy.* Jason Aronson.

Schleider, J. L., Dobias, M., Sung, J., Mumper, E., & Mullarkey, M. C. (2020). Acceptability and utility of an open-access, online single-session intervention platform for adolescent mental health. *JMIR Mental Health, 7*(6), e20513.

Segal, Z., Williams, M., & Teasdale, J. (2018). *Mindfulness-based cognitive therapy for depression.* Guilford Publications.

Shen, J., Rubin, A., Cohen, K., Hart, E. A., Sung, J., McDanal, R., & Schleider, J. L. (2023). Randomized evaluation of an online single-session intervention for minority stress in LGBTQ+ adolescents. *Internet Interventions, 33*, 100633.

Skinner, B. F. (1957). The experimental analysis of behavior. *American Scientist, 45*(4), 343–371.

Tang, Y. Y., Hölzel, B. K., & Posner, M. I. (2015). The neuroscience of mindfulness meditation. *Nature Reviews Neuroscience, 16*(4), 213–225.

Teasdale, J. D., Segal, Z. V., Williams, J. M. G., Ridgeway, V. A., Soulsby, J. M., & Lau, M. A. (2000). Prevention of relapse/recurrence in major depression by mindfulness-based cognitive therapy. *Journal of Consulting and Clinical Psychology, 68*(4), 615.

Tolin, D. F. (2024). *Doing CBT.* Guilford Publications.

van der Kolk, B. A. (2003). *Psychological trauma.* American Psychiatric Pub.

van Zoonen, K., Buntrock, C., Ebert, D. D., Smit, F., Reynolds III, C. F., Beekman, A. T., & Cuijpers, P. (2014). Preventing the onset of major depressive disorder: A meta-analytic review of psychological interventions. *International Journal of Epidemiology, 43*(2), 318–329.

Wachtel, P. L. (2011). Inside the session: What really happens in psychotherapy. American Psychological Association.

Wampold, B. E., Flückiger, C., Del Re, A. C., Yulish, N. E., Frost, N. D., Pace, B. T., ... & Hilsenroth, M. J. (2017). In pursuit of truth: A critical examination of meta-analyses of cognitive behavior therapy. *Psychotherapy Research, 27*(1), 14–32.

Watson, J. B., & Rayner, R. (1920). Conditioned emotional reactions. *Journal of Experimental Psychology, 3*(1), 1-14. https://doi.org/10.1037/h0069608

Weaver, A., Zhang, A., Xiang, X., Felsman, P., Fischer, D. J., & Himle, J. A. (2023). Entertain me well: an entertaining, tailorable, online platform delivering CBT for depression. *Cognitive and Behavioral Practice, 30*(1), 96–115.

Wolpe, J. (1968). Psychotherapy by reciprocal inhibition. *Conditional reflex: A Pavlovian Journal of Research & Therapy, 3*, 234–240.

Young, J. E., Klosko, J. S., & Weishaar, M. E. (2003). *Schema therapy: A practitioner's guide.* Guilford.

5

Historical and current innovations in integrative psychotherapy

Introduction

We have discussed in detail two major theoretical schools that have influenced clinical practice in the United States—psychodynamic and cognitive behavioral—and the research that has examined their effectiveness. By now, it should be clear that we do not believe an either/or approach to treatment is the best route to take. It would be simpler to choose one theory over another to guide your practice, but which one? The temptation is to choose a model of practice without understanding the theory(ies) behind them, or cherry-picking techniques from different models. Schact's (1984) analogy demonstrates the dangers of doing so: "Salt in one's soup is quite different from salt in one's gas tank" (p.121), for example, an exposure technique that may be quite helpful in cognitive behavioral therapy can serve as an empathic failure if mixed with a therapy that utilizes the transference in more direct ways. We value both psychodynamic and CBT for their strengths and find that they can complement each other in the real world of practice, as has also been reflected in psychotherapy research that has drawn from multiple theoretical frameworks.

Early in the field of psychotherapy research, practice with clients that met narrow criteria (one diagnosis or symptom picture) was studied (e.g., depression *or* anxiety *or* substance use). In the less-controlled world of practice, most clinicians rarely meet clients that fit such a narrow diagnostic perspective with only one focal problem. Because of this ambiguity, they may seek out the latest therapeutic model in a search for clarity. Though there is much value in packaged approaches, they are often divorced from their theoretical foundations and consequently lack a framework that guides clinicians to understand how and when the model is or is not working. Likewise, a packaged approach does not allow for understanding the subjectivities of multiple identities prevalent in our world today.

Psychodynamic and Cognitive Behavioral Theory and Practice. Terry B. Northcut and Shveta Kumaria, Oxford University Press. © Oxford University Press (2025). DOI: 10.1093/9780197508404.003.0005

The rapid rise of teletherapy and telehealth has contributed to this push to have a map or protocol for certain treatments that can be managed quickly and remotely. Adding to this confusion is the sheer volume of research and experts available online and in person, all prepared to offer quick or "thin" (Geertz, 1973) answers. Practitioners are left struggling to understand and work with complex cases that challenge the most seasoned clinicians to respond in a timely manner with the sometimes ambiguous guideline of choosing "evidence-based" interventions.

Qualitative studies have consistently reported common relational factors such as warmth, empathy, encouragement, and interest as the most beneficial across therapies, with quantitative and qualitative studies emphasizing the therapeutic alliance as the strongest predictor of positive therapy outcome (Fluckiger et al., 2020). However, identifying the ingredients and overall picture of a "successful" psychotherapy requires a "thicker" (Geertz, 1973) understanding that includes client satisfaction and common factors but also findings from research and clinical experience. Historically, there has often been a disconnection between what is practiced every day in the "real" world and the psychotherapy process and outcome research, which has clouded the quest for answers to the question of "what makes therapy work." Greater specificity about these qualities that contribute to success is important for practitioners to understand, which is why this chapter closely examines what we have learned from psychotherapy research and what we still need to learn. For too long, psychotherapy research has been divorced from social work practice experience and clinical wisdom out of concern that this branch of research fails to take into account the biopsychosocial-spiritual context and the critical need for action (outside of the therapy room and within it) to eradicate social injustices. We hope to bridge that historical division, but this requires clinicians to leave their comfort zone and examine broader research results rather than relying on how they were trained, professional ideology, or solely on their own practice wisdom. We will discuss the factors that contribute to a positive outcome in treatment and the limitations of those studies and will also briefly cover the body of literature that speaks to efforts to integrate multiple theoretical frameworks. The conclusion of the chapter will highlight our takeaways from this review of the literature that we think can guide practice and our case illustrations in subsequent chapters.

Integration efforts

The struggle to reconcile the "cool logic of science" with the "spirit of humanistic activism" (Marquis et al., 2021) has yielded integrated approaches that attempt to resolve the either/or dilemma. The term "integration" implies approaches to therapy that are not wedded to a single school or theory and seeks to choose, blend, innovate, and/or combine therapy approaches to find a more effective approach with diverse clients while still maintaining an understanding of the pros and cons in doing so. Since the 1940s, there have been rebels that have attempted to be atheoretical (Sol Garfield, Carl Rogers, and Jerome Frank, to name a few), and these theoretician-practitioners tried to distill the core elements of what worked successfully to help clients with mental illness in clinical practice and remove it from theoretical silos. Fredrick Thorne (1957), considered the founder of eclecticism, argued for practitioners to have more than one kind of "tool" in their toolbox. However, having multiple tools does not necessarily come with instructions for when and how to use them or prevent the dangers of using multiple tools at once. On the other hand, the integration movement evolved within the context of a variety of issues, some of which were outlined in Chapters 1 and 2. Diverse settings and changing economic and political cultures push for shorter, problem-focused treatments that have even greater emphasis than when Fredrick Thorne was practicing. In this chapter, we are also focusing on findings from outcome research in psychotherapy and the shift that has occurred from looking at specific treatments for specific diagnoses to looking at change mechanisms inherent in the treatment context (Castonguay & Goldfried, 1994; Imel & Wampold, 2008; Wampold, 2000). Theoretical integration efforts have moved hand in hand with psychotherapy and neurobiological research (especially work with trauma), with each pushing the other to even more refinements and revisions. Unfortunately, however, some of these results published in more academic circles have not always reached clinical practitioners in their day-to-day world of negotiating agency, insurance, and societal pressures.

Psychotherapy outcome research does provide empirical evidence of factors that cut across theoretical divides and how critical these factors are to the successful outcome of psychotherapy. These results often confirm what clinicians already know from experience, for example, that the therapeutic alliance is critical for successful outcomes (Cameron et al., 2018;

Gianotti & Danielian, 2014, 2017; Gianotti, 2022). However, results have also emphasized the importance of the client's environment or the client's beliefs about illness and cure (Ahn & Wampold, 2001; Elkin et al., 1989; Norcross & Wampold, 2011). In addition, these research findings point out that techniques specific to theoretical schools are less of a contributor to successful outcomes than theoretical purists would perhaps like to admit. One caveat to keep in mind in examining research results, however, is that researcher bias and clinician idiosyncrasies often shade results where researchers proclaim to "scientifically" prove the efficacy of the theoretical school they espouse over other theoretical models (Leichsenring et al., 2017; Luborsky et al., 1999; Wampold, 2001). This is one reason it is so important in looking at evidence-based models that we remember our clients' values and circumstances, empirically supported evidence, and clinician experience (Drisko & Grady, 2018). Clinicians need to regularly maintain their awareness of what all kinds of research tell us, not just what is trending in the marketplace or what confirms our own biases, which is the reason we wrote this chapter. The integration movement shifted the dictates or confines of a single model of doing therapy to embracing more than one theoretical model, technique, or sensibility of delivering therapy efficiently. Some theorists also refer to this as "transcending" constructs associated with divergent schools (Castonguay et al., 2015). Cooper (2016), a relational psychoanalyst, used the term "bridge theory" to address the numerous concepts that cross boundaries and become integrated into different orientations" (as described in Kuchuck, 2021), a term that we find more accurate to describe our attempts to integrate, hence the title of the book. Integration has been attempted in a multitude of ways, and technical eclecticism, assimilative integration, theoretical integration, and common factors are the most distinctive attempts at doing so.

Technical eclecticism

Technical eclecticism refers to using techniques or procedures from many theoretical schools with a focus on pragmatism and what works best for a client, as described above. However, this does not mean that eclectic therapists are antitheoretical (Lazarus et al., 1992). A better way of describing this is that "eclecticism can be better understood for what it is not (nonadherence to a specific school) than for what it is" (Feixas & Botella, 2004, p. 193).

Technical eclecticism brings the clinician's experience into research to reveal the kinds of therapy most effective with clients with similar diagnoses or similar personality characteristics.

Beutler and Clarkin (1990) proposed a systematic treatment selection (STS) approach to matching clients to treatment strategies based on their state and trait characteristics. One example is matching the therapist's involvement style (directive/non-directive) based on the client's level of reactance, that is, clients' reactions to others attempting to control them. The higher the client's reactance level, the better the client does with therapists who are less directive, and vice versa. Another way is based on the client's coping style. The more clients internalize or blame themselves or ruminate as a way of coping with stressful times, the more responsive these clients will be to treatments that encourage self-exploration. On the other hand, clients who blame their situations or others or act out to cope with stressful events, that is, externalize, tend to do better in treatments that are more symptom-focused and/or focused on behavioral change. These principles that propose that one can systematically match clients to treatments and therapists are great in theory; they overlook the barriers posed by economics and culture that restrict a perfect clinical roll-out based on these principles. Likewise, we cannot overlook that a client perceived as "reactive" may very well be showing good judgment in the face of a racist behavioral health care system. The context of the client, the clinician, and the therapeutic milieu must be considered.

Another example of technical eclecticism that has a theoretical basis is the multimodal therapy proposed by Lazarus (1981). Multimodal therapy is a psychoeducational framework, largely resting on a CBT background, which begins by assessing seven different modalities captured by the acronym BASIC ID, which stands for Behavior, Affect, Sensation, Imagery, Cognition, Interpersonal factors, and Drug/biological considerations. The understanding behind this model is that there are atypical presentations or comorbidities of diagnostic categories. Folks experiencing depression may have behavioral inhibition, depressed mood, and difficulty problem-solving: for example, Zimmerman et al. (2015) showed that there are 227 possible presentations of major depressive disorder based on the symptom criteria. These symptoms are present with other diagnostic categories as well, and applying a single theoretical school or technique to treating depression, for example, is a disservice to the client. This broad spectrum of assessment captures the ways that make a particular client's diagnosis unique, allowing a therapist to choose areas to focus on with a particular client that may be different from another client with the same diagnostic disorder. It is also a framework that includes medication, family, and interpersonal work as part of the treatment options that are offered. This framework prioritizes relapse prevention as one of its central goals. For example, in working with a client with recurrent depression, identifying factors that lead to depression and may keep this episodic pattern in place (e.g., precarious financial circumstances or abusive relationships) is critical.

The challenge for technical eclecticism is the difficulty in training young practitioners, as the heuristics for choosing the techniques are context-dependent. Ramsey (2001) illustrates this difficulty by using the sports metaphor of pulling star players from many teams to build one's own team. Individually skilled players do not guarantee a win, as the chemistry between the players may or may not work, and understanding this chemistry requires skill and wisdom that is difficult to teach. The rapid development of improved simulation models raises important questions, and hopefully some answers, about how this chemistry between clients, clinicians, and context can be taught. Time and further research can do much to clarify the role that simulation can play in determining helpful, pragmatic, and culturally attuned assessments and interventions without minimizing the original theoretical foundations or losing the essential characteristics of in-person clinical internships.

Assimilative integration

Assimilative integration refers to an approach where there is a strong commitment, grounding, and training in a particular approach/school/theory of doing therapy, often called the "home theory" (Stricker & Gold, 2005), yet where there is still flexibility to incorporate techniques from other therapeutic approaches to be responsive and adaptive to the unique needs of individual clients. Messer (1992) stated that it is difficult, and almost impossible, to be atheoretical in choosing the therapeutic approach. Every choice of technique, direction, and procedure is informed by a view of change or growth in humans, which may or may not be explicit to the therapist. Therapists should ideally be able to provide a rationale for incorporating the techniques they do and an outcome that they want to achieve. In addition, the technique or therapy elements that are being brought into therapy by the therapist should be congruent with the beliefs and values of the client for the treatment to be effective (Whalley & Hyland, 2010). The critical questions for clinicians to answer that we will also discuss in subsequent chapters are as follows:

1. What is the theoretical framework with this client and why?
2. What is the reasoning for bringing in other approaches?
3. How will effectiveness of the intervention or variation from their approach be measured or understood?

Challenges in using assimilative integration lie in including the contextual factors brought in by the client and the client's previous experience with a particular type of therapy. For example, a client that I (SK) worked with would get triggered by the word "exposure" due to a prior experience with a behaviorally oriented therapist. While exposure would be a good fit for this client, who presented with avoidance of biking following a road accident, it would have caused challenges in the alliance. The first eight sessions of the therapy were spent building trust, understanding the client's definition of what constitutes a cure for them, and building a case for introducing exposure nontraditionally later in the therapy, as well as exploring other contextual factors of the presenting symptom. Therapist flexibility with an understanding of the context in which the client has entered therapy has been critical for our work and aids us in figuring out what to do and when. A "fuller" understanding of context includes understanding the client's subjective experience of potential therapeutic models and their values as well as therapists' knowledge of the research on the client's symptomatology.

Another somewhat related challenge is making sure that the interventions match the goals that the client has for that phase of therapy. Clients may enter treatment with clear goals that may reflect a narrow understanding of their presenting problems. Over the course of treatment, these goals must be respected even if the therapeutic work brings a "thicker" understanding of the problem. For example, an emerging adult may want to focus on difficulty communicating with peers during the transition into college. The clinician may observe that these difficulties may be rooted in patterns established in the client's family. This should be discussed with the client, with attention to whether the client wants to further understand those subjective experiences. Research by Delboy and Michaels (2023) indicates that many people want deeper work; however, this cannot be assumed to be the case. Additionally, the "No Surprises" Act requiring disclosure of potential costs and length of treatment must be complied with National Association of Social Workers (2022).

An important part of assimilative integration is also knowing when certain parts of your "home theory" need to be dropped because they may not work for the client. Pragmatically, this does not mean that you need to continually add more and more theories that can only be known on a surface level, which raises the question of how many schools of therapy a clinician must be skilled in to be "good enough." The answer here is twofold: It is not the quantity of therapies or techniques that is critical, it is being skilled in the ones you know and having self-awareness to be clear about what you can and cannot do. Additionally, a clinician's humility makes it essential to appropriately use referrals when the expertise required is not in one's wheelhouse.

A few obvious examples from the evolution of CBT and PDT typify assimilative integration in practice and clarify what is meant by this term. The addition of behavioral activation to supplement cognitive restructuring for a client with depression illustrates this point. Cognitive restructuring operates to help clients identify how their cognitions affect their emotions. The work lies in identifying patterns of maladaptive cognitions and working to reframe them in a way that is more adaptive. On the other hand, behavioral activation helps clients understand how their behaviors can influence their emotions (moods). Positive actions such as taking a shower, going for a short walk, keeping an appointment to see a physician, and so on can provide a sense of accomplishment to a person with depression. Completing these tasks can improve self-worth, and engaging in them presents opportunities for relational exchanges that can be rewarding to the client who is depressed. Assimilative integration combines cognitive and behavioral techniques to better alleviate the experienced depression.

The addition of attachment work in psychodynamic therapy for chronic and complex anxiety is another type of assimilative integration (Gold, 2011). The focus in treatment then goes beyond understanding the symptoms of anxiety to examining early attachment injuries that restrict clients' relationships with others and their explorations of the world. This process is anchored in the therapist serving as a safe attachment base for the client, which supports the client forming new attachments (Shilkret & Shilkret, 2022). In addition, homework tasks in psychodynamic-interpersonal psychotherapy for depression (Nelson & Castonguay, 2017; Stricker, 2006) can range from simple requests that clients record or note their fluctuations in mood to encouraging clients to try out a new behavior and note associated feelings and fears related to that, which may or may not be as formal as a therapy journal.

One final, important example of assimilative integration comes from the field of social work. The cognitive-integrative model was developed by Sharon Berlin (2002) by integrating elements of the current cognitive models of practicing psychotherapy with practitioner wisdom and research. Berlin, in her conversations with other practitioners, realized that Beck's cognitive theory did not emphasize the role of sociocultural factors in the creation, maintenance, and exacerbation of negative cognitions assumed to be at the core of mental health issues such as depression. She also believed that cognitive theorists assumed that negative cognitions would be available to the client through words, while these cognitions are often not verbal and not available to the conscious mind. Similarly, the role emotions play pre-cognition was not being emphasized (e.g., early trauma). Mental health issues often arise from current life stressors (systemic and interpersonal) as well as from the memories of past stressors (developmental) (Berlin, 2010). Berlin attempted to bridge the gap between the focus on the person or the environment. Human experience is guided by the information a person gets from the inner workings of the mind, the relational self, the social environment, and the mental schemas through which this information is processed. This process of meaning-making makes this unique for each person, as it determines which aspects we elaborate on or focus on. In her model of intervention, she outlines two levels of change: one focused on sources of information (environmental) and the other focused on schemas (internal). In practice, if the social worker determines that the barrier to change is a skill deficit arising from limited knowledge or oppressive circumstances, then the role of the clinician is to locate new sources of information or create them for the client so the client can assimilate and integrate them into their existing schemas. If the other barrier to change is rigid, restrictive, and mental schemas, then the role of the clinician is to help the client reorganize these schemas by making use of new information, which leads to change in feelings, thoughts, and behaviors and eventually "a more able and versatile and stronger self" (Berlin, 2002, p. 349).

In creating change, Berlin also recognizes the prominent role of the therapeutic relationship as a provider of new sources of information that highlight maladaptive cognitive-relational patterns and facilitate schemas that lead to new meaning-making (Borden, 2010). Borden (2010) spoke of the therapeutic relationship as a form of exposure for clients whose experience in the world was toxic, traumatic, and violent. Sometimes, beginning contact with the caregiving environment requires an "over exposure" to a system that may have helped traumatize and exacerbate the trauma. For example, military sexual trauma can be exacerbated when the source of treatment is through the VA (Northcut & Kienow, 2014), which is part of the system that has created an environment of violence. In this case, an assimilative form of integration allows us to recognize that the therapeutic relationship may be a form of exposure that a client finds difficult, if not impossible, to negotiate. The therapist must be able to reconceptualize the therapeutic action to include awareness of internal and external factors that are not discrete and inhibit any ability to make use of traditional therapy, whether CBT or PDT.

Theoretical integration

Theoretical integration is the ultimate utopian quest for therapy where two or more different therapies are conceptually united to create a new one that is theoretically sound and can guide research and practice (Lampropoulos, 2001). Paul Wachtel (1991) has summed this up well by saying that "[e]clecticism in practice and integration in aspiration is an accurate description of what most of us in the integrative movement do much of the time" (p. 44). There are passionate advocates who see theoretical integration as the only worthy form of integration, and others who warn us about theory smushing (Norcross, 2005) or mere conceptual transposition.

There are several clinical researchers who demonstrate forms of integration. For example, in Linehan's Dialectical Behavior therapy discussed in the previous chapter, CBT is combined with the Eastern influence of radical acceptance, attachment facilitation (to the therapist), skills training, and exposure. The CBT theory is expanded by including contributions from other fields. Wachtel's Cyclical Psychodynamic is another approach that melds psychodynamic, cognitive behavioral, systemic, and experiential perspectives (Wachtel, 2008). This theory is a response to the constructivist epistemological turn in the field to a more social, relational approach. The attention to the relationship (as a foundational piece in psychodynamic theory) is balanced by the attention to the relationships that the client has outside the therapy room so that the corrective emotional experiences inside the therapy room can be carried out into the client's social world, making it more rewarding, and therefore, therapeutic. While there is a focus on early childhood experiences, they are seen as precursors to current dysfunctional intrapersonal and interpersonal patterns in adult life. A client can be stuck in a vicious cycle of trying to avoid anxiety and yet have their security and belonging needs met which leaves them continually frustrated. The role of the therapist is to interrupt these relational cycles by any techniques possible, including interpretation or exposure. The therapeutic relationship is warm and supportive, using transference to show the client how the vicious relational cycles operate. Countertransference is acknowledged silently by the therapist and is used occasionally to give feedback to clients on how their behavior affects other people (Gold & Wachtel, 1993). What is important to emphasize is that, like many theories and models, cyclical psychodynamic theory has not remained static and is responding to changes in society and in the field. Wachtel's more recent push has been to focus on communication in the therapy room, both in-the-moment responses and metacommunication (Wachtel, 2014, 2017; Wachtel & Gagnon, 2019).

Theoretical integration is difficult, and difficult to do well because it requires understanding that if you bring in one theory you may be minimizing important aspects of another theory. For example, in Wachtel's early work, he had to minimize or omit the influence of drives to bring in the focus on behaviors. Though this was necessary, he then needed to come up with an explanation for how other aspects of psychodynamic theory (e.g., defenses) still had operational value. Wachtel was able to do so in his Cyclical Dynamic approach by, in a sense, maintaining a 30,000-foot view of the theories while also focusing on the near- and midlevel experience perspectives. As clinicians, we often find it easy to focus on what is happening with the client in the present, but it is difficult to view the macro-, mezzo-, and microlevels of understanding of the theories being integrated and how they are being altered. Unfortunately, in addition to there not being a common language between therapeutic schools, there are also philosophical differences that must be considered when designing and understanding the impact of integrating different theories.

Common factors

The common factors model of integration, which is perhaps the most famous in psychotherapy integration, proposes that there are some commonalities that therapies share, and that it is possible to make efficacious and parsimonious treatments based on these commonalities (Norcross, 2005). Some theorists have stated that looking at common factors allows us to really get to what practitioners actually *do* in therapy, rather than what *they say they do* in therapy. Here, we examine the history of common factors to understand that this is not a new concept.

Commonality across schools of therapy and various healing settings has been proposed by theorists for close to a century now. The idea of common factors was first put forward in 1936 by Saul Rosenzweig, who stated that clients may find success in different forms of healing due to common factors such as the personality of the healer (e.g., if it is inspiring or charismatic). He said that catharsis also plays an important role in helping people heal as they talk about deep conflicts and feelings that were not articulated until now, processing events that are causing them distress, and understanding why they are reacting in a certain way or why a particular event triggers a distressing emotional response.

In 1957, Carl Rogers published his pathbreaking paper titled "The Necessary and Sufficient Conditions of Therapeutic Personality Change," which led to the client-centered framework. These necessary and sufficient conditions were a setting where two people are in psychological contact, one of which is a client who is distressed, and the other is an invested, empathic therapist who is attempting to understand the client's inner world and communicate positive regard to the client. This paper gave centrality to the therapist as a common factor as well as to the therapeutic relationship. This idea was also echoed by Sol Garfield in 1957, who emphasized the same factors as Rosenzweig and Rogers.

Jerome Frank's (1973) book *Persuasion and Healing* was the first entire text devoted to commonalities across therapies. Frank identified four aspects common to all therapeutic endeavors: an emotionally charged, confiding relationship with a healer (e.g., a therapist, a shaman); a healing setting; a rationale or myth that provides an explanation for the client's symptoms; and a ritual prescribed by the healer that both parties believe is curative and aligned with the explanation for the client's distress. Frank, and even Rosenzweig, believed that these common factors were found across treatment settings (e.g., psychoanalysis, traditional healing in churches or other religious settings) as long as the healing myth and accompanying rituals are adhered to with consistency by the therapist and accepted by the client.

The concept of common factors received another boost with the research on psychotherapy outcome. These multi-study research papers showed that therapies, irrespective of theoretical allegiances, had equivalent results/caused equivalent change (Luborsky et al., 1975). This result of outcome research has been referred to more commonly as the dodo bird verdict, or as "all have won, and all must have prizes." Wampold (2001) carried out a meta-analysis showing that differences among theoretical models only accounted for 1 percent of variance in outcome. And today, after fifty years of robust psychotherapy research, researchers have declared that "the existence of specific psychological treatments for specific disorders are a myth" (Duncan et al., 2010, p. 28).

There have been many attempts by researchers to classify common factors into categories, or even to enumerate them, though unfortunately, this has resulted in too many common factors. Grencavage and Norcross (1990) listed these factors, dividing them into labeled categories: client factors, therapist factors, change processes, treatment structure, and lastly, the therapeutic relationship. So, for example, qualities characterized as *client factors* are commonalities across client behaviors and characteristics such as positive expectation of cure, hope, and faith that the client will get better. *Therapist characteristics* are warmth and a therapist personality that inspires hope for cure, acceptance, and other positive outcomes. *Change processes* most commonly include an opportunity for catharsis, to acquire and practice new behaviors, and the provision of a rationale for the illness and "cure." In this research, change processes received the highest endorsement as points of agreement among therapists from different theoretical orientations. The fourth identified category was *treatment structures*, which included techniques/rituals, exploration of emotional issues and the client's inner world, and adherence to a theory. The last category was the *therapeutic relationship*, with the commonalities of building an alliance, engagement, and analyzing transference. Further analysis by Tracey et al. (2003) yielded two other dimensions of commonalities among Grencavage and Norcross's common factors, namely, activities that were related to thinking or feeling, along with process elements such as the therapist–client bond, receiving and giving information, and the therapeutic role. These myriad ways of classifying or bucketing common factors have led to the same problems as with theories of psychotherapy: There are so many of them, not all of them are tied to interventions, and all yield equivalent results. At this point, clinicians and our readers may lose any interest or hope that psychotherapy research offers a means to understand what they can do or offer clients to get better. It is easy to become overwhelmed from just the sheer volume of characteristics or qualities that can be considered helpful. We don't specifically know why or how a particular intervention works, and neither the common factors nor specific factors provide causal evidence for client change (Cuijpers et al., 2019; Huibers et al., 2021).

More recent research has fortunately begun to examine common factors from a client's perspective of what is helpful (Wucherpfennig et al., 2020). We cannot emphasize this contribution enough: It seems so natural for social workers accustomed to "beginning where the client is," yet we often forget this, or find it difficult to assess clients' understanding of what works. The factors identified in all forms of therapy related to positive outcomes reported by clients were activating resources, motivational clarification, coping via social competence, coping via self-management and emotion regulation, and the therapeutic relationship. These researchers furthered their

Table 5.1 Common factors from the client perspective

Common factor	Definitions
Activating resources	Purposefully considering the patient's positive potential, unique characteristics, and abilities that support the healing process. Therapy helps to recognize, use, and strengthen existing resources.
Motivational clarification	Patients become aware of the meaning of their experience and behavior regarding their conscious and unconscious motives. Therapy helps patients to gain insight and develop a new and consistent version of their life story.
Self-management and emotion regulation	Therapy helps patients to develop functional strategies to regulate emotions, motivate themselves, and independently plan and take action to follow their goals. The patient can competently deal with intense feelings such as anger and sadness as well as stress.
Social competence	Therapy helps the patient to behave in a socially competent fashion. Patients can assert themselves, engage in positive contact, and form intense attachments to others. The patient has strategies to solve interpersonal conflicts constructively.
Therapeutic relationship	The patient experiences the relationship with the therapist as healing. The relationship is characterized by empathy, authenticity, and positive regard. The therapist is a positive identification figure that takes an interest and gives advice.

Notes Cited from Wucherpfennig et al., 2020, p.744–745.

study to show what techniques match those common factors, and we have included their summary for clarity and efficiency in. This research is an important step in moving toward a model of therapy based on common factors that go beyond vague concepts such as therapists' warmth or bond with a client.

Critique of common factors

Critiques of common factors lie in the definition and understanding of what constitutes common factors, along with how to operationalize them to show a causal link with outcome. Common factors are phenomena that cut across theoretical orientations and may in fact be the curative factors inherent in therapy (Ahn & Wampold, 2001; Garfield, 1980; Grencavage & Norcross, 1990; Messer & Wampold, 2002). However, these are not stand-alone elements that can be incorporated into therapy as the therapist sees fit. It is a misrepresentation of the research on common factors to state that the therapeutic relationship is curative in itself. For example, it would be difficult to imagine the therapeutic alliance independent of the therapist and client contexts as the cause of change. The common variables are nonspecific, unscientific, more of an art of therapy rather than the skill, a starting point but not the whole, necessary but not sufficient (Sexton & Ridley, 2004).

Another criticism of the sole focus on common factors is the relative lack of attention to both therapist and client social-cultural locations and their intersectional identities, as well as the context of current practice. This is especially significant to us as clinical social workers and as researchers who know that a large part of the client change has to do with the client's life experiences outside of therapy (also called extratherapeutic or client factors). What is worrying is that besides client expectations, motivations, and hope, few other variables of clients' lives and context make it to research models of intervention success.

Lastly, common factors do not lend themselves to an understanding of causality about illness or wellness. Goldfried (2018; 1980) suggested using the transtheoretical term "principles of change" to describe what happens in therapy instead of focusing on common factors and emphasized that it is not possible to achieve consensus at the theoretical level or the lowest level of techniques. Goldfried (1982) identified five principles of change:

- Fostering hope, expectation, and client motivation
- Facilitating the therapeutic alliance

- Increasing client's awareness and insight around the problem
- Encouraging corrective experiences for the client (in-session relationally or outside of sessions, which can include different types of exposure)
- Emphasizing ongoing reality testing.

These change principles have been supported by research as essential in successful psychotherapies (Carey, 2011; Castonguay et al., 2019; Twomey et al., 2023) such as supporting structure and focus (Castonguay & Beutler, 2006), client insight (Castonguay & Hill, 2007), corrective experience (Castonguay & Hill, 2012), client expectations (Norcross & Lambert, 2019), and the therapeutic alliance (Norcross & Lambert, 2019).

Summary of integration efforts

So far in this chapter, we have summarized almost one hundred years of study about what makes good, effective therapy. A brief summary is in order to help us retain the most important points in this chapter for our purpose of laying the foundation for how we think PDT and CBT can be bridged. The evolution of psychotherapy research yields several ways to integrate diverse theoretical schools and frameworks. We learn from technical eclecticism about the need for a broad spectrum of assessment, which includes identifying behavioral or relational patterns that contribute or reinforce symptoms that are unique to individuals and may require diverse forms of interventions. However, such a smorgasbord approach is difficult to teach and reproduce, given the lack of clarity about what combinations work with which clients and the fact that no two clients are alike.

Assimilative integration highlights the need for clarity about which theoretical framework is being utilized, the reasoning for bringing in other approaches, and the importance of knowing when you've got it right. It is not the quantity of tools or theories that clinicians should worry about, rather it is important to be skilled at what you do know, and to have the humility and self-awareness to know what you don't know. What is not so clear in assimilative models is how, when, and where clients' goals and values are considered. Theoretical integration attempts to focus on theory expansion, such as by identifying and understanding relational cycles and communication, but makes it difficult to account for the underlying changes essential in that theory to develop an effective approach for change.

One other major area of focus in psychotherapy research is on the common factors approaches, including client factors, therapist characteristics, the change process, treatment structures, and the therapeutic relationship. Also relevant to understanding essential common factors are those qualities identified by clients as helpful: activating resources, motivational clarification, self-management and emotional regulation, social competence, and the therapeutic relationship. Again, however, the concepts can be fuzzy to teach and generalize in training clinicians and attempting to reproduce effective therapeutic efforts.

Current attempts at theoretical integration

It would be fair to call the four methods of integration discussed above the first wave of psychotherapy integration. However, the story of integration seems to have been so focused on these four ways that it has given the impression that there is nothing new to be said (Constantino et al., 2017; Gaines at al., 2021). In this section, we preview more promising approaches to integration that are both exciting at the theoretical level and hold a promise of innovative practice models in the future.

As clinical social workers, it is exciting to see the Unification movement, which at long last brings in the bio-psycho-social perspective that has been scantily addressed in integration. The unification theorists believe that unless we have a systems lens to understanding psychopathology, our understanding of etiology, perpetuating factors, and treatment for our client is limited. Based on the systems approach, the "access points" of the intervention change with each client (Wolfe, 2008). This means that with one client, the intervention level might be at the social level, and interventions would be specific to that; for another client, the intervention might be on the interpersonal level and based on the perpetuating factors or etiology of the problem; while for a third client, it might be at two levels of bio and social. This means that integration will be tailored to each client as opposed to integration as a static concept applied to a client.

Another way that theorists have envisioned moving integration forward is by offering guiding principles and knowledge about factors for therapists to consider while making judgments and decisions and choosing a course of action with a client. These principles of change are broad, abstract, atheoretical principles that offer guideposts rather than rules for treatment planning and clinical work. There is a similarity with Garfield's principles of change (mentioned on page 14), but also a difference, as Goldfried's principles also try to explain how change occurs. There are thirty-eight evidence-based principles of change that Castonguay et al. (2019) delineate, which are grouped into five broad categories: client prognostic factors, treatment/provider moderating principles, client process variables, therapy relationship principles, and therapist intervention principles. Principles of change have been used to bridge the research–practice gap by identifying which of these principles are used by practitioners when working with clients with different symptom presentations. It was found that these principles are used by clinicians in unique combinations, emphasizing the particular style of each clinician, which has often been implicit. Focusing on the principles of change has made these combinations and choices of interventions used by practitioners explicit. One example from Castonguay et al. (2019) regarding therapy relationship principles is that clients who experience alliance rupture and are with therapists who are trained in how to deal with ruptures are more likely to benefit from the therapy.

Our criticism of these principles is that they offer a bleak outcome for the clients that clinical social workers often work with, clients with a higher level of baseline impairment, clients with low intrinsic motivation, or clients who may be unemployed or come from a lower socioeconomic status and therefore are often considered poor candidates for psychotherapy. This brings us to *mechanisms of change*, which are focused on how change occurs in a client, so that the mechanisms of change are more client-focused, while principles of change could be thought of as more therapist-focused. Principles of change offer guidelines for the therapist on how to proceed, while mechanisms of change explain how change occurs as a result of certain interventions in psychotherapy. From a psychotherapy integration perspective, this approach seeks to identify the mechanisms of change that underlie two or more psychotherapy approaches.

To understand mechanisms of change further, let us revisit the concept of hope. Hope was earlier referenced as a common mechanism by Frank (1973), who wrote that client expectations and hope about treatment accompany any treatment that provides a rationale and a ritual for the client's problems. Newer research by Gallagher et al. (2020) shows that hope mediates the pathway between treatment and changes in anxiety, and that changes in hope predict changes in both the client's and the clinician's anxiety. Hope involves both the cognitive and the emotional mechanisms in the treatment of anxiety disorders. This understanding of hope as a mechanism of change is meaningful because it brings practitioner wisdom into research, offering legitimacy to what centuries of clinicians know as true: that hope is a powerful common variable that cuts across therapies and predicts success. This is an important step forward in psychotherapy research as we gain further clarity on the pathways through which hope operates, along with an empirical validation (i.e., a sanctioning) of variables that practitioners and researchers know are important.

Another mechanism of change that has understandably received a great deal of focus is emotional regulation (Palmieri et al., 2022). Emotional regulation is a pan-theoretical variable that operates across various therapeutic approaches and is consistent with findings in interpersonal neurobiology. In both CBT and PDT, the work of the therapy is to improve the ability to regulate emotions and ultimately impact thoughts in relation to emotions. Emotions are seen as excessive or restricted (broad or narrow), intrapersonally or interpersonally, causing problems in the biopsychosocial-spiritual functioning of the individual. The current understanding of psychopathology and problematic mental health behavior is based on issues in an individual's behaviors, emotion regulation, or cognition, viewed particularly as experienced within the individual (APA, DSM- 5 TR 2022).

We have spoken about the context of service delivery of psychotherapy in earlier chapters, and a cautionary note is needed here to remind us that there is an entire industry of mental health workers and pharmaceuticals attempting to manage and restrict emotions to an acceptable band. This means labeling those people outside of this narrow band with a mental health diagnosis (as dysfunctional) and medicating or managing them to fit within this subjectively defined band. The inability to regulate emotions is seen as unfavorable and located in the person, or generalized as representative of the person's culture rather than representative of who has power and who has a stake in retaining that power. Generally speaking, the lack of control of emotions is often attributed to marginalized populations, with women being seen as having too many emotions compared to men and derogatory stereotypes such as the "angry Black woman" prevalent for African American women in the United States. It is worth considering what (if any) function it serves to have an entire population emoting within a narrowly defined band of acceptability. Colonization of mental health means that in a hierarchy, the mental health of the one at the top is better than of those at the bottom. There are ways this hierarchy is maintained to sustain the production of cheap, reliable labor for a hypercapitalistic society. In the United States, the carceral system and the current mental health diagnostic system are used by the privileged few in power within this hierarchical system.

With that cautionary note setting the context for how we think about emotion regulation in psychotherapy, let's think about how different perspectives in PDT and CBT may approach this mechanism of change. In PDT, for example, defenses, including denial, repression, or isolation of affect, are several ways of coping with unmanageable affect arising from a conflict or a relational deficit that may or may not be known to the client. The work of the therapy is to provide a safe enough environment for the client and the therapist to access the emotion associated with this conflict or relational deficit that is known to the client and experienced or grieved in the present with a therapeutic other to minimize the impact on current and future interpersonal functioning.

In CBT, the client is seen as using maladaptive coping, which affects cognitive appraisal of situations (threat perception), emotions (such as anger or fear), and behavior (avoidance). Ellis (1999) said that when we have feelings, it necessarily implies that some appraisal or evaluation has occurred. The work in CBT then involves the reappraisal of situations and their emotional and behavioral consequences. Experiential action, such as exposure, learning new skills, or role-play situations, is an integral part of this reappraisal of situations and beliefs. In this sense, CBT focuses on explicit tools and learning to help clients appraise their world more adaptively.

To cope with all of these different forms of integration and the ongoing results of quantitative and qualitative psychotherapy research, several theorists have come up with metamodels. Because there is no single unified model that serves all people of all cultural backgrounds with all problems, researchers have begun putting forth metamodels of how psychotherapy works by placing the common factors in context and showing how integral they are to the change process. These overarching models show how psychotherapy works and is effective. They are not meant to be practice models; rather, they provide a helicopter view of the rapidly changing landscape of psychotherapy. We will briefly discuss here the contextual model (Wampold & Imel, 2015) and the unification model (Marquis et al., 2021).

Contextual model

Wampold and Imel (2015) have extended the common factors model to include the importance of the therapeutic relationship and the social cultural contextual factors. They have also referred to their model as a metamodel of psychotherapy, which means a model of how psychotherapy works or is effective that cuts across all theories. We can also see it as a move away from enumerating common factors across therapies—which had started to feel cumbersome and numerous to the point of losing focus—and building on research on common factors. A metamodel includes all the elements of what we know of psychotherapy and the skills that make it effective. The basic premise of the model is that psychotherapy is a relational enterprise and that the benefits arise out of this relational process. In this metamodel, psychotherapy is seen as working through three pathways that ideally should all go together: *the therapeutic alliance*, which includes aspects of a real relationship between the therapist and the client but is conducted in a professional, boundaried manner; an *adaptive explanation for the distress* that the patient is coming with that includes an explanation of the process by which this distress can be alleviated; and lastly, the *tasks and goals needed to achieve success*, including health-promoting actions. The outcome of this model, then, are the interrelated factors of symptom reduction and a better quality of life. The model makes space for the client's beliefs, lived experiences, experiences with healers, about distress and cure, the role of the therapeutic relationship, and the place of the healer, and these are taken into account while delivering a particular kind of therapy. The contextual model has embraced routine monitoring and using deliberate practice procedures in their more recent evolution (Wampold, 2017).

Unfortunately, the assumption that the therapeutic relationship, viewed as the linchpin of change, is uniform in all therapies is bogus (Bell, 2022). Everyone agrees that the relationship is central to change, but practitioners differ about how that relationship affects different therapies. For example, in psychodynamic therapy, the relationship is the cornerstone of working through the transference and countertransference reactions; in fact, some even call it "the work." It is more than a warm, fuzzy, platform of connection in which the specific ingredients of therapy are delivered. In contrast, the humanistic school emphasizes the Rogerian conditions of empathy, nonjudgmental stance, and positive regard, which clearly differs both structurally and theoretically from the psychodynamic treatment of the relationship. The relationship has often been called the common factor of all psychotherapies, which it is, but it is not uniformly common.

Unification

The Unified framework is a relatively new addition to psychotherapy integration. Its value for our work is the focus on larger systemic structures that clients and clinicians live in. Unification approaches psychological constructs from a metamodern perspective, which is a perspective that follows modernism and postmodernist perspectives (Marquis et al., 2021). The metamodern perspective attempts to both include and transcend positivist and constructivist epistemologies. The researchers associated with unification have used the term "zooming in and zooming out" (Magnavita & Anchin, 2014) and examine both the big picture and the specifics to see what commonality underlies psychotherapy rather than what divides them.

The broad principles that underlie the unification wave include the following:

- The importance of the relational matrix that humans are born into, including only the familial, but also the larger systems that influence them
- The centrality of working with emotions and affect in the change process, the primacy of the therapeutic relationship
- Working with avoidance and defensiveness of affect to understand psychopathology
- Identifying vicious cycles of emotions, behaviors, self-identity, and relationships, that keep psychopathology in place and the work of reversing them.

In practice, the therapists who work from a unified framework zoom out to understand the problem from a systemic perspective as well as from a personality perspective, and they zoom in on how this plays on with this particular client. In conjunction with the client, these therapists then understand the motivations for engaging in treatment and the hopes and expectations the client brings to the treatment. They take a developmental perspective to understand the problems that clients are presenting with and work on them, providing corrective emotional experiencing in the therapeutic relationship. As strategies, they employ techniques that focus on habits, cognitions, emotions, and being present to reality (mindfulness), all the while engaging emotions, which is seen as necessary for change. For social workers trained in a biopsychosocial-spiritual framework, this "new" development may seem so obvious that it is almost comical. While none of these broad, core principles are new, they do shed light on ways in which researchers are trying to bridge the seemingly varied fields of psychopathology, attachment work, theories of psychotherapy, personality theories, emotions, and cognition, in the context of the unique systems that the client is embedded in.

Critiques of psychotherapy integration research

There are many ways to integrate skills and theories of psychotherapy, as the previous sections make apparent, and we have only given an overview. This can leave clinicians confused as to what is really integrative and cause them to question whether there are any rules or boundaries around a so-called good integration. Most critical is the question "Does any of this matter?" One of my doctoral research teachers (TN) used to emphasize the question "Is this trip necessary?" from the days of gas rationing, which has been one of our guiding principles in this chapter. To put this question a different way, what is most important for clinicians to understand and remember from examining all of these methods to bridge PDT and CBT?

An important conclusion of our "necessary trip" in psychotherapy integration is realizing how much psychotherapy research have evolved over time in terms of using what is found in a particular study—or perhaps in cognitive science or neurobiological research on trauma—to move the field forward. What is particularly glaring and troublesome, however, is the long road it has taken to reach the realization that context matters, and that it is critical to include our clients in our attempts to understand what works (Magnavita & Anchin, 2014; Marquis et al., 2021; Norcross & Wampold, 2019). Social work has been at the forefront in considering the contexts of clients, though unfortunately, attempts to be "scientific" and quantifiable have at times stood in the way of capturing nonspecific and even specific factors.

Qualitative studies, on the other hand, that are focused on psychotherapy outcomes find that clients can give a more "nuanced appraisal of the helpfulness of the therapy. In general, when clients are given time and space to talk at length about the outcomes of their therapy, they tend to offer a somewhat more critical account, when contrasted with the findings of quantitative outcome studies that merely report changes in levels of functioning" (Dale et al., 1998; Howe, 1996; McLeod, 2013, p. 66; Morris, 2005). The critical ingredient here is that clients must be given the opportunity to tell their perspective, rather than simply utilizing a quantifiable measure such as pre- and post-test symptom relief or assessments of the relationship at predetermined points in treatment. Symptom relief is important but "it may not be the truth arrived at as much as the manner of arriving at the truth which is the essence of therapy" (Edgar Levenson, 1978, p. 16).

Similarly, what seems to be most critical is clients and clinicians are active agents in the treatment, rather than the techniques provided or the "concrete operating procedures" (e.g., providing information, clarifying roles, and giving advice or suggestions) that are designed to produce certain client behaviors (Bohart, 2007). Likewise, the totality of therapists and their ability to engage in ongoing reflexivity about their own biases, schemas, experiences, and so on needs to be held as a critical variable, particularly when interacting with clients who have been underserved, marginalized, and who have differing beliefs about what is helpful or therapeutic. These factors related to both the client and the therapist are situated in a cultural and societal context that can empower or disempower its participants. These contextual factors need to be prioritized in future studies. Also, it is important to consider the type of research being utilized to examine these dynamic variables. For example, qualitative research may be best at trying to answer how clients experience the moment-by-moment process of therapy, what clients consider to be significant in their treatment, and how they have integrated or assimilated difficult experiences within the time span of their therapy (Mcleod, 2013). Process and outcome research for the therapeutic alliance has indicated that for different types of therapy, different variables are measured: emotional arousal during behavior therapy for anxiety disorders, the use of "concrete" techniques for cognitive therapy, and gains in self-understanding in psychodynamic therapy (Crits-Christoph et al., 2013). These differences are important, particularly when training clinicians and evaluating competency in the practice of psychotherapy. Utilizing the appropriate form of measurement with the appropriate treatment is critical when examining the question of what is helpful in therapy. In addition to the results of quantitative and qualitative research, it is also important to remain cognizant of the pragmatic necessity to utilize many ways of knowing to examine all aspects of the therapeutic process and to apply a critical lens to all of these ways (Anastas, 2014; Hill, 2012; Stiles, 2002, 2010). In the words of William James, pragmatism about what works should be key; however, how we define "works" must be broadened to include what is being learned about how our brain changes and processes experiences through the course of therapy. Our brains continually need to adapt to a world influenced by massive technological advances that, at times, short-circuit relationships of depth.

Conclusion

Our next step is to focus on the guiding practice principles resulting from our summary and critique of psychotherapy research which we hope will demonstrate why it is important to examine psychotherapy research. In our opinion, we can extrapolate the following guiding principles from current and past psychotherapy research:

1. Applying a single theoretical school or technique is a disservice to clients who bring to treatment a complex intersectional history and biopsychosocial-spiritual context (as does the therapist). However, integration should not be done without awareness of the changes to foundation theories that can occur when one imports a different framework into the treatment.
2. It is critical to have a broad spectrum of assessment that allows one to assess variables that cross theoretical schools, such as affect, cognition, behavior, interpersonal patterns, historical antecedents, and the sociocultural, economic, and political environments. Treatment will likely address different components of the constellations of our clients' lives, whether that be emotional regulation or the ability to activate goal-directed behavior such as interpersonal changes.
3. When attempting to integrate/bridge/assimilate different theoretical models, it is important for therapists to ask themselves these questions: What is the theoretical framework with this particular client and why? What is the reasoning for bringing in other approaches? How will the effectiveness of the intervention or the variation from the approach be measured or understood?
4. The process of therapy is a form of exposure therapy rather than a separate intervention and can be experienced by clients as important for

identifying their strengths and serve as a source for understanding the meaning of their experiences.

5. Therapists need to be aware of the limitations of the theoretical schools they are trained in and consider those limits when discussing potential avenues for growth with clients. Likewise, professional and cultural humility each requires knowing one's own limitations and skillsets as a therapist. Having more tools in the toolbox can result in convoluted or misattuned work rather than improvement for the client. "More" may not always be better; however, at a minimum it is essential for clinicians to be trained in several theoretical frameworks.
6. The therapeutic relationship is unique to each therapeutic dyad and is essential but insufficient on its own to effect change.
7. Decisions about interventions must be based on more than empirical evidence and include client needs, preferences, and values in addition to professional expertise.

Our next chapter will outline the helpful ways we have found to bridge PDT and CBT in a manner that is consistent with our understanding of psychotherapy research, the theories themselves, our clinical experiences, and our understanding of the current sociocultural, political, and economic realities impacting practice.

References

Ahn, H.-n., & Wampold, B. E. (2001). Where oh where are the specific ingredients? A meta-analysis of component studies in counseling and psychotherapy. *Journal of Counseling Psychology*, *48*(3), 251–257. https://doi.org/10.1037/0022-0167.48.3.251

American Psychiatric Association. (2022). *Diagnostic and statistical manual of mental disorders* (5th ed., text rev.). https://doi.org/10.1176/appi.books.9780890425787

Anastas, J. W. (2014). The science of social work and its relationship to social work practice. *Research on Social Work Practice*, *24*(5), 571–580. https://doi.org/10.1177/1049731513511335

Bell, C. R. (2022). Beyond the specific factors versus common factors debate: Lacan's four discourses informing Wampold and Imel's contextual model of psychotherapy efficacy. *Theory & Psychology*, *32*(3), 423-442. https://doi.org/10.1177/09593543221083580 (Original work published 2022)

Berlin, S. B. (2012). The applied-science approach and the cognitive-integrative perspective. In T. L. Rzepnicki, S. G. McCracken, & H. E. Briggs (Eds.), *From task-centered social work to evidence-based and integrative practice* (pp. 40–64). Lyceum.

Berlin, S. B. (2002). *Clinical social work practice: A cognitive-integrative perspective*. Oxford.

Berlin, S. B. (2010). Why cognitive therapy needs social work? In W. Borden (Ed.), *Reshaping theory in contemporary social work: Toward a critical pluralism in clinical practice* (pp. 31–50). Columbia Press.

Beutler, L. E., & Clarkin, J. F. (1990). *Systematic treatment selection: Toward targeted therapeutic interventions.* Brunner/Mazel.

Bohart, A. C. (2007). An alternative view of concrete operating procedures from the perspective of the client as active self-healer. *Journal of Psychotherapy Integration, 17*(1), 125–137. https://doi.org/10.1037/1053-0479.17.1.125

Borden, W. (Ed.). (2010). *Reshaping theory in contemporary social work: Toward a critical pluralism in clinical practice.* Columbia Press.

Cameron, S. K., Rodgers, J., & Dagnan, D. (2018). The relationship between the therapeutic alliance and clinical outcomes in cognitive behavior therapy for adults with depression: A meta-analytic review. *Clinical Psychology & Psychotherapy, 25*(3), 446–456. https://doi.org/10.1002/cpp.2180

Carey, T. A. (2011). Exposure and reorganization: The what and how of effective psychotherapy. *Clinical Psychology Review, 31*, 236–248.

Castonguay, L. G., & Beutler, L. E. (2006). Principles of therapeutic change: A task force on participants, relationships, and techniques factors. *Journal of Clinical Psychology, 62*(6), 631–638. https://doi.org/10.1002/jclp.20256

Castonguay, L. G., & Goldfried, M. R. (1994). Psychotherapy integration: An idea whose time has come. *Applied & Preventive Psychology, 3*(3), 159–172. https://doi.org/10.1016/S0962-1849(05)80068-X

Castonguay, L. G., & Hill, C. (Eds.). (2007). *Insight in psychotherapy.* American Psychological Association. https://doi.org/10.1037/11532-000

Castonguay, L. G., & Hill, C. E. (Eds.). (2012). Corrective experiences in psychotherapy: An introduction. In L. G. Castonguay & C. E. Hill (Eds.), *Transformation in psychotherapy: Corrective experiences across cognitive behavioral, humanistic, and psychodynamic approaches* (pp. 3–9). American Psychological Association. https://doi.org/10.1037/13747-001

Castonguay, L. G., Constantino, M. J., & Beutler, L. E. (2019). *Principles of change: How psychotherapists implement research in practice.* Oxford University Press. https://doi.org/10.1093/med-psych/9780199324729.001.0001

Constantino, M. J., Coyne, A. E., & Gomez Penedo, J. M. (2017). Contextualized integration as a common playing field for clinicians and researchers: Comment on McWilliams. *Journal of Psychotherapy Integration, 27*, 296–303. https://doi.org/10.1037/int0000067

Castonguay, L. G., Eubanks, C. F., Goldfried, M. R., Muran, J. C., & Lutz, W. (2015). Research on psychotherapy integration: Building on the past, looking to the future. *Psychotherapy Research, 25*(3), 365–382. https://doi.org/10.1080/10503307.2015.1014010

Cooper, S. (2016). *The analyst's experience of the depressive position: The melancholic errand of psychoanalysis.* Routledge.

Crits-Christoph, P., Gibbons, M. B. C., & Mukherjee, D. (2013). Psychotherapy process-outcome research. In M. Barkham, W. Lutz, & L. G. Castonguay (Eds.), *Bergin and Garfield's handbook of psychotherapy and behavior change* (6th ed., pp. 298–340). John Wiley & Sons.

Cuijpers, P., Reijnders, M., & Huibers, M. J. H. (2019). The role of common factors in psychotherapy outcome. *Annual Review of Clinical Psychology, 15*, 207–231. https://doi.org/10.1146/annurev-clinpsy-050718-095424

Dale, P., Allen, J., & Measor, L. (1998). Counselling adults who were abused as children: Clients' perceptions of efficacy, client-counsellor communication, and dissatisfaction. *British Journal of Guidance & Counselling, 26*, 141–158.

Delboy, S. & Michaels, L. (2023). Going beneath the surface: What people want from therapy. In L. Michaels, T. Wooldridge, N. Burke, & J. R. Muhr (Eds.), *Advancing psychotherapy for the next generation* (211–239). Routledge.

American Psychiatric Association. (2022). *Diagnostic and statistical manual of mental disorders* (5th ed., text rev.). https://doi.org/10.1176/appi.books.9780890425787

Drisko, J., & Grady, M. D. (2018). Teaching evidence-based practice using cases in social work education. *Families in Society, 99*(3), 269–282. https://doi.org/10.1177/1044389418785331

Duncan, B. L., Miller, S. D., Wampold, B. E., & Hubble, M. A. (Eds.). (2010). *The heart and soul of change: Delivering what works in therapy* (2nd ed.). American Psychological Association. https://doi.org/10.1037/12075-000

Ellis, A. (1999). Why rational-emotive therapy to rational emotive behavior therapy? *Psychotherapy: Theory, Research, Practice, Training, 36*(2), 154–159. https://doi.org/10.1037/h0087680

Elkin, I., Shea, M. T., Watkins, J. T., Imber, S. D., Sotsky, S. M., Collins, J. F., Glass, D. R., Pilkonis, P. A., Leber, W. R., & Docherty, J. P. (1989). National Institute of Mental Health Treatment of Depression Collaborative Research Program. General effectiveness of treatments. *Archives of General Psychiatry, 46*(11), 971–983. https://doi.org/10.1001/archpsyc.1989.01810110013002

Feixas, G., & Botella, L. (2004). Psychotherapy integration: Reflections and contributions from a constructivist epistemology. *Journal of Psychotherapy integration, 14* (2), 192–222.

Fluckiger, C., Del Re, A. C., Wlodasch, D., Horvath, A. O., Solomonov, N., & Wampold, B. E. (2020). Assessing the alliance-outcome association adjusted for patient characteristics and treatment processes: A meta-analytic summary of direct comparisons. *Journal of Counseling Psychology, 67*(6), 706–711. https://doi.org/10.1037/cou0000424

Frank, J. D. (1973). *Persuasion and healing: A comparative study of psychotherapy.* The Johns Hopkins University Press.

Gaines, A. N., Goldfried, M. R., & Constantino, M. J. (2021). Revived call for consensus in the future of psychotherapy. *BMJ Mental Health, 24*(1), 2–4. https://doi.org/10.1136/ebmental-2020-300208

Gallagher, M. W., Long, L. J., Richardson, A., D'Souza, J., Boswell, J. F., Farchione, T. J., & Barlow, D. H. (2020). Examining hope as a transdiagnostic mechanism of change across anxiety disorders and CBT treatment protocols. *Behavior Therapy, 51*(1), 190–202. https://doi.org/10.1016/j.beth.2019.06.001

Garfield. S. L. (1980). *Psychotherapy: An eclectic approach.* Wiley.

Garfield, S. L. (1957). *Introductory clinical psychology: An overview of the functions, methods, and problems of contemporary clinical psychology.* Macmillan.

Geertz, C. (1973). *The interpretation of cultures: Selected essays.* Basic Books.

Gianotti, P. (2022). *Embracing therapeutic complexity: A guidebook to integrating the essentials of psychodynamic principles across therapeutic Disciplines.* Routledge

Gianotti, P., & Danielian, J. (2014). *Listening with purpose: Entry points into shame and narcissistic vulnerability.* Jason Aronson.

Gianotti, P., & Danielian, J. (2017). *Uncovering the resilient core: A workbook on the narcissistic defenses, shame, and emerging authenticity.* Routledge.

Gold, J. (2011). Attachment theory and psychotherapy integration: An introduction and review of the literature. *Journal of Psychotherapy Integration, 21*(3), 221–231. https://doi.org/10.1037/a0025490

Gold, J. R., & Wachtel, P. L. (1993). Cyclical psychodynamics. In G. Stricker & J. R. Gold (Eds.), *Comprehensive handbook of psychotherapy integration.* Springer. https://doi-org.libproxy.smith.edu/10.1007/978-1-4757-9782-4_5

Goldfried, M. (2018). Obtaining consensus in psychotherapy: What holds us back? *American Psychologist, 74*(4), 484–496.

Goldfried, M. R. (1980). Toward the delineation of therapeutic change principles. *American Psychologist, 35*(11), 991–999. https://doi.org/10.1037/0003-066X.35.11.991

Goldfried, M. R. (1982). *Converging themes in psychotherapy: Trends in psychodynamic, humanistic, and behavioral practice.* Springer.

Grencavage, L. M., & Norcross, J. C. (1990). Where are the commonalities among the therapeutic common factors? *Professional Psychology: Research and Practice, 21*(5), 372–378. https://doi.org/10.1037/0735-7028.21.5.372

Hill, C. E. (Ed.). (2012). *Consensual qualitative research: A practical resource for investigating social science phenomena*. American Psychological Association.

Howe, D. (1996). Client experiences of counselling and treatment interventions, a qualitative study of family views of family therapy. *British Journal of Guidance and Counselling, 24*, 367–376.

Huibers, M. J. H., Lorenzo-Luaces, L., Cuijpers, P., & Kazantzis, N. (2021). On the road to personalized psychotherapy: A research agenda based on cognitive behavior therapy for depression. *Frontiers in Psychiatry, 11*, 607508. https://doi.org/10.3389/fpsyt.2020.607508

Imel, Z. E., & Wampold, B. E. (2008). The importance of treatment and the science of common factors in psychotherapy. In S. D. Brown & R. W. Lent (Eds.), *Handbook of counseling psychology* (4th ed., pp. 249–266). John Wiley & Sons.

Kuchuck, S. (2021). *The relational revolution in psychoanalysis and psychotherapy*. Confer Books.

Lampropoulos, G. K. (2001). Bridging technical eclecticism and theoretical integration: Assimilative integration. *Journal of Psychotherapy Integration, 11*(1), 5–19. https://doi.org/10.1023/A:1026672807119

Lazarus, A. A. (1981). *The practice of Multimodal therapy*. McGraw-Hill.

Lazarus, A. A., Beutler, L. E., & Norcross, J. C. (1992). The future of technical eclecticism. *Psychotherapy: Theory, Research, Practice, Training, 29*(1), 11–20. https://doi.org/10.1037/0033-3204.29.1.11

Leichsenring, F., Abbass, A., Hilsenroth, M. J., Leweke, F., Luyten, P., Keefe, J. R., Midgley, N., Rabung, S., Salzer, S., & Steinert, C. (2017). Biases in research: Risk factors for non-replicability in psychotherapy and pharmacotherapy research. *Psychological Medicine, 47*(6), 1000–1011. https://doi.org/10.1017/S003329171600324X

Levenson, E. A. (1978). Two essays in psychoanalytic psychology-I. Psychoanalysis: Cure or persuasion. *Contemporary Psychoanalysis, 14*, 1–17.

Luborsky, L., Singer, B., & Luborsky, L. (1975). Comparative studies of psychotherapies. Is it true that "everyone has won and all must have prizes"? *Archives of General Psychiatry, 32*(8), 995–1008. https://doi.org/10.1001/archpsyc.1975.01760260059004

Luborsky, L., Diguer, L., Seligman, D. A., Rosenthal, R., Krause, E. D., Johnson, S., Halperin, G., Bishop, M., Berman, J. S., & Schweizer, E. (1999). The researcher's own therapy allegiances: A "wild card" in comparisons of treatment efficacy. *Clinical Psychology: Science and Practice, 6*(1), 95–106. https://doi.org/10.1093/clipsy.6.1.95

Magnavita, J. J., & Anchin, J. C. (2014). *Unifying psychotherapy: Principles, methods, and evidence from clinical science*. Springer Publishing Company.

Marquis, A., Henriques, G., Anchin, J., Critchfield, K., Harris, J., Ingram, B., Magnavita, J., & Osborn, K. (2021). Unification: The fifth pathway to psychotherapy integration. *Journal of Contemporary Psychotherapy, 51*(4), 285–294. https://doi.org/10.1007/s10879-021-09506-7

McLeod, J. (2013). Increasing the rigor of case study evidence in therapy research. *Pragmatic Case Studies in Psychotherapy, 9*(4), 382–402. https://doi.org/10.14713/pcsp.v9i4.1832

Messer, S. B. (1992). A critical examination of belief structures in integrative and eclectic psychotherapy. In J. C. Norcross & M. R. Goldfried (Eds.), *Handbook of psychotherapy integration* (pp. 130–165). Basic Books.

Messer, S. B., & Wampold, B. E. (2002). Let's face facts: Common factors are more potent than specific therapy ingredients. *Clinical Psychology: Science and Practice, 9*(1), 21–25. https://doi.org/10.1093/clipsy.9.1.21

Morris, B. (2005). *Discovering bits and pieces of me: Research exploring women's experiences of psychoanalytical psychotherapy*. Women's Therapy Centre.

National Association of Social Workers. (2022, January 3). *NASW guidance on No Surprises Act*. https://naswnys.org/nasw-guidance-on-no-surprises-act

Nelson, D. L., & Castonguay, L. G. (2017). The systematic use of homework in psychodynamic-interpersonal psychotherapy for depression: An assimilative integration approach. *Journal of Psychotherapy Integration, 27*(2), 265–281. https://doi.org/10.1037/int0000063
Norcross, J. C. (2005). A primer on psychotherapy integration. In J. C. Norcross & M. R. Goldfried (Eds.), *Handbook of psychotherapy integration* (2nd ed., pp. 3–23). Oxford University Press. https://doi.org/10.1093/med:psych/9780195165791.003.0001
Norcross, J. C., & Lambert, M. J. (2019). Evidence-based psychotherapy relationships: The third task force. In J. C. Norcross & M. J. Lambert (Eds.), *Psychotherapy relationships that work: Evidence-based therapist contributions* (3rd ed., pp. 1–23). Oxford University Press. https://doi.org/10.1093/med-psych/9780190843953.003.0001
Norcross, J. C., & Wampold, B. E. (2019). Personalizing psychotherapy: Results, conclusions, and practices. In J. C. Norcross & B. E. Wampold (Eds.), *Psychotherapy relationships that work: Evidence-based therapist responsiveness* (3rd ed., pp. 329–341). Oxford University Press. https://doi.org/10.1093/med-psych/9780190843960.003.0011
Norcross, J. C., & Wampold, B. E. (2011). What works for whom: Tailoring psychotherapy to the person. *Journal of Clinical Psychology, 67*(2), 127–132. https://doi.org/10.1002/jclp.20764
Northcut, T. B., & Kienow, A. (2014). The trauma trifecta of military sexual trauma: A case study illustrating the integration of mind and body in clinical work with survivors of MST. *Clinical Social Work Journal, 42*(3), 247–259. https://doi.org/10.1007/s10615-014-0479-0
Palmieri, A., Fernandez, K. C., Cariolato, Y., Kleinbub, J. R., Salvatore, S., & Gross, J. J. (2022). Emotion regulation in psychodynamic and cognitive-behavioral therapy: An integrative perspective. *Clinical Neuropsychiatry, 19*(2), 103–113.
Ramsey, R. (2001). The clinical challenges of assimilative integration. *Journal of Psychotherapy Integration, 11*(1), 21–42.
Rogers, C. R. (1957). The necessary and sufficient conditions of therapeutic personality change. *Journal of Consulting Psychology*, 21, 95–103. http://dx.doi.org/10.1037/h0045357
Rosenzweig, S. (1936). Some implicit common factors in diverse methods of psychotherapy. *American Journal of Orthopsychiatry, 6*(3), 412–415. https://doi.org/10.1111/j.1939-0025.1936.tb05248.x
Schact, T. E. (1984). The varieties of integrative experience. In H. Arkowitz & S. B. Messer (Eds.), *Psychoanalytic therapy and behavior therapy: Is integration possible?* (pp. 107–131). Plenum.
Sexton, T. L., & Ridley, C. R. (2004). Implications of a moderated common factors approach: Does it move the field forward? *Journal of Marital and Family Therapy, 30*(2), 159–163. https://doi.org/10.1111/j.1752-0606.2004.tb01231.x
Shilkret, B., & Shilkret, C. (2022). Attachment theory. In J. Berzoff, L. M. Flanagan, & P. Hertz (Eds.), *Inside out and outside in: Psychodynamic clinical theory and psychopathology in contemporary multicultural contexts* (5th ed, pp. 169–187). Rowman & Littlefield.
Stiles, W. B. (2002). Assimilation of problematic experiences. In J. C. Norcross (Ed.), *Psychotherapy relationships that work: Therapist contributions and responsiveness to patients* (pp. 357–365). Oxford University Press.
Stiles, W. B. (2010). Theory-building case studies as practice-based evidence. In M. Barkham, G. E. Hardy, & J. Mellor-Clark (Eds.), *Developing and delivering practice-based evidence: A guide for the psychological therapies* (pp. 91–108). Wiley-Blackwell. https://doi.org/10.1002/9780470687994.ch4
Stricker, G. (2006). Using homework in psychodynamic psychotherapy. *Journal of Psychotherapy Integration, 16*(2), 219–237. https://doi.org/10.1037/1053-0479.16.2.219
Stricker, G., & Gold, J. (2005). Assimilative psychodynamic psychotherapy. In J. C. Norcross & M. R. Goldfried (Eds.), *Handbook of psychotherapy integration* (2nd ed., pp. 221–240). Oxford University Press. https://doi.org/10.1093/med:psych/9780195165791.003.0010

Thorne, F. (1957). An evaluation of eclectically oriented psychotherapy. *Journal of Consulting Psychology*, *21*(6), 459–464. https://doi.org/10.1037/h0045258

Tracey, T. J. G., Lichtenberg, J. W., Goodyear, R. K., Claiborn, C., & Wampold, B. E. (2003). Concept mapping of therapeutic common factors. *Psychotherapy Research*, *13*(4), 401–413. https://doi.org/10.1093/ptr/kpg04

Twomey, C., O'Reilly, G., & Goldfried, M. R. (2023). Consensus on the perceived presence of transtheoretical principles of change in routine psychotherapy practice: A survey of clinicians and researchers. *Psychotherapy*, *60*(2), 219–224. https://doi.org/10.1037/pst0000489

Wachtel, P. L. (2014). An integrative relational point of view. *Psychotherapy*, *51*(3), 342–349. https://doi.org/10.1037/a0037219

Wachtel, P. L. (2014). *Cyclical psychodynamics and the contextual self: The inner world, the intimate world, and the world of culture and society*. Routledge.

Wachtel, P. L. (1991). From eclecticism to synthesis: Toward a more seamless psychotherapeutic integration. *Journal of Psychotherapy Integration*, *1*(1), 43–54. https://doi.org/10.1037/h0101201

Wachtel, P. L. (2008). *Relational theory and the practice of psychotherapy*. Guilford Press.

Wachtel, P. L. (2017). The relationality of everyday life: The unfinished journey of relational psychoanalysis. *Psychoanalytic Dialogues*, *27*(5), 503–521.

Wachtel, P., & Gagnon, G. (2019). Cyclical psychodynamics and integrative relational psychotherapy. https://doi.org/10.1093/med-psych/9780190690465.003.0009

Wampold, B. E. (2000). Outcomes of individual counseling and psychotherapy: Empirical evidence addressing two fundamental questions. In S. D. Brown & R. W. Lent (Eds.), *Handbook of counseling psychology* (3rd ed., pp. 711–739). John Wiley & Sons.

Wampold, B. E. (2001). *The great psychotherapy debate: Models, methods, and findings.*

Wampold, B. E. (2017). What should we practice?: A contextual model for how psychotherapy works. In T. Rousmaniere, R. K. Goodyear, S. D. Miller, & B. E. Wampold (Eds.), *The cycle of excellence: Using deliberate practice to improve supervision and training* (pp. 49–65). Wiley Blackwell. https://doi.org/10.1002/9781119165590.ch3Lawrence Erlbaum Associates Publishers.

Whalley, B., & Hyland, M.E. (2010). One size does not fit all: Motivational predictors of contextual benefits of therapy. *Psychology and Psychotherapy: Theory, Research and Practice*, *82*, 291–303. https://doi.org/10.1348/147608309X413275

Wampold, B. E., & Imel, Z. E. (2015). *The great psychotherapy debate: The evidence for what makes psychotherapy work*. Routledge.

Wolfe, B. E. (2008). Toward a unified conceptual framework of psychotherapy. *Journal of Psychotherapy Integration*, *18*(3), 292–300. https://doi.org/10.1037/1053-0479.18.3.292

Wucherpfennig, F., Boyle, K., Rubel, J. A., Weinmann-Lutz, B., & Lutz, W. (2020). What sticks? Patients' perspectives on treatment three years after psychotherapy: A mixed-methods approach. *Psychotherapy Research: Journal of the Society for Psychotherapy Research*, *30*(6), 739–752. https://doi.org/10.1080/10503307.2019.1671630

Zimmerman, M., Ellison, W., Young, D., Chelminski, I., & Dalrymple, K. (2015). How many different ways do patients meet the diagnostic criteria for major depressive disorder? *Comprehensive Psychiatry*, *56*, 29–34. https://doi.org/10.1016/j.comppsych.2014.09.007

6

The therapeutic relationship as a crucible for integration

Introduction

We have covered the contextual and historical factors influencing the theoretical frameworks of PDT and CBT and considered the results of psychotherapy research relevant for our attempts at bridging the two schools. In this chapter, we want to build on the summary of the process and outcome research from Chapter 5 and move to more specific clinical priorities for integration. Our goal is to connect implicit clinical wisdom with theoretical concepts and practices supported by qualitative and quantitative research in developing and managing the most critical variable in psychotherapy: the therapeutic relationship.

In our understanding of the practice and the teaching of integrative psychotherapy, we work hard to steer our students away from the idea that there is one best way to practice or integrate different theories and techniques—that there is no perfect integrative approach. Just as "the uniqueness of every person makes it impossible ever to be fully prepared for the next new client" (McWilliams, 2004, p. 47), there cannot be one type of integration that fits perfectly with every clinician and every client. The ability to sit with the ambiguity of not knowing, not falling into standard ways of operating in therapy, and, most importantly, not endorsing any one method as "the way to integrate" is the hallmark of an integrative mindset. However, this does not mean that new graduates and students are asked to go into practice without any tools; on the contrary, there must be grounding in "home theories" such as CBT and psychodynamic, with ample training in relational skills.

In line with the contextual and common factors models discussed in Chapter 5, we want to emphasize the therapeutic relationship as the "flagship common factor" in integration (Anchin et al. 2024, p. 234; Flückiger et al., 2018). The therapeutic relationship is the hallmark of all psychotherapy, especially integrative psychotherapy (Boswell et al., 2021). It is also

Psychodynamic and Cognitive Behavioral Theory and Practice. Terry B. Northcut and Shveta Kumaria, Oxford University Press. © Oxford University Press (2025). DOI: 10.1093/9780197508404.003.0006

true that the therapeutic relationship is a function of both the therapist and the client, which changes from moment to moment based on the responsiveness of both parties. Psychotherapy is, after all, not about the tools we use but about two people (or more) working together. This relationship occurs between a helper and a client, where the helper has some legitimacy, such as a license or a culturally bestowed healer status. The client's experience and perspective are paramount; however, the person of the therapist is an essential tool. This relationship is emotionally charged and provides clients at different times with hope, motivation, and an understanding of why they are suffering. Based on this relationship and understanding of the problem, the clinical dyad or group agrees on goals and corresponding changes in behavior, affect, and thought to achieve these goals. This goal setting is consistent with a CBT emphasis on the therapeutic relationship that includes collaborative empiricism and Socratic dialogue (Kazantzis & Dobson, 2022; Kazantzis et al., 2017). From a psychodynamic perspective, focusing on the therapeutic relationship allows the client and the therapist to remain experientially grounded in the present while exploring the impact of the past on current functioning and experiences. Both CBT and PDT bring important relational emphases that include a focus on emotional regulation (Palmieri et al., 2022) in the context of the therapeutic relationship that also emphasizes the action of both parties (Gaztambide, 2020).

We learned from our last chapter that therapist flexibility, personal and professional awareness, theoretical and cultural humility, dyadic attunement, and responsiveness to the context are some of the most critical variables contributing to this essential relationship (Constantino et al., 2021). The source of relief from suffering is not a therapeutic model, but a healing relationship in which stories are heard, truths acknowledged, and feelings shared, offering new ways of "living in the world" (Wachtel, 2020).

Home theory

Whether we can articulate it or not, we all have a theory in our minds about the development of distress and how change occurs. We consciously and unconsciously use this lens to filter clients' data and social context in or out. These ideas influence clients' openness to therapist interventions while also influencing the interventions offered by the therapist, the relationship offered by the therapist, the listening ear, and the moments of the therapist's absence and presence in the therapeutic relationship. These implicit ideas undergo assimilation and accommodation with education, supervision, training, personal therapy, life experiences, and years of experience with clients. In the following paragraphs, we explain our personal theoretical evolution to offer readers a perspective on why we evolved as integrative practitioners.

As our home base, we have evolved theoretically to embrace a social justice-focused relational integrative approach grounded in the current psychodynamic understanding of attachment. When we use the term *attachment*, we want it to be clear that we are thinking about Bowlby's focus on the *process* of attachment dynamics as opposed to the *categories* that have historically received so much focus. Wachtel's (2017) theoretical perspective of cyclical psychodynamics focuses on how early internal working models are continually confirmed or revised over time, creating feedback loops that maintain certain patterns. It is the process of exploring these patterns and how they are maintained in the present that allows us to bridge PDT and CBT. The exploration of these patterns is conducted within the context of a therapeutic relationship, which undergirds the work of emotional regulation in therapy, a common factor or mechanism of change that underlies how change occurs in multiple forms of therapy (Palmieri et al., 2022). Accessing and modifying emotional schemas lies at the heart of relational clinical work.

In addition to our relational focus, we believe our personal and professional values of social justice necessitate an awareness of the power differential between clinicians and clients and recognize that we are not the experts on the client; instead, we have knowledge and training in facilitating a helpful therapeutic relationship and possible avenues of growth. We have learned that we can never assume that all presenting problems clients bring to therapy are isolated and lie solely within the individual. On the contrary, there are always larger oppressive systems in which we all live and work. Farrar and Hanley (2023) argue that all therapy is political, given these contextual factors. Politics determines access to rights and resources, and even how we define what constitutes human "rights" or "problems." Our ability as clinicians to recognize our own experiences with oppression and the ways in which we are also the oppressed or the oppressors grounds our clinical work and must continually be brought into awareness as we interact with clients and the greater social surroundings in which we practice. Along with our awareness of the need for ongoing efforts to challenge social injustice in our therapeutic work, we also need to recognize the ways in which these contextual experiences impact relational past, present, and future mental health. The healing of the past in the present can only happen in relationship with others, which may often require working on the social structures that are made to benefit the few and oppress the many, especially those who seek help from social workers. While the past carries a heavy presence, the nature of ongoing oppression requires balancing historical and current relational factors with the ever-present reality of discrimination as we work therapeutically and as advocates. We, and our clients, live in the world—a world that also provides feedback loops confirming or disconfirming our internal working models, beliefs, and cognitions, which in turn impacts our behavior in that world.

Contemporary relational psychoanalytic theory is a post-constructionist lens that focuses on contextual factors that influence relationships and intersecting identities. The emphasis is on a "three-person" relationship (see Chapter 3) in the therapeutic space, with the third "person" being the dynamic relationship between client and therapist and the sociocultural–political–economic context that continually impacts that relationship. Wachtel (2020) used the phrase "living-in-the-world" to convey "the seamlessness of person and context (the dashes in the phrase pointing to their being not fully separate or separable; like Winnicott's baby and mother) and to the *activity* of living" (p. 322). Bowlby's working models, or use of terms such as *emotion schema*, convey more than a static, representational entity. Rather, they are interactive and need to be dynamically explored and experienced both in therapy and outside the therapy relationship.

Any such exploration of emotional schemas requires the building and solidifying of a therapeutic relationship. In the language of electronics, the relationship is the power strip in which you can plug in multiple devices: a phone charger, a computer, and a lamp to light the way. You need the power strip of the relationship to be up and running before you can run any applications, that is, before you can attempt symptom relief, problem-solve, or explore the impact of oppression. The relationship is necessary but insufficient for change. In Chapters 7 and 8 and our discussion below, we will demonstrate our home theory in action; in a sense, the "plug-ins" we think are critical to successful practice. Unlike electronics and a power strip, these aspects of the relationship overlap and are sometimes indistinguishable. We are separating them for clarity, but they operate simultaneously. Barsness

(2021) sought to clarify what "relational" actually looks like in practice by conducting a qualitative study to find the commonalities between psychoanalytic therapists who identify as relational. His findings echo the psychotherapy research we have discussed in prior chapters and are consistent with the components we emphasize in the therapeutic relationship: personal and professional awareness, attuned flexibility, appropriate responsiveness, and a broad spectrum of assessment that includes case conceptualization and treatment planning.

The therapeutic relationship

Personal and professional awareness

In a social justice relational approach (and in good practice in general) it is essential for clinicians to be aware of their implicit and explicit beliefs, attributions, and assumptions that lead them to process client information uniquely in sessions. A holistic and open therapeutic stance with the ability to continually maintain self-awareness allows us to pick up more cues than are possible from a single theoretical focus. Reflective practice is grounded in the never-ending cycle of experience, reflection, and action, including understanding and learning from our mistakes (Sicora, 2017). We discussed in Chapters 3 and 4 some of the biases and values within PD and CBT, including assumptions about the therapeutic actions that change affect, behavior, and thoughts; however, it is up to all clinicians to do their own work to understand their own assumptions in addition to the theoretical ones. Supervision, consultation, and personal therapy can help monitor and shape these perceptions by serving as a supportive community for the reflexive process. For example, potential clients may not find an individualized perspective on mental health syntonic to their way of being in the world. "Identity" may mean "we" rather than an "I." Efforts to focus on the individual may at the very least be met with confusion, leading to a sense of disempowerment and even oppression that can be interpreted by the therapist as "resistance" or a lack of insight. Supervision can shed light on the dynamic occurring in the therapeutic relationship as opposed to assuming the problems are clients' alone. Reflexivity, whether with others or individually, can provide the space to consider alternative explanations. Engaging in practice means recognizing that even the idea of psychotherapy may be counter to a cultural or religious value held by the individual, family, or community of our clients.

For example, I (SK) come from a collectivist culture and am conflict-avoidant. This shows up in my relationship with clients around boundary setting. When I fail to set appropriate boundaries, I feel resentment, which can show up in my clinical work and impact the therapeutic alliance. I also tend to use humor as a defense. When I find myself colluding with the client and laughing over a traumatic past event, I have to pause, reflect, bring it to my awareness, and sometimes even bring it up in the relationship to uncover what feelings the client and I are trying to avoid. Other contextual factors must also be considered with our professional and personal awareness, such as illness or loss in the therapist's life or family when seeing clients with similar issues. I remember that during a time when my father was unwell, if a client brought up an ill parent, I would ask too many questions about the parent's illness and care in ways that soothed my anxiety but took attention away from the client. Recognizing this, it was vital for me to tune back to my clients and consider taking a leave of absence until my father's health had improved and I was not doing so much caregiving outside of therapy. This example highlights how the healing of the "Other "is so intimately tied to the healing of the "Self" (Kumsa, 2007).

> For me (TBN), a problematic issue that requires a great deal of reflexivity is the impact of current political issues and the anxiety clients and I have felt in recent months. Increasing culture wars have led to clients and practitioners inevitably discussing political issues in therapy (TS (Global): Please link all the unlink cross-references.), and I have found myself displaying nonverbal expressive reactions when clients report being anxious about the national election and changing social policies. My bias overrides any attempts to be bipartisan. I may make suggestions about limiting exposure to the news: interventions that are not necessarily bad, but often not in tune with the client's needs in the moment and reflect more of how I myself try to cope with political uncertainty. When clients share my same political beliefs or values, I have tended to relax into a somewhat "we have the real truth" smugness that interferes with the emergence of any diverging opinions. What is important to recognize here is that what we choose to reflect on and/or probe about indicates our personal, political, and professional values. Years ago, I had a client who told me I perked right up whenever he talked about dreams. Just that nonverbal response highlighted for him that

dreams were important to me (not necessarily to the treatment). The integrative practitioner, however, tries to monitor personal subjective states to make choices based on an openness to multiple perspectives. We want to be able to comfortably question the well-trod clinical path to explore other possible biases or values (Bhola et al., 2022). Participating in a therapeutic relationship also requires us to be continually tuned into changes in the profession and our own world, as emphasized in the code of ethics that guides our practice.

A particular and necessary form of self-awareness is professional self-doubt, which has been an important aspect of research on therapist factors in psychotherapy. In my training (SK), it was often stressed that as a therapist, I needed to be confident and portray myself as an expert. Newer research from the field of wisdom, process research in psychotherapy, and research on humility emphasize professional self-doubt. Self-doubt is not under confidence but having a healthy doubt about whether the therapist can effectively help the client (Nissen-Lie et al., 2017). Moderate or healthy self-doubt helps therapists to be reflexive, non-defensive, and flexible when they recognize their limitations in helping clients and yet have the confidence to figure out how to meet the client's needs differently. Of course, it can additionally be true that therapists must also examine whether their rush to refer might reflect a relational enactment in their clinical work with a particular client.

While we have cautioned extensively about much-needed humility in practice, we do not mean to imply that we are to be blank slates. To the contrary, our "use of self" utilizes this humility as a divining rod that allows us to judiciously know when and how to self-disclose or use our subjective experience during the session to engage the client's emotional life further. Use of self is a common factor of therapy, that is, it is so intrinsic to psychotherapy that it cuts across all theoretical schools and is seen as critical to the therapeutic relationship (Aponte, 2022). We form therapeutic relationships with clients with our full humanity, our lived experiences, our vulnerabilities and psychological wounds, with all aspects of our selfhood: those that are expressed and those that are hidden, including the social and contextual factors that make us human. Aponte (2017) used the term "signature theme" to help his students identify their life's core personal struggle (and issues related to it) as an emotional vulnerability. We encourage students and beginning clinicians reading this text to reflect on how this vulnerability can play out in the session with clients. It is important to identify how our individual vulnerability can also be a source of strength that helps develop empathy for the client but can also confound or obfuscate our assessment and choice of intervention with clients. We will demonstrate the use of individual vulnerability in case illustrations in subsequent chapters.

Attuned flexibility and responsiveness

As we tune in to the client with humility and openness, we must also be prepared to respond flexibly. Terms such as *attunement* and *responsiveness* are similar to the term *relational*, where we think we all agree on what they mean but have a hard time defining them. Attunement is the crucible where psychodynamic theory, attachment work, and CBT come together. Developmentally, we understand that a child–caregiver dyadic attunement is related to the child's personality development and ability to relate to others. Similarly, our ability to be attuned to clients provides the "enlivening experience of being responded to and understood by the attachment object creates an important need in its own right, powerfully shaping our behavior, experience, and sense of self" (Wachtel, 2017, p. 334). The hope is that this experience in therapy is experienced as a positive change that leads to changes in the client's behavior even outside therapy, which changes how the world reacts to the client, thus initiating a healthier cycle of interpersonal and intrapersonal interactions rather than the repetitive pattern of relating to the self, others, and the world (Wachtel, 2017).

Implicit in empathic attunement is the ability to respond therapeutically. Processes that facilitate therapist responsiveness and encourage integrative shifts in sessions can be linked to the work of Anchin et al. (2024), who emphasize that the grounding in more than one theoretical framework allows us to understand the language of client communications and symptoms more widely. Our ability to attune to multiple levels of communication lets us consider different kinds of responses, whether exploring the relational pattern that may represent a client's effort to protect against historical injuries or helping to facilitate a client's movement out of the affective realm and into cognitive interventions to manage a narrow window of tolerance. At times, this may mean responding to parts of the client that the client is not proud of, that have never been seen, or that the client has not even been aware of. As mentioned in Chapter 5, we see clients with complex presentations, histories of complex traumas, and possible repetitions of the traumas in their relationships. The work of therapy becomes interrupting those patterns with choices made moment to moment in how we respond to the clients to interrupt these maladaptive cycles, relationally, to provide an "exposure" to a new relational possibility that soothes the nervous system instead of activating it. With a wider understanding of what clients may be communicating, we enhance our ability to make judgments and decisions about how to respond.

A caveat is also in order here: When talking about "appropriate responsiveness," we don't mean to imply that there is one right way to respond. What is more important is the flexibility that allows us to pivot as needed by the client instead of being locked into one pathway of exploration. Kramer and Stiles (2015) have said that "appropriate responsiveness" is difficult to capture, as it is not a specific behavior but instead an attempt to optimize interventions according to emerging circumstances in a session, which makes it a "fluid, adaptive process" (p. 289). Responsiveness is seen as the "very sine qua non of integrative practice" (Anchin et al., 2024, p. 240), which involves action rather than an attitude. However, the behavioral aspect of responsiveness can be as slight as a nonverbal gesture, expression, or even a verbal response or choosing not to respond overtly. The key is that this responsiveness can enhance the therapeutic relationship (Eubanks et al., 2021) and have a positive effect on the psychotherapy outcome (Zuroff et al., 2010). The challenge lies in knowing what kind of responsiveness is most beneficial.

Optimal responsiveness is shaped by the kinds of listening we engage in. Every clinician at some time or another has been asked, "What do you do all day—just listen to people talk?" with the implicit message that it is easy, passive, and perhaps dull and/or traumatic. On the contrary, listening well is a complex process that is often a lost art. In our day-to-day life, most people often only listen to bide time until they can talk again; but for the therapist, listening is our best tool that is often undervalued and misunderstood, yet it forms the backbone of our ability to flexibly respond therapeutically.

Pulling from narrative therapy and our psychodynamic forebears, we want to focus on the purpose of different forms of listening and how they influence our choice of when to utilize CBT techniques. For example, Nwoye (2006) highlighted four different forms of listening in his narrative work with families: *empathic, credulous, deconstructive, negative, and hermeneutic.* Good clinicians certainly understand the importance of *empathic* listening and showing "solidarity with client's feelings of pain" (Nwoye, 2006, p. 10);

however, we know that empathy is necessary but not sufficient for a positive outcome. Unfortunately, with the external economic constraints on our practice and perhaps impacted by our own anxiety, we often jump to problem-solving short-circuiting empathy. The most helpful guiding principle is to "empathize first and problem solve second," which inevitably leads to the question of "how much empathy is enough?" Nwoye answers that question with *credulous* listening, which encourages clinicians to not bombard clients with questions—a behavior that we have all been guilty of at one time or another. It helps to acknowledge this by being transparent with clients when you observe this in yourself, and to say something to the effect of, "I've been asking so many questions that I think it may have not given you the space to tell me more. Can we go back to what you were saying about." Clients need our ongoing interest and patience, which makes room for the "sustaining echoes of empathic resonance" (Kohut, 1984, p. 78). Credulous listening requires us to believe what our clients are saying: Their stories are credible until proven otherwise. They need time and space to tell their stories with our engaging and encouraging interest expressed both verbally and nonverbally.

As we listen to our clients, we also engage in *deconstructive* listening, in which we notice gaps, assumptions, and ambiguities in the story being told. We are trying to open up the client's narrative as Freedman and Combs (1996) describe, in which we want to make room for narratives that have not yet been "storied." We notice the cast of characters in the client's life—"accomplices," as Wachtel (2014) calls them—and the role they serve in maintaining the schemas or beliefs in a client's life. We also notice the characters that always leave or those that are yearned for. We all believe in our own stories and often think that they tell the whole story. The challenge is to help our clients move beyond this bias or cognitive distortion and become aware of the strange in their stories. As clients become aware of the gaps or assumptive leaps they are making, "the original story starts to lose its grip of restrictive meaning on the client and, with this, the distress that is inflamed by it" (Nwoye, 2006, p. 11). In my clinical work (TBN), I often hear about restrictive religious beliefs and accompanying guilt. Just raising the question about the possibility of religion as different from spirituality can allow for envisioning acceptance of actions that may have been condemned in a client's prior religious upbringing.

It is during this process that we can also begin to engage in *negative* listening as we notice the contradictions and inaccuracies in clients' thinking.

For example, as we explore the presenting issues with clients, we also take notice of what is not talked about, such as missing information about family, a lack of friendships or other forms of support, sexual identities and orientations, religious or spiritual background, or gaps in history. We begin to see parts of their selves that are exaggerated or "liked" and shown more readily, and parts that are shameful, unacceptable, and sometimes even hidden from the client's view. We are able to relate this information back to the clients to connect it to their developmental past to understand their interactions with their caregivers, the dyadic needs that were met, and those that were not even seen or acknowledged by the caregivers.

Social learning theory developed by Bandura (1977) described how we make assumptions and cognitive leaps in our attempts to understand the world around us. Naturally, those inferential learning leaps are not always accurate, and lead to cognitive distortions, which CBT emphasizes. It is during this form of listening that we can return to Langs's (1978) and even Reik's (1948) emphasis on listening for encoded communications, which can lead to exploration of latent experiences and perceptions. By listening for unconscious or hidden meanings in what our clients tell us, we are engaging in *hermeneutic* listening, as labeled by Tomm (1993). We are expanding our understanding with clients to ascertain the meanings of their pain and distress, as well as examining their understanding of their own strengths. Listening in these ways allows us to "widen our ears" to encompass the many layers of communications in the therapy room (ours, and that of our clients), which expands our understanding that goes far beyond a focus on the symptom. Such a broad picture allows us to make decisions about what and how to intervene that are so essential in forming an integrative assessment.

Years ago, I (TBN) had a client who was desperate for her mother's attention and approval. As an artist, she made extremely large paintings. She had used the phrase "See me, Mommy" when describing early childhood deprivation. The connection between her paintings and her experiences as a neglected daughter allowed her emotional relief. This recognition of the meaning did not alter the size of her art; rather, it expanded the vividness with which she could express herself. Listening to client stories and bringing issues to their awareness could be enough for some clients and client systems to give them hope to change or move. For some clients and systems, awareness may be the first step, while the second step is tackling the larger system that is oppressive. The issue could also lie within the individual as a skill deficit. Support for clients may mean taking the client outside the therapy room to carry out an exposure exercise, or it may look like helping the client figure out how to apply for temporary housing, or helping them to negotiate through destabilizing emotions.

As we listen to our clients, we also notice the shifts in sessions where a client's affective or cognitive process changes. These signal in the PDT and CBT world that therapeutic work is being undertaken, as we know that changes in affective processes predict and precede cognitive distortions, and that changes in cognitive distortions predict and precede affective symptoms (Persons et al., 2023). In the words of Virginia Demos (2001), we "track the trigger" within the therapeutic session. When there is a shift, we need to engage the client in reflecting upon what transpired just before that shift. How could our statements or questions have triggered dysregulation, or facilitated the consolidation of affective states? Tracking the triggers to shifts in the client's narrative enables the client and the therapist to bring the dynamic process between them into the room and into the present. The dynamic interchange becomes the focus.

"Serve and return" is another term utilized in child development to refer to the process in which the caregiver and child engage in a "back and forth" of communication, which is known to foster brain development, particularly in the area of cognition and language. Based on psychodynamic intersubjectivity theories and interpersonal neurobiology research, we know that the negotiated joint space between therapist and client can serve to coregulate each participant. When there is a shift in this process, it can indicate a critical area for focus.

Therapists are responsible for monitoring their role in the dynamic space and monitoring shifts between them and their clients. Fortunately, Winnicott reassured us, along with current interpersonal neurobiological research results, that we do not have to be perfect, just "good enough" (Applegate & Bonovitz, 1995). We make mistakes or enact empathic failures and basically "miss the mark" just like in relationships external to the therapeutic relationship. However, what is most critical is our ability to make space for the repair of any empathic failures and even the microaggressions that can occur in treatment. In this repair, we provide the client with a corrective emotional experience, an experiential exposure to a new relational pattern to change the client's emotional schema, and an opportunity to disconfirm the old, known, painful, emotional patterns (Wachtel, 2020).

There can also be errors when we shift theoretical frameworks in response to our own internal states. For example, when I (TBN) first began exploring when and how to utilize CBT techniques within psychodynamic therapy, I brought in a cognitive restructuring technique in the middle of a session when a client was discussing grief and a sense of loss in a recent relational encounter. The client was accessing important affect and sharing it in the present. In my efforts to avoid the intense feelings occurring in the session, I switched to problem-solving interventions designed to minimize the affect he was expressing and "rescue" him from his pain. The client became very quiet, and his talking became stilted. Wachtel (2020) noted that as therapists we also have an unconscious meaning we are capable of distorting, deflecting, selectively listening to, and misinterpreting what is being presented by the client. It slowly dawned on me that something significant had occurred, and when I asked him if we could talk about what had shifted, he was able to tell me that he felt as if I (TBN) had left the room. I was using an intervention defensively as opposed to in the service of furthering our relationship and deepening his experience, and we were subsequently able to repair that disruption/rupture and talk about when problem-solving interventions were more helpful. Therapeutic repairs are a large part of our work, as the process allows us to join the client in this experience of disappointment and hurt. We model for our clients that frustration, pain, and even anger are tolerable and inevitable, but they can be shared with an attuned other. That shared process knits a stronger relationship and fosters psychic integration for the client. For the clinician, this experience can also facilitate our own professional and personal identities around the necessary humility and confidence.

Attuned flexibility and responsiveness also require us to pay attention to issues related to client distress and when a change in the treatment structure is needed (e.g., the health of the client, the timing of termination, temporary external crises, and affective dysregulation). Clients' relational patterns may also indicate when to provide reassurance or when it is contraindicated. For example, in the case of a client with an anxious attachment style, reassurance may be a greater need, with an eventual exploration of relational anxiety. For clients with dismissive attachment styles, reassurance may likely increase avoidance or emotional withdrawal in sessions (Wu & Levitt, 2020). As mentioned above, because of the power imbalance in the therapeutic relationship in Western medicine, it is also important that therapist responsiveness includes initiating dialogue with the client about cultural factors, including misunderstandings that can occur. Communication styles, the use of metaphors, and religious and spiritual beliefs are all important components in our lives, and vary within and between cultures. A therapist's internalized racism is also essential to consider, and how that may show up in the therapeutic relationship and impact the ability of the therapist to discuss the client's experience of racism (Smith, 2022).

Case conceptualization, assessment, and treatment planning

Case conceptualization is often seen as the second most crucial step, following the focus on the therapeutic alliance that most mental health professionals are expected to master (Sperry & Sperry, 2020). It bridges the theory–real-world practice gap to guide the clinician's decision-making to allow the tailoring of the treatment to the unique needs of the client. Case conceptualization has a lengthy history, some of which has been covered in prior chapters. Many research practitioners and clinicians have provided formats of a formulation that fits within a variety of integrative perspectives (e.g., Eells, 2022a; 2022b; Gilboa-Schechtman, 2024; Sperry & Sperry, 2020) that attempt to summarize demographic information, core strengths, challenges, maintaining factors of symptoms, and a developmental timeline of presenting issues and precipitating factors (Beck, 2020). Likewise, there are numerous case formulation guidelines as representative of singular theoretical frameworks whether it be psychodynamic (Cabanis et al., 2013; McWilliams, 1999, 2004) or CBT (Beck, 2020; Persons, 2023, 2022). We are assuming readers have experience in writing atheoretical conceptualizations that provide relevant information for treatment planning; however, in the next two chapters, we will utilize aspects of both types of case formulations to illustrate how they can inform treatment interventions.

In this text, we use case conceptualization as an example to show how incorporating the essential markers of a good therapeutic relationship can assist therapists in assessing, planning, and intervening in the most client-centered way possible. Case conceptualization refers to the therapist's assessment of presenting symptoms and understanding of the client's unique bio-, psycho-, racial, social, and cultural context to *collaboratively develop* an intervention strategy best suited to the client. This essential assessment informs the hypothesis of why this client is suffering from this particular constellation of symptoms of distress. Such a hypothesis is collaborated on with clients, and based on their feedback is then used to craft an individualized treatment plan. We use the phrase "collaboratively develop" purposively in that this is not a process we engage in without the client, but rather one that we work together to establish a process that is ongoing and evolves over time. The dynamic process of collaborative formulation can support our ongoing efforts to keep in mind the micro-, mezzo-, and macro-issues that continue to impact our clients and ourselves as we move through time.

The first step in case conceptualization is an initial intake assessment. A therapist with an integrative relational approach understands the presenting issues through many lenses, including PDT and CBT. The assessment seeks to understand why the client is coming into therapy and why now. When did the symptoms begin, and what precipitating events led to this initial contact? Why do these symptoms persist, what is their impact, what maintains them, and what meaning do they have for the client? This approach is similar to Macneil et al.'s (2012) Five P's case formulation: presenting issues, predisposing issues, precipitating factors, perpetuating factors, and protective factors. Viewing the presenting issues through multiple theoretical lenses or a transtheoretical lens opens several ways to intervene that may best suit the client's social and cultural location, in addition to remembering to explore the potential impact of oppression and marginalization that may have played a role in the cause or perpetuation of the symptoms.

To show the process of case conceptualization, we offer a case composite. A former client of mine (SK) presented with panic attacks. As a part of the initial assessment, I checked for other symptoms that might be present in addition to panic attacks, such as generalized anxiety disorder, depression, or other physical symptoms, if any. I checked whether the client was in crisis and why the client was choosing therapy now. This comprehensive assessment is also reflective of my training in a medical model of psychological distress. The assessment of the level of urgency or crisis was critical, as it allowed me to assess the client's current ability to affectively regulate and process cognitive information. As mentioned earlier in this chapter, I was assessing whether the client's "window of tolerance" was broad enough to tolerate the level of arousal in therapy and outside the therapy setting. Did the client need emotional regulation skills, a referral to a psychiatrist or a social agency, or perhaps psychoeducation?

The precipitating factor for the client's symptoms was the sudden demise of his older sister. The client believed that he might also die early, and these symptoms of panic could be indicative of a heart attack. This belief, along with his visits to the ER every time he had a panic attack, served to perpetuate his symptoms. In the broad assessment of this client, I was also looking for support structures that buoyed him and strengths or protective factors that he might not have been aware of. I found out that one place where he felt confident in life was sports, which served as a source of esteem and made him feel good physically. However, the client was now avoiding sports because when his heartbeat went up with exertion, he feared it would signal an impending heart attack, and he would have a panic attack despite being given a clean bill of health.

The client was married and had a child for whom he had much affection but also a great sense of responsibility, so parenting was both a protective factor and a stressor. His father had been emotionally abusive of his mother throughout the client's childhood years. His mother had stayed with his father but often used somatization to express her psychological and social distress. The client was also close to his mother and saw her as a confidante.

The client was living in America with his family and doing well financially and socially. He sent money back home, enabling his family to better their life circumstances and build a safety net. The client rushed to India to see his father, who had been hit by a moving vehicle and was now bedridden. He planned to be in India for a month or so and then return to the United States, relinquishing the parental caregiving to his sister. However, when he was in India, his sister passed away suddenly, and now his family expected him to take care of his parents. He was angry about the relentless day-to-day care he had to provide for his father, while a very different life waited for him in America. Because he was the oldest son in a collectivist culture, he was assumed to be the primary caregiver. However, his elder sister was doing these duties, enabling him to build a different life in the United States. The client fulfilled this role of caregiving but began feeling that his resentment would cause him bad karma (i.e., guilt) and that he would consequently die without loving caregivers. The client and I shared a hypothesis that the etiological basis of the symptoms could be connected to his sister's death, which had exacerbated his resentment about caring for his ill father and increased his feeling of being trapped in this role more than it had previously.

As an integrative therapist, ongoing assessment may look different from other mono-lens theoretical therapists. I simultaneously assessed the developmental attachment patterns and listened to the attributions the client made regarding the challenges in his life. I was listening for a history of trauma and patterns of relationship dynamics that were getting played out interpersonally and intrapersonally, with the understanding that they could also play out between us in the therapeutic relationship. In addition, I was gathering information for pan-theoretical variables such as emotional accessibility, rigidness or inflexibility in personality, cognitive distortions or impairments, developmental contextual factors such as poverty and deprivation, and lastly, assessing whether the client's personality would be able to tolerate interpretations or worldviews that were very different from his own. This pan-theoretical assessment does not preclude considering clients with more particular theoretical constructs such as defenses or schemas that we will illustrate in subsequent chapters; however, we want first to illustrate those variables that bridge theories and impact the initial engagement with a client.

This client and I shared a similar cultural background: We were both from a collectivist culture, immigrants who were miles away from our families of origin, and shared the cultural guilt of not being able to give our best support to our aging parents and extended families. Because of this, he did not have to over-explain his guilt, resentment, and shame in taking care of his father (whom he saw as abusive toward his mother) or the concept of karma. However, all assumptions aside, I had to check with him about his subjective experience of our common cultural identities. He shared that I was similar in age to his only sister, who had passed away recently and suddenly in the precipitating event that triggered his panic. As an integrative therapist using a PDT lens, I wondered how that would play out in the transference-countertransference dynamics. What affective triggers should I be watching for in the alliance? What were the somatic markers of distress or well-being that are culturally informed and permissible for this client (Kaiser & Jo Weaver, 2019)? What were the "idioms of distress' that exist beyond the DSM-prescribed language of symptoms that the client is expressing? For clients from the Indian subcontinent, these could include complaints of a pulling sensation in the limbs, a sinking feeling in the stomach, constipation/bowel issues, a redness of the cornea, a feeling of electric current in the scalp/head, and other symptoms (Desai & Chaturvedi, 2017).

As I was thinking of a treatment/intervention plan, I kept listening and monitoring the relationship for ruptures and shifts that signal disengagement or a change in the therapeutic relationship's "flow." For example, while working with the client above, I found that his window of tolerance was narrow, and my attempts to increase self-awareness around his self-sabotage were getting him to disengage. Because of this tracking, I realized that exploring his disengagement would not be fruitful in this situation. I suggested a mindfulness-based third wave CBT intervention before more insight-oriented work, which was culturally aligned with the client.

Alternatively, had the client not been open to mindfulness or thought it was a "fad," I would have solicited his support in analyzing what options might work for him to stay in the session rather than disengaging emotionally.

As such, this example of an ongoing, dynamic, collaborative assessment illustrates options and markers to determine whether we should proceed with one set of interventions or try a newer one. My grounding in psychodynamic theory allowed me to consider internal and relational patterns that might emerge, the client's concerns about guilt and the factors contributing to those feelings, and ultimately, the decision to utilize a CBT intervention to be less emotionally dysregulating at the beginning of therapy by keeping focus on cognitions.

Using my reflexivity, a social justice perspective, and openness to many theoretical perspectives helped me map many paths to intervention, such as working with bodily symptoms to teach the client deep breathing or using psychoeducation to demystify panic attacks and explain the mind-body connection. I had the option to explore whether the client was open to discussing the feelings of resentment against his father and how they might have been re-triggered when his older sibling passed away suddenly, or even the fear of his own mortality. I also employed the technique of cognitive restructuring to examine the beliefs underlying his avoidance of sports as one pathway to examine evidence contrary to the belief that he has a heart condition. As the client's symptoms stabilized, we could then talk about whether to focus more on relational patterns that may exacerbate symptoms or cause further distress and/or the cultural constraints that placed a heavy burden on him as the eldest male child exploring his resentment and anger further.

The therapist's therapeutic flexibility in conceptualizing this case offers the client choice, agency, and control starting from the beginning of treatment. It lets clients know that their story is being heard, and their distress is understood. The challenge lies in which theoretical lens to use, how to use it, and when. Using this case composite allows us to see how we prioritize the different information that we have learned from using diverse frameworks.

Conclusion

Beginning with the understanding that the grounding of therapeutic work is in the relationship calls us to reexamine what components comprise and impact that relationship. We share our home theory that builds on our social work commitment for social justice and a relational model that draws on personal and professional reflexiveness and attuned, flexible responsiveness. It is essential that all clinicians be cognizant of their home theories even if—and especially if—they think they don't have one. Doing so allows us the necessary perspective to modify or pull from other frameworks in a thoughtful and effective way, which then lays the foundation for developing a case conceptualization that informs and empowers therapeutic collaboration. Our next two chapters will further illustrate how we implement our framework with clients.

References

Anchin, J. C., Řiháček, T., Roubal, J., & Boswell, J. F. (2024). Psychotherapy integration: History, current status, and future directions. In F. T. L. Leong, J. L. Callahan, J. Zimmerman, M. J. Constantino, & C. F. Eubanks (Eds.), *APA handbook of psychotherapy: Theory-driven practice and disorder-driven practice* (pp. 231–255). American Psychological Association. https://doi.org/10.1037/0000353-014

Aponte, H. J. (2017). The philosophy of the person-of-the-therapist training model: The underlying premises. *Seminare: Learned Investigations, 38*(4), 57–67. https://doi.org/10.21852/sem.2017.4.05

Aponte, H. J. (2022). The soul of therapy: The therapist's use of self in the therapeutic relationship. *Contemporary Family Therapy, 44*, 136–143. https://doi.org/10.1007/s10591-021-09614-5

Applegate, J. S., & Bonovitz, J. M. (1995). *The facilitating partnership: A Winnicottian approach for social workers and other helping professionals.* Jason Aronson.

Bandura, A. (1977). *Social learning theory.* Prentice

Barsness, R. E. (2021). Therapeutic practices in relational psychoanalysis: A qualitative study. *Psychoanalytic Psychology.38*(1), 22–30. https://doi.org/10.1037/pap0000319

Beck, J. (2020). *Cognitive behavior therapy: Basics and beyond* (3rd ed.). Guilford.

Bhola, P., Duggal, C., & Isaac, R. (2022). *Reflective practice and professional development in psychotherapy.* Sage Publications.

Boswell, J. F., King, B. R., Schwartzman, C. M., Wasserman, R. H., & Constantino, M. J. (2021). Responsiveness in integrative therapies. In J. C. Watson & H. Wiseman (Eds.), *The responsive psychotherapist: Attuning to clients in the moment* (pp. 277–296). American Psychological Association. https://doi.org/10.1037/0000240-008

Constantino, M. J., Goodwin, B. J., Muir, H. J., Coyne, A. E., & Boswell, J. F. (2021). Context-responsive psychotherapy integration applied to cognitive behavioral therapy. In J. C. Watson & H. Wiseman (Eds.), *The responsive psychotherapist: Attuning to clients in the moment* (pp. 151–169). American Psychological Association. https://doi.org/10.1037/0000240-008

Demos, E. V. (2001). Psychoanalysis and the human sciences: The limitations of cut-and-paste theorizing. *American Imago, 58*(3), 649–684.

Desai, G., & Chaturvedi, S. K. (2017). Idioms of distress. *Journal of Neurosciences in Rural Practice, 8*(1), 94–97. https://doi.org/10.4103/jnrp.jnrp_235_17

Eells, T. D. (Ed.). (2022a). *Handbook of psychotherapy case formulation* (3rd ed.). Guilford.

Eells, T. D. (2022b). History and current status of psychotherapy case formulation. In T. D. Eells (Ed.), *Handbook of psychotherapy case formulation* (3rd ed., pp. 1–35). Guilford.

Eubanks, C. F., Sergi, J., & Muran, J. C. (2021). Responsiveness to ruptures and repairs in psychotherapy. In J. C. Watson & H. Wiseman (Eds.), *The responsive psychotherapist: Attuning to clients in the moment* (pp. 83–104). American Psychological Association. https://www.jstor.org/stable/j.ctv1r4xcwf.9

Farrar, N., & Hanley, T. (2023). Where "culture wars" and therapy meet: Exploring the intersection between political issues and therapeutic practice. *Counselling and Psychotherapy Research, 23*, 593–597. https://doi.org/10.1002/capr.12623

Flückiger, C., Del Re, A. C., Wampold, B. E., & Horvath, A. O. (2018). The alliance in adult psychotherapy: A meta-analytic synthesis. *Psychotherapy, 55*(4), 316–340. https://doi.org/10.1037/pst0000172

Freedman, J., & Combs, G. (1996). *Narrative therapy: The social construction of preferred realities.* W. W. Norton & Co. NY.

Gaztambide, D. (2020). From Freud to Fanon to Freire: Psychoanalysis as a liberation method. In L. Comas-Díaz & E. Torres Rivera (Eds.), *Liberation psychology: Theory, method, practice, and social justice* (pp. 71–90). American Psychological Association. https://doi.org/10.1037/0000198-005

Gilboa-Schechtman E. (2024). Case conceptualization in clinical practice and training. *Clinical Psychology in Europe, 6*(Spec Issue), e12103. https://doi.org/10.32872/cpe.12103

Kaiser, B. N., & Jo Weaver, L. (2019). Culture-bound syndromes, idioms of distress, and cultural concepts of distress: New directions for an old concept in psychological anthropology. *Transcultural Psychiatry, 56*(4), 589–598. https://doi.org/10.1177/1363461519862708

Kazantzis, N., & Dobson, K. S. (2022). Therapeutic relationships in cognitive behavioral therapy: Theory and recent research. *Psychotherapy Research, 32*(8), 969–971. https://doi.org/10.1080/10503307.2022.2124047

Kazantzis, N., Datillio, R. M., & Dobson, K. S. (2017). *The therapeutic relationship in cognitive behavior therapy: A clinician's guide.* Guilford.

Kohut, H. (1984). *How does analysis cure?* University of Chicago Press.

Kramer, U., & Stiles, W. B. (2015). The responsiveness problem in psychotherapy: A review of proposed solutions. *Clinical Psychology: Science and Practice, 22*(3), 211–316.

Kumsa, M. K. (2007). Encounters in social work practice: Trying out the "use of self." In D. Mandell (Ed.), *Revisiting the use of self: Questioning professional identities* (pp. 87–103). Canadian Scholars' Press.

Langs, R. (1978). *The listening process.* Jason Aronson.

Macneil, C. A., Hasty, M. K., Conus, P., & Berk, M. (2012). Is diagnosis enough to guide interventions in mental health? Using case formulation in clinical practice. *BMC Medicine, 10*(111), 1–3. https://doi.org/10.1186/1741-7015-10-111

McWilliams, N. (2004). *Psychoanalytic psychotherapy: A practitioner's guide.* Guilford.

McWilliams, N. (1994). *Psychoanalytic case formulation.* Guilford Press.

Nissen-Lie, H. A., Rønnestad, M. H., Høglend, P. A., Havik, O. E., Solbakken, O. A., Stiles, T. C., & Monsen, J. T. (2017). Love yourself as a person, doubt yourself as a therapist? *Clinical Psychology & Psychotherapy, 24*(1), 48–60. https://doi.org/10.1002/cpp.1977

Nwoye, A. (2006). A narrative approach to child and family therapy in Africa. *Contemporary Family Therapy, 28*(1). 1–23 https://doi.org/10.1007/s10591-006-9691-6

Palmieri, A., Fernandez, K. C., Cariolato, Y., Kleinbub, J. R., Salvatore, S., & Gross, J. J. (2022). Emotion regulation in psychodynamic and cognitive-behavioural therapy: An integrative perspective. *Clinical Neuropsychiatry, 19*(2), 103–113. https://doi.org/10.36131/cnfioritieditore20220204

Persons, J. B., Marker, C. D., & Bailey, E. N. (2023). Changes in affective and cognitive distortion symptoms of depression are reciprocally related during cognitive behavior therapy. *Behavior Research and Therapy, 166*, 1–8. https://doi.org/10.1016/j.brat.2023.104338

Persons, J. B., & Tompkins, M. A. (2022). Cognitive-behavioral case formulation. In T. D. Eells (Ed.), *Handbook of psychotherapy case formulation* (3rd ed., pp. 252–286). Guilford.

Reik, T. (1948). *Listening with the third ear; the inner experience of a psychoanalyst.* Farrar, Straus & Co.
Sicora, A. (2017). Reflective practice, risk and mistakes in social work. *Journal of Social Work Practice, 31*(4), 491–502. https://doi.org/10.1080/02650533.2017.1394823
Smith, L. L. (2022). Speaking the unspoken: Understanding internalized racial oppression from the perspective of Black women psychotherapists. *Smith College Studies in Social Work, 92*(1), 48–72. https://doi.org/10.1080/00377317.2022.2026855
Sperry, L., & Sperry, J. (2020). *Case conceptualization: Mastering this competency with ease and confidence* (2nd ed.). Routledge.
Tomm, K. (1993). The courage to protest: A commentary on Michael White's works. In S. Gilligan, & R. Price (Eds.), *Therapeutic conversations* (62–80). Norton.
Wachtel, P. L. (2014). *Cyclical psychodynamics and the contextual self: The inner world, the intimate world, and the world of culture and society.* Routledge/Taylor & Francis Group.
Wachtel, P. L. (2017). Attachment theory and clinical practice: A cyclical psychodynamic vantage point. *Psychoanalytic Inquiry, 37*(5), 332–342. https://doi.org/10.1080/07351690.2017.1322431
Wachtel, P. L. (2020). Representations, schemas, and living-in-the-world. *Psychoanalytic Perspectives, 17*, 318–329. https://doi.org/10.1080/1551806X.2020.1801041
Wu, M. B., & Levitt, H. M. (2020). A qualitative meta-analytic review of the therapist responsiveness literature: Guidelines for practice and training. *Journal of Contemporary Psychotherapy: On the Cutting Edge of Modern Developments in Psychotherapy, 50*(3), 161–175. https://doi.org/10.1007/s10879-020-09450-y
Zuroff, D. C., Kelly, A. C., Leybman, M. J., Blatt, S. J., & Wampold, B. E. (2010). Between-therapist and within-therapist differences in the quality of the therapeutic relationship: Effects on maladjustment and self-critical perfectionism. *Journal of Clinical Psychology, 66*(7), 681–697. https://doi.org/10.1002/jclp.20683

7

Negotiating complex trauma with integrative psychotherapy

In this chapter, we want to illustrate how our discussions of PDT and CBT, the therapeutic process, and research in psychotherapy and neurobiology contribute to guiding our interventions with clients. We have developed case composites in this chapter and in Chapter 8 to protect clients' confidentiality and anonymity in our practices and to adhere to a consistent outline of information. These are not client scenarios where everything works beautifully; we want to demonstrate the untidy aspects of practice and potential avenues forward. Specifically, with this case illustration of Rachel, we will highlight a history of complex relational trauma and an understanding of its impact from the perspective of both theoretical frameworks, resulting in panic attacks and affective dysregulation.

Setting of Tx

The client is presenting to a community mental health center, which has an early psychosis unit, services for neurodivergent children, a trauma center that offers outpatient services, and a substance use unit that provides both inpatient and outpatient services. They have one psychiatric nurse practitioner who rotates on different days of the week through the agency. The service provider team comprises psychologists, social workers, mental health counselors, and interns from all three professions. The client was referred from the substance use unit in the community mental health agency to the trauma unit for one-on-one outpatient counseling.

The therapist is a fifty-year-old Caucasian, university-educated, cisgender female who is licensed as a clinical social worker. She is a single mother with two children who are both preparing to go off to college.

Psychodynamic and Cognitive Behavioral Theory and Practice. Terry B. Northcut and Shveta Kumaria, Oxford University Press. © Oxford University Press (2025). DOI: 10.1093/9780197508404.003.0007

Client description

Demographic data

The client (Rachel) is a twenty-year-old Caucasian, able-bodied, heterosexual, cisgender female who is separated from her partner. She is the mother of a four-year-old who was taken away from her by the Department of Children and Family Services (DCFS) on the grounds of neglect and violence in the home. The client is not married but is partnered with Colin, whom she met in a foster home when she was twelve and has been in an on-and-off relationship with since then. The client has not been in touch with her parents since she was twelve years of age (when she was sent to foster care).

Rachel grew up in rural West Virginia in a very impoverished community; she describes her mother as an alcoholic and her father as an addict. Her parents were abusive toward each other and toward Rachel and her siblings. Rachel was the oldest of four children and, as far back as her memory goes, had taken on the caretaking role of her siblings. Her parents were often absent from home for days, and she was "in charge."

Rachel was fifteen when she and Colin boarded a bus to escape foster care. She became pregnant with their child, Adrian, when she was sixteen. Since then, they have lived in many cities in the Midwest, alternating between shelters and apartments or being unhoused, depending on Rachel's employment and financial support from local and state resources. Childcare has been haphazard, but it appears that she and Colin have managed to share those responsibilities despite their volatile relationship.

Precipitating issue

Rachel said that she and Colin have had a strained relationship since Adrian was born, characterized by violence and abuse, often precipitated by substance use (alcohol and opiates) by one or both of them. This most recent episode occurred three weeks ago and was particularly violent. It is unclear how it started, but it ended when Colin choked Rachel until she passed out. A neighbor called the police, who then had her transported to the emergency room and subsequently to the substance use inpatient unit. DCFS was called to care for Adrian, as Colin had disappeared when Rachel was being transported to the clinic. When Rachel was discharged from the inpatient unit, she began living in a short-term residential program for homeless individuals with a major mental illness, many of whom also have substance abuse issues.

Presenting issues

Rachel said that she has been having intrusive memories of the most recent incident where Colin choked her. She reports insomnia and an inability to sleep at night. There are periods during the day when she dozes off but has great difficulty relaxing. She says that she can't seem to slow her mind down to think. She has described up to five episodes of panic attacks per day for the past three weeks. These are worse late at night and in the early hours of the morning. Rachel says she needs help managing the panic attacks and needs to "get her shit together" to get Adrian back from DCFS. Upon further questioning, she said that this means managing her temper, panic attacks, and drug use.

Strengths and vulnerabilities, including intersectional issues

Rachel has a number of strengths that help motivate her involvement with therapy. She has a definite goal of reuniting with her son, though her goals with Colin are less clear. She has some history of stability with employment, even when she misuses substances. Both Rachel and Colin appear to be "street smart," which helps them survive. Interpersonal interactions with Rachel show her biting wit, intelligence, and sensitivity to perceptions of criticism or judgment.

As a Caucasian, able-bodied, heterosexual, young cisgender female, she is negotiating a treatment facility that has historically treated White patients, which is consistent with the demographics of many service providers. However, her current and past economic class make it difficult for her to feel that the staff will understand her and what she has had to do to survive. She believes the staff are "tools of the system" who are far removed from the reality of her past and daily life. Her history of substance misuse/abuse presents a well-traveled path of vulnerability, despite her being currently stable on naltrexone, and she is sporadically attending several AA groups. As mentioned, there is a history of complex relational and physical trauma from her parents, Colin, and perhaps other people she has encountered throughout her short life. Currently, she is unemployed and living in a short-term residential facility, which raises the stakes for not only her own care and sobriety but also her ability to be reunited with Adrian. Given her living situation and history of impulsivity, there are concerns about a possible opioid overdose while on naltrexone.

There are many gaps in Rachel's memory of her childhood. Her strategy seems to have been that it is better not to think about the past. One of her more complex issues relates to her and Colin's isolation from others: it is unclear whether Colin played a major role in keeping them from forming other supports or whether this resulted from their lack of economic stability, difficulty with interpersonal skills, and/or erratic and conflictual home life. While their communication at the moment is intermittent, it is apparent that Rachel considers Colin her family, given that they have had the most consistent relationship in both of their lives for the past eight years. While she is not currently living with Colin, it is unclear whether that will happen in the future; Colin has not made any attempts to get her to leave her current housing setup. Neither has filed any complaints with police about domestic violence, given their mistrust of police and concerns about losing custody of Adrian.

History and current context of treatment

While some information is missing in Rachel's history, we do know that in the past she called a domestic violence helpline and talked with a social worker. Rachel was compliant with the treatment plan during her inpatient substance abuse treatment, though she reportedly had difficulty with other patients on the unit, getting into frequent disagreements with them. Medication has helped eliminate the instability related to her drug and alcohol use, but consistent adherence may be difficult. While it seems unlikely that Colin will support her sobriety and abstinence given their history of violence, it is too early in the therapeutic relationship to assess how he may impact Rachel's struggle to regain custody of their son.

Theoretical contributions to understanding

Psychodynamic

While we have emphasized the attachment *process* in this text over particular attachment *styles*, Rachel's chaotic background and current behavior lead us to think she does not have a secure attachment style, which influences her engagement with others. Despite its volatility, given the length of their relationship, Colin has been her most meaningful attachment. Rachel has great difficulty identifying and managing affect: if she is feeling anxious (often outside of her awareness), she becomes dysregulated, and in the past, she has used substances to cope. Repression, denial, projection, dissociation, and isolation of affect are predominant intrapsychic measures she utilizes to cope with anxiety and fears related to potential and past losses, as well as to cope with triggers related to extensive trauma. When she becomes anxious or angry, she demonstrates poor impulse control and becomes argumentative, which results in conflicts or disengagement with others. While she can acknowledge tremendous grief and shame over being separated from Adrian, she is unable to reflect on any of the other losses in her life. The relational patterns that have emerged are chaotic yet repetitive of her early life. Her longing for connection makes her anxious and panicked that she will be rejected or abandoned, which leads to outbursts and impulsive behavior that furthers her disconnect with others.

Rachel's relational themes are evident in the narratives she describes and in her interactions with others at the treatment center. This pattern, from either a PDT or CBT perspective, will be important for the therapist to keep in mind when initiating action and reacting to Rachel's emotions, thoughts, and behaviors.

CBT

Rachel's schemas about self, others, and the world are essential to identify and understand in order to make a plan with Rachel collaboratively. Rachel's self-schema is that she is unlovable and bad; otherwise, why would her parents neglect and abuse her and seemingly forget all about her after she left? Given her life experiences, it is not hard to understand why Rachel assumes the worst and makes faulty attributions about the motives behind the actions of others. As a result of these schemas and attributions, Rachel is exquisitely focused on any indication that people in her world will fulfill her expectations of malintent or rejection and that the world is not a safe place; consequently, she screens out any disconfirming information. When she perceives that her beliefs about the world and/or herself are being confirmed, she becomes dysregulated, acts impulsively, or disappears. These protective mechanisms make it difficult for her to get her needs met.

Rachel has great difficulty knowing what her thoughts, feelings, and behaviors are, much less seeing the connections between them or being able to stay in the moment to figure them out. When she is triggered in any way, her panic ensues, and she resorts to her limited repertoire of behaviors, which then reinforce her fears and beliefs, confirming her sense of badness and leading to more disruptive behaviors. In anticipation of a panic attack, Rachel tends to avoid certain situations that she fears will result in an attack, which increases her sense of isolation and stuckness, adding to her self-criticism.

Empirical and clinical contributions to interventions

Rachel has many issues requiring attentive and necessary interventions to ensure her safety and mental health. Significant problems include emotional dysregulation, negative self-concept, disturbances in relationships, and ongoing panic attacks. Her substance abuse, housing, and economic insecurity are also essential to address. Rachel's trauma history necessitates beginning with how to help her manage those experiences that are triggered in the present because they significantly impair her functioning when coupled with her panic attacks. They also impact her ability to engage interpersonally so that no further work can be accomplished unless she develops skills to manage the panic and complex post traumatic stress disorder (CPTSD) symptoms.

We can draw on both empirical and clinical research to guide us further in attempting to understand and focus therapy on managing Rachel's CPTSD. Alan Schore's (2012) extensive work on traumatic dissociation, the inability to "co-regulate external stimuli with internal emotional experience" (Gianotti, 2022, p. 160), describes Rachel's experience when she can't manage overwhelming affect or external stimulation. Her capacity to mentalize is diminished, as Bateman & Fonagy (2013) describe this process as the ability to cognitively process our internal state, including emotions, thoughts, desires, and beliefs, and reflect on the mental states of others (Jansen et al., 2023). When experiences in childhood are not modulated by a caregiver who can soothe the child or help to integrate affective arousal, the child is unable to consciously process experiences, and the attachment is compromised (Asen & Fonagy, 2012). An additional impact of this lack of attunement and reassurance is that these children do not have language for their internal states, as they have had to be cut off from awareness and remain outside explicit memory (Gianotti, 2022). Putting affective unformulated experiences into words (a cognitive function) facilitates the integration of affect and cognition, which can then reduce fragmentation or dissociation, including the impact on the body (van der Kolk, 2014). The challenge arises when these misattuned experiences are repeated and become generalized to interpersonal patterns throughout adulthood (Stern, 1985), which then act to interfere with attempts to get needs met. The dynamic, back-and-forth aspect of interpersonal relationships is, at the very least, shaped by miscuing from either partner's efforts to connect. In clinical work, helping clients develop tools that can sustain them when they are overstimulated and dysregulated in interpersonal interactions becomes a critical goal, especially when they have experienced profound, complex trauma (Herman, 1992, 1997).

In addition to Rachel's current and historical trauma history, we know there is additional substance misuse. There are decades of research on treating substance abuse and misuse, though we know that Rachel has already opted for naltrexone combined with AA. Over time, her thoughts and feelings about this treatment course may reveal pros and cons related to research around diverse methods; however, she is adamant about wanting to get her son back, and this seemed to her like the best course of action given her circumstances. Of course, with any kind of addiction, there are chances of relapse, though this medication carries an additional danger of unintentional overdoses due to the increased sensitivity to opioids at the dose used before the beginning of the medication (Substance Abuse and Mental Health Services Administration, 2024). Of particular concern for Rachel are the dangers of overdose when she is feeling panicky or dysregulated, which can be easily stimulated in transitional housing, with her missing her son, during disagreements with Colin, and in other stressful instances.

CBT has a demonstrated positive track record of research with panic disorder, specifically with techniques that utilize cognitive restructuring, interoceptive exposure (symptom induction), SMART (Specific, Measurable, Achievable, Relevant, Time-bound) goals, muscle relaxation, mindfulness, grounding exercises, and/or exposure therapy (Curtis et al., 2021; Duprey, 2024). While PDT does not have as much research focused on particular symptomatology, we do know that it is effective, particularly in the areas of interpersonal difficulties associated with trauma. Lilliengren (2023) came to the conclusion that PDT and CBT yield comparative results in his overview of research on Randomized Control Trials (RCTs). Leichsenring et al. (2014, 2019, 2020, 2023) have provided analyses and summaries of the efficacy of psychodynamic treatments for common mental health disorders, PTSD, and the impact of short-term treatment, and findings indicate that PDT is especially well-suited for the attachment issues and interpersonal patterns that Rachel is grappling with. Fechau et al. (2024) also highlight the need for clients' perspectives, particularly with CPTSD. There will undoubtedly be relational ruptures with the therapist and other members involved in Rachel's health and mental health care, and both CBT and PDT frameworks should provide scaffolding for the clinician not only to monitor these inevitable disruptions but also to continue to prioritize Rachel's perspective combined with the clinician's experience.

In terms of diagnostic labels, CPTSD, panic attack disorder, and substance use disorders explain many of Rachel's symptoms; however, it must be held in the context of ongoing factors, including ongoing external variables (e.g., regulations with DCFS, housing, or fees for service) that impact Rachel, Colin, and their child. It is striking that while CBT has been the gold standard in terms of evidence-based treatment, the American Psychological Association (2024) recently issued its report on "Guidelines for Working with Adults with Trauma Histories" and found that "not all persons who participate in such treatment benefit to the same degree. It is possible thus that one size does not fit all (Cloitre, 2015; Courtois, 1999; Greenberg, 2020) and that arguably, psychology often neglects a personalized approach to professional practice that includes individualized and contextually focused interventions for specific persons" (Courtois & Marotta-Walters, 2021) (APA, p. 8).

While this pronouncement is unsurprising for social workers who have been seeing clients with complex diagnoses—especially in oppressed and economically depressed environments—it does remind us of the need to broaden our understanding of research with empirical support for our particular clients.

Treatment plan

So, returning to the research and our discussion of findings from neurobiology discussed in Chapter 2, we know that when there is trauma, the brain is primed to react with fight, flight, freeze, and, in some cases, "fawn" (Walker, no date) when it perceives danger. It is critically important to provide a safe, consistent, undisturbed psychotherapy space that allows the client to have as much control as possible (Schäfer et al., 2019) and to minimize overstimulation.

As discussed in Chapter 6, the case conceptualization, i.e., the therapist's understanding of Rachel's symptoms, was shared with Rachel. The therapist posed the question that with all of the issues Rachel is facing right now (e.g., Adrian being away at a DCFS facility and her wanting to see him, her panic attacks, her conflict with Colin, being unhoused, and not receiving any state benefits), which one seemed to her the most urgent to attend to at first? Rachel said that she was so overwhelmed that she found herself "paralyzed" and "unable to slow her mind to think." The panic attacks were so unpredictable that she couldn't even decide what the most pressing problem was.

With an understanding of CPTSD and the recent violence in Rachel's life, including her son being taken away from her, the therapist focused on creating a sense of safety. In Rachel's case, safety looks like providing clear information about housing, medication, the care team, and the treatment plan, as well as being a predictable, consistent presence with regular appointments. Safety also looks like helping her feel safe in her body. This means managing the panic attacks, which would then assist in helping her have access to the executive functioning part of her brain to plan the next step of her care more collaboratively.

The therapist shared the treatment plan with Rachel, suggesting they start with some techniques from mindfulness-based CBT that will help slow down her mind to think and also help her manage the panic attacks. These techniques aim to build clients' agency and sense of control in calming themselves down. The choice to start using breathing or other mindfulness techniques was carefully considered, as sometimes breathing techniques can be terrifying for clients with panic attacks because they fear it might trigger a panic attack. Likewise, with trauma that may have included sexual abuse, some methods of mindfulness might be experienced as overwhelming and dysregulating, particularly if the therapist is not trained in somatic experiencing or embodied interoception. This means that with clients who have a history of trauma, the ability to process and interpret bodily signals (interoception) has been truncated by fear (Levine, 2010).

The therapist also provided some psychoeducation about mindfulness and the brain and normalized that some techniques work better with certain clients, while others may have different reactions. Together, they would find the one most helpful to Rachel. Based on the therapist's understanding of empirical and clinical wisdom, the therapist began using a guided box breathing technique (also called 4×4 x 4×4 breathing; Cleveland Clinic, 2021) to offer Rachel a simple tool that might be easiest to remember. She encouraged Rachel to keep her eyes open and focus on something in the office that was pleasing or calming, or to just lower her gaze.

During another session, the therapist used visualization techniques by asking Rachel to talk about a place or time when she felt calmer and then describe it. Rachel was able to talk about a childhood swing that she loved at a park that gave her the best feeling of flying and escape. She and the therapist could talk about that sensation and gradually include more of Rachel's bodily sensations as Rachel's trust in the therapist and herself grew.

Course of treatment

Therapeutic process

Once Rachel was able to do guided box breathing in sessions without panic, and she and the therapist had a common image or metaphor for a feeling she treasured but had forgotten about (the swing), the therapist explained that panic attacks are a misinterpretation of bodily symptoms. This misinterpretation leads us to avoid these feared situations, cognitions, feelings, or sensations (Beck & Cottrell, 2024). Rather than these feared stimuli, the fear of panic attacks keeps a person stuck in place. Our window of tolerance for these situations, thoughts, and sensations can be expanded by tracking the triggers—what precedes these feelings—and gradually exposing ourselves to those feared stimuli. Rachel and the therapist began work on identifying the thoughts, feelings, and sensations that trigger her panic attacks. This meant a shift into an explorative stance, giving her a space to speak about her worries, then using the CBT downward arrow technique flexibly to help her identify her beliefs that get triggered and lead to panic. The flexibility here is critical because, inevitably, Rachel will become overwhelmed and anxious. In ego psychology terms, the therapist is lending her "observing ego" to Rachel so she can indicate when she is beginning to get dysregulated so that emotional schemas that get activated can be discussed or managed.

In a sense, the therapist and Rachel are building a house: before pulling off the scaffolding, one must ensure that the structure is strong enough to stand. The "house" must be strong enough to withstand the removal of the scaffolding and stand alone. Likewise, schemas are deep, implicit structures that process information from the environment. They are resistant to change and need to be approached cautiously. Disrupting them too soon could cause relational impasses or ruptures with clients, leaving them feeling unsafe with the therapist. We referred to some attributes, attitudes, and behaviors therapists can adopt in Chapter 6, such as moment-to-moment attunement to respond empathically and flexibly to clients' needs as they do this work. Likewise, internal working models of relationship patterns, such as with Rachel, are easily activated to ward off anxiety and fear.

Through the course of exploring triggers for Rachel's panic attacks, the therapist observed that some of her relational schemas, "I am unlovable" and "The world is not a safe place," were formed developmentally with the experiences she had with her parents and were reinforced by the social environment that she lived in: foster homes, the streets, and her relationship with Colin. Rachel had enough evidence to support these beliefs, but the schemas also filtered out information that could provide disconfirming evidence for them. She and the therapist reached a point where the therapist felt she was working harder than Rachel in the therapy. After several sessions of this, the therapist asked if they could pause to observe what was happening between them. The therapist stated that it seemed she was making too many suggestions and asked if Rachel felt the same way. Rachel seemed confused and didn't respond. The therapist then stated that she felt she had not been able to understand how terrifying it must be for Rachel to live with these overwhelming feelings. Rachel became significantly dysregulated when the therapist said this and said: "You think, with your PhD, you know all about my life and what I have been through. I have lived on the streets and in train cars, where I dare not sleep for fear of being robbed or raped. People are untrustworthy, they will cheat you for a hit. Clearly, you don't understand." She then stormed out of the session.

The therapist felt deep shame for pushing an agenda and not responding empathically to the client's emotional experience. The therapist had made a good course correction by acknowledging the impasse; however, she had overestimated how much calling attention to and problem-solving those patterns of behavior could be tolerated this early in the treatment relationship. In a sense, the therapist's countertransference was that she was "arm-wrestling" the client to get her to see the self-destructiveness of her behaviors and attitudes. This was a pivotal moment for the therapist to see how she had "lost" the client, just like Rachel had lost Adrian. They were united in their shared feelings of grief, sadness, and self-criticism, and had much to unpack if Rachel would give her another chance. She left Rachel a voicemail explaining that she had made a mistake and invited her to return for their next scheduled session.

In the next session, the therapist acknowledged that their previous session had been a tough one. Rachel said that it was all her fault, and she lost her cool and had no idea how to stop herself. She said this was why she and Colin would fight so often and why she had no friends. The therapist reassured her that it was a natural response to feeling unheard and unseen in a relationship and commended her for coming back, even though it was uncomfortable and anxiety-provoking. She further connected it to a similar pattern Rachel had gone through in her childhood, which is why there was anger (possibly rage) and grief when she felt this in the therapeutic relationship. The therapist told Rachel that coming to the session that day was a step toward changing her relational pattern, as she had not given up on the therapist or their relationship. Paul Wachtel (2020) and, earlier, Alexander and French (1946) said that for a relationship to be corrective, it must be emotional. This process of rupture and repair is the hallmark of the corrective experience in therapy, which disrupts the maladaptive relational patterns that tend to be reenacted with the therapist.

Over time, Rachel started to trust the therapeutic bond, and the panic attacks decreased; however, she was still only getting out to come to therapy and AA meetings (all within the agency setting). The therapist brought an experiential aspect to their work by suggesting they do a walking meditation/mindfulness exercise as a form of exposure. Rachel was apprehensive that being outside might bring about a panic attack, even though, at this point, she had not had a panic attack for close to ten days. The therapist offered to do a breathing exercise with her if the panic set in and offered her presence as a reassurance that they would be okay. Walking outside was both an exposure to getting Rachel out in the world again and a positive reinforcement that the panic attacks had decreased with her daily breathing and visualization practices. Rachel responded well to the introduction of walking mindfulness and was able to incorporate it into her daily schedule.

During her next session, Rachel mentioned that she was out doing her walking meditation when she saw a mother and child walking to their car. This triggered her anxiety about Adrian, and she asked for the therapist's help in figuring out how to be with Adrian again. The therapist tried to understand what had gotten in the way of Rachel getting Adrian back. Rachel did not have a state ID, and getting one seemed too overwhelming. The therapist used a behavior therapy technique (graded task assignment) to break down the task into small steps to help Rachel with feeling overwhelmed and anxious. The therapist printed out the application form for her and had the organization arrange transport to take her to the state motor vehicle agency. Despite this, Rachel procrastinated at each step of getting a state ID. She felt shame when she admitted that she had not filled out the form, creating a dynamic where she regressed to a more childlike state. While she enjoyed the caregiving the therapist was providing in the maternal transference, she also felt deep shame around the "enjoyment" of the caregiving the therapist provided. The therapist brought this dynamic to Rachel to explore the meaning further. Rachel said that she was not feeling ready to be a single parent and was unsure whether she wanted to be with Colin since he had not reached out to see how she and Adrian were doing. At times, she felt her experience with the therapist was "too rich" and difficult to swallow. She was also envious that Adrian seemed to be in a DCFS facility that was different from what she had experienced.

In an ideal world, Rachel would be able to stay in therapy with this therapist until she was ready to terminate. However, the paradox of getting better meant that she was not going to be eligible for therapy at the center where the therapist worked. Over the period Rachel stayed at the agency, the therapist was able to ensure that she remained on the path of sobriety, gained a state ID, was free of panic attacks, and started to form friendships with other patients at the agency. Rachel had not yet regained custody of Adrian but could have supervised visits with him weekly, which she looked forward to.

Therapeutic relationship

As described above, at times, the therapist felt as if she were a "bad mother," aggressively trying to get Rachel to change or frustrated by her frequent verbal attacks. However, Rachel's sense of humor and scrappiness, in some ways, endeared her to the therapist. By reflecting on her own subjective experiences and consulting with others, the therapist began to gain a better understanding of what it must have been like for Rachel growing up in an unstable and volatile home. She was able to use that insight to help repair relational ruptures with Rachel and titrate specific techniques to moments when Rachel felt understood and was more able to initiate changes or respond well to suggestions. The context of the therapeutic relationship was that the therapist had economic and educational privilege compared to Rachel's life as a homeless, unemployed woman whose child was in foster care. While Rachel did not know particulars about the therapist's life circumstances, it was automatic for her to assume that the therapist would abandon her or harm her, or at the very least, be unable to understand her. At times, Rachel was angry and envious of her therapist, and these periods vacillated with times when she wished the therapist could have been her "better" mother. Rachel had experienced enormous loss: her child, her childhood, her parents, and possibly her partner. She identified with her own "bad" mother, feeling shame and guilt about her failures. Rachel and her therapist learned to follow each other's lead and negotiate the path forward, deciding when to problem-solve more directly and when to process feelings, as her window of tolerance increased.

Conclusion

We have discussed Rachel's case to highlight the interwoven work of clinical social workers in agency practice. There are real-life demands of getting a state ID, figuring out housing, and enrolling someone for health insurance, which have to be balanced with the work of managing the symptoms of anxiety, depression, and substance use in the context of a therapeutic relationship. In this case, we have understood the client's anxiety, panic, and substance use as a means to regulate herself, a skill she did not learn in the crucible of a loving caregiver relationship. Trauma has instilled negative schemas about Rachel's sense of self and others. To help her learn the skills of emotional regulation, the therapist provided a client-centered relationship characterized by the classic Rogerian qualities of nonjudgment, positive regard, and genuineness, to provide a foundation for exploring and re-experiencing, in the moment, affects and cognitions.

In parallel, the client was taught mindfulness skills to regulate her body and mind by learning the connection between the two and giving her control over her emotional responses. The client was encouraged to talk and share her life story with the therapist so that she could change the narrative of herself as not being good or loved and that the world was an unsafe place to a narrative that is empowering and a story where she still has some agency, whether it be in getting a state ID, managing her symptoms of panic, or choosing whether to be with Colin or raise Adrian without him. The case of Rachel also illustrates the reality that for some clients, the best treatment may be serial psychotherapy as opposed to a "one and done." Clients may make changes, have a positive experience in therapy, then choose (or have it chosen for them by economics or agency policies) to leave therapy, returning when new insights or hurdles are experienced. This ongoing process would inevitably bring many impasses and empathic failures that would need to be worked through over time within the context of a safe environment with a consistently attuned therapist—an empathic therapist who doesn't come with pre-set ideas of what models work best with a particular set of symptoms but has sufficient skills to utilize them as needed in response to clients' needs and contexts (Segalo et al., 2007).

References

Alexander, F., & French, T. (1946). *Psychoanalytic therapy: Principles and application.* Ronald Press

American Psychological Association. (2024). *Guidelines for working with adults with complex trauma histories.* https://www.apa.org/practice/guidelines/adults-complex-trauma-histories.pdf

Asen, E., & Fonagy, P. (2012). Mentalization-based therapeutic interventions for families. *Journal of Family Therapy, 34*(4), 347–370. https://doi.org/10.1111/j.1467-6427.2011.00552.x

Bateman, A., & Fonagy, P. (2013). Mentalization-based treatment. *Psychoanalytic Inquiry*, 33(6), 595–613. https://doi.org/10.1080/07351690.2013.835170

Beck, J. S., & Cotterell, N. (2024) *The price of freedom.* Beck Institute. https://beckinstitute.org/blog/the price of freedom/?_gl=1*1cn3m4j*_up*MQ..*_ga*MTM4OTYzMDMxLjE3MzczOTg3NDU.*_ga_61J27G9LMB*MTczODI1NzUzNC4xLjEuMTczODI1NzU1Mi4wLjAuMTA4MDc4MDM2Nw.

Cleveland Clinic. (2021, August 17). *How box breathing can help you destress.* Cleveland Clinic. https://health.clevelandclinic.org/box-breathing-benefits

Cloitre, M. (2015). The "one size fits all" approach to trauma treatment: Should we be satisfied? *European Journal of Psychotraumatology*, *6*(1), 27344–27344. https://doi.org/10.3402/ejpt.v6.27344

Courtois, C. A. (1999). *Recollections of sexual abuse: Treatment principles and guidelines*. W. W. Norton. https://wwnorton.com/books/9780393703979

Courtois, C. A., & Marotta-Walters, S. A. (2021). The contemporary study of adult survivors of interpersonal violence and the development of mental health treatment. In R. Geffner, J. W. White, L. K. Hamberger, A. Rosenbaum, V. Vaughan-Eden, & V. I. Vieth (Eds.), *Handbook of interpersonal violence and abuse across the lifespan: A project of the National Partnership to End Interpersonal Violence Across the Lifespan* (pp. 4183–4208). Springer Nature.

Curtiss, J. E., Levine, D. S., Ander, I., & Baker, A. W. (2021). Cognitive-behavioral treatments for anxiety and stress-related disorders. *Focus (American Psychiatric Publishing)*, *19*(2), 184–189. https://doi.org/10.1176/appi.focus.20200045

Duprey, S. (2024). *Cognitive behavioral therapy for panic disorder: How it works & what to expect*. Choosing Therapy. https://www.choosingtherapy.com/cbt-for-panic-disorder

Fechau, E. I., Siebert, M., Beutel, M. E., Gündel, H., Hermann, A., Hoyer, J., Knaevelsrud, C., Kolassa, I.-T., Kruse, J., Leichsenring, F., Niemeyer, H., Salzer, S., Weidner, K., Witthöft, M., & Steinert, C. (2024). The balancing act of fitting in: A grounded theory study on how patients with posttraumatic stress disorder following childhood maltreatment experience participating in a randomized controlled psychotherapy study. *Qualitative Psychology*. Advance online publication. https://doi.org/10.1037/qup0000304

Gianotti, P. (2022). *Embracing complexity: A guidebook to integrating the essentials of psychodynamic principles across therapeutic disciplines*. Routledge.

Greenberg, T. M. (2020). *Treating complex trauma: Combined theories and methods*. Springer.

Herman, J. L. (1992). Complex PTSD: A syndrome in survivors of prolonged and repeated trauma. *Journal of Traumatic Stress*, *5*(3), 377–391. https://doi.org/10.1002/jts.2490050305

Herman, J. L. (1997). *Trauma and recovery: The aftermath of violence: From domestic abuse to political terror*. Basic Books.

Jansen, N., Kühl, J., Eller, N., Kingdon, P., & Firk, C. (2023). Mentalizing capacity partially mediates the relationship between attachment and stress, depression, and anxiety in social work students. *Clinical Social Work Journal*, *51*(4), 339–353. https://doi.org/10.1007/s10615-023-00882-2

Leichsenring, F., Abbass, A., Heim, N., Keefe, J.R., Kisely, S., Luyten, P., Rabung, S. and Steinert, C. (2023). The status of psychodynamic psychotherapy as an empirically supported treatment for common mental disorders: An umbrella review based on updated criteria. *World Psychiatry*, *22*, 286–304. https://doi.org/10.1002/wps.21104

Leichsenring, F. & Klein, S. (2014) Evidence for psychodynamic psychotherapy in specific mental disorders: a systematic review. *Psychoanalytic Psychotherapy*, *28*(1), 4–32. https://doi.org/10.1080/02668734.2013.865428

Leichsenring, F., & Steinert, C. (2019). The efficacy of psychodynamic psychotherapy: An up-to-date review. In D. Kealy & J. S. Ogrodniczuk (Eds.), *Contemporary psychodynamic psychotherapy: Evolving clinical practice* (pp. 49–74). Academic Press. https://doi.org/10.1016/B978-0-12-813373-6.00004-0

Leichsenring, F., Steinert, C., Beutel, M. E., Feix, L., Gündel, H., Hermann, A., Karabatsiakis, A., Knaevelsrud, C., König, H.-H., Kolassa, I. T., Kruse, J., Niemeyer, H., Nöske, F., Palmer, S., Peters, E., Reese, J.-P., Reuss, A., Salzer, S., Schade-Brittinger, C., ... Hoyer, J. (2020). Trauma-focused psychodynamic therapy and STAIR Narrative Therapy of post-traumatic stress disorder related to childhood maltreatment: Trial protocol of a multicentre randomised controlled trial assessing psychological, neurobiological and health economic outcomes (ENHANCE). *BMJ Open*, *10*(12). https://doi.org/10.1136/bmjopen-2020-040123

Levine, P. A. (2010). *In an unspoken voice: How the body releases trauma and restores goodness*. North Atlantic Books.

Lilliengren, P. (2023). A comprehensive overview of randomized controlled trials of psychodynamic psychotherapies. *Psychoanalytic Psychotherapy, 37*(2), 117–140. https://doi.org/10.1080/02668734.2023.2197617

Schäfer, S. K., Becker, N., King, L., Horsch, A., & Michael, T. (2019). The relationship between sense of coherence and post-traumatic stress: a meta-analysis. *European Journal of Psychotraumatology, 10*(1), 1562839–1562839. https://doi.org/10.1080/20008198.2018.1562839

Schore, A. N. (2012). *The science of the art of psychotherapy.* W.W. Norton & Company.

Segalo, P., Kruger, D. J., Fourie, E., & Terre Blanche, M. (2007). Re-imagining community: The Unisa community psychology experience. In M. Anderson (Ed.), *Journey to Freedom Narratives* (pp. 41–53). Unisa Press.

Stern, D. N. (1985). *The interpersonal world of the infant.* Basic Books.

Substance Abuse and Mental Health Services Administration (SAMHSA). (2024, March 29). https://www.samhsa.gov/substance-use/treatment/options/naltrexone

van der Kolk, B. (2014). *The body keeps the score: Brain, mind, and body in the healing of trauma.* Penguin Books.

Wachtel, P. L. (2020). Representations, schemas, and living-in-the-world. *Psychoanalytic Perspectives, 17*(3), 318–329. https://doi.org/10.1080/1551806X.2020.1801041

Walker, P. (no date) *The 4 Fs: A trauma typology in complex PTSD.* Pete Walker.com. https://www.pete-walker.com/fourFs_TraumaTypologyComplexPTSD.htm

8

Negotiating intrapsychic and interpersonal worlds with integrative psychotherapy

The case of Marcus allows us to focus on the inherent difficulties with most, if not all, clients, where intersecting identities and social and economic stressors interact with mental health difficulties, making it difficult to know where to begin. Social workers learn to "start where the client is," but usually clients present with complex issues that leave clinicians feeling a bit like they are searching for handholds as they try to scale a mountain. Working with Marcus offers potential gripping points around the areas of depression while negotiating race, sexuality, and the avoidance of potentially disappointing relationships.

Setting of treatment

The client is coming into the VA in the borough of the Bronx in New York City. The VA offers health care and allied services to veterans and their families, including physical health, mental health, prescriptions, radiology and diagnostics, substance abuse help, homeless programs, outreach, and community programs such as banking, education, and others. This is the client's first time engaging in outpatient psychotherapy. The therapist is a Jewish, cisgender male in his early thirties, licensed in New York with three years of practice in the VA system.

Psychodynamic and Cognitive Behavioral Theory and Practice. Terry B. Northcut and Shveta Kumaria, Oxford University Press. © Oxford University Press (2025). DOI: 10.1093/9780197508404.003.0008

Client description

Demographic data

The client, Marcus, is a forty-two-year-old Latine able-bodied gay cisgender male single veteran. Marcus receives VA benefits for his time in the service, which allowed him to finish his associate's degree and find employment in security. He has an apartment that he shares with two roommates to help cover costs. Marcus describes their relationship as friendly, albeit like "ships passing the night."

Precipitating issue

Marcus initially presented with low mood, low self-esteem, loneliness, and a past history of passive suicidal ideation. His PCP recommended that he see a therapist within the VA when he was seen for his annual check-up eight months ago. At that time, the PCP prescribed an antidepressant and made the referral to the therapist. While the medication has been helpful with his overall mood, Marcus still doesn't feel motivated to make any changes or seek out any new relationships. He has been consistently attending his therapy appointments for the last eight months.

Presenting issues

Marcus expresses futility about seeking romantic relationships, although that is what he most wants to have in his life. He believes any attempts to meet someone is spoiled by the relentless insecurity that permeates his interpersonal interactions, so he gives up trying. Strikingly, despite wanting intimate relationships, Marcus has initiated all of his breakups. One relationship was with a married man who promised to leave his wife to be with him. Marcus waited for two years for this to happen before finally giving up and ending the relationship. Another relationship involved excessive drinking and arguing on both of their parts until Marcus decided to walk away to try and get his drinking under control. A third relationship was the most recent and ended a year ago when Marcus's partner wanted him to meet his family and make more of a commitment. Disappointing relationships are a theme in both friendships and more intimate relationships. Marcus reports that he has no friendships that last, nor does he have any friends who are LGBTQIA+.

While Marcus has always felt lonely, this feeling was exacerbated this birthday week when he realized no one had remembered his birthday or apparently even thought of him. His family lives in Texas and has never visited him in New York. Given what he believes is a conservative political climate in the area where his family lives, Marcus is not keen to visit them. He is an only child, but has two older stepsiblings from his father's first marriage. These stepsiblings live near his parents in Texas and have grown children of their own. As he feels like an outsider even in his own family, he reports, "I don't think I have ever been loved well."

Marcus describes chronic insomnia and says that alcohol and exercise are the only things that help him fall asleep. He often does not feel like doing any form of physical activity. The antidepressant he was prescribed has helped with his insomnia, although he thinks he should be able to manage it on his own without needing medication. Physically, his health is good, and with his VA status, he has been able to maintain and meet all of his annual medical care needs.

Strengths and vulnerabilities

Marcus is an able-bodied cisgender man who has housing and access to health care. Given his education, training, and military service, he is employable and has no difficulty getting jobs. He is bright and can be engaging when talking about activities he cares about. While Marcus is able to form relationships, both romantic and platonic, he has difficulty maintaining them. He tends to avoid social interactions that could offer opportunities for positive, affirming interactions, for example, he is not part of the larger LGBTQIA+ community, the veteran community, or the Latino community. Although he reports a good relationship with his parents, they live far away, rarely travel, suffer from a variety of health challenges, and often do not speak to each other for weeks or months at a time. There seems to be a silent pact in his family that no one ever talks about Marcus being gay. His family maintains their conservative Catholic beliefs and attends church in their parish. Despite these important cultural connections, Marcus does not have strong familial ties that he can draw on for support. While Marcus rarely attends religious services, he goes through phases where he will sneak in after a service begins and leave before it is over. He isolates and avoids meeting people, including the church community, when things are not going well. When he was younger, he was more active on social media and in meeting for hookups, but he does not have much interest in that world or in sexual activity currently. He has also lost interest in exercise, which previously bolstered his self-esteem.

Marcus believes that because he has intersecting identities as a gay, Latine male, he is often overlooked for job-related promotions at his workplace or is subject to verbal microaggressions and insulting innuendos at his job. One way he manages his painful experiences at work is to accentuate a stereotypical image of machismo that allows him to sidestep questions about his sexuality, a pattern he established while in the military. Unfortunately, this also requires him to avoid most personal conversations at work, which increases his experience of loneliness and separateness from everyone else. Marcus reports that he realized he was gay as a prepubescent boy, which he feels emphasized his sense of being different in the small town where he and his family lived. Mental health was not talked about or considered, and it was easy for him to "hide in plain sight."

History and current context

Marcus describes his childhood as uneventful. His father worked long hours as a mechanic and did repair jobs for others to supplement his income. Marcus's mother worked as a childcare worker and took in sewing in the evenings and on weekends. While he reports a positive relationship with his mother, Marcus describes her as having had frequent migraines that meant he often had to play quietly or watch TV by himself. His father's long hours of work and after-work hours at the local bar left him little time to interact with Marcus, who did not feel that his father ever intentionally wanted to be with him, and thus avoided him. He believes some of that avoidance was related to his being gay, but he also felt that his father was never really interested in him, instead preferring Marcus's stepsiblings. School was a challenge given his lack of confidence and his sense of isolation; he dated a few girls briefly, but found it hard to keep up the pretense of a straight relationship. Without a sense of purpose, he decided that the Army seemed to be a good way to get away from home. During Marcus's seven years in the Army, he was not actively involved in combat but worked in security at military airports worldwide. He does not maintain contact with any of the other enlisted men he knew. Since his retirement, he has been working security for various businesses in New York City. He usually works one job for a while, then leaves due to feeling passed over for promotions or that others are being given better opportunities.

Theoretical contributions to understanding

Psychodynamic

Based on what Marcus has told us and on his history of disappointing and perpetual losses in relationships, it seems that his parents were good enough in terms of meeting basic needs but were absent in ways that left Marcus feeling unseen and chronically lonely. His internal working model of attachment is a well-worn path that perceives people and relationships as unavailable and, therefore, rejecting. The internal working model of attachment also dictates the security functions an individual uses for emotional regulation. In Marcus's case, distance from others fits his developmental experiences, making him feel safe yet yearning for something more. The messages he received from the social world about his sexuality and love made him feel different, affected his self-worth, and made him hide this part of himself for a long time. This hiding and shame led to anger against the world and at himself for being gay and contributed to his depression and rejection of others. Economic realities and an environment that did not support authenticity and his strivings for relationships have led to difficulty initiating relationships with partners that can affirm his sense of self-worth. Instead, relationships that offer greater closeness are destabilizing, leading him to pull away and then vacillate between shame for wanting more and anger at the disappointing other. Cyclical psychodynamic therapy offers one perspective of Marcus's subjective experience of the world, and is

> thus strongly based on an ironic perspective that suggests that people unwittingly recreate pathogenic childhood experiences despite their earnest intentions to find new sorts of relationships, because these early experiences skew and limit their ability to make new and better choices.
>
> (Gold & Wachtel, 1993, p. 81, cited in Stricker & Gold, 2006)

In addition to a cyclical psychodynamic perspective, self psychology sheds additional light on the complexity of Marcus's intersectional identities in relation to others. Chapter 3 highlighted the importance of empathic resonance for being able to experience a sense of aliveness and an ability to seek out important selfobject relationships for mirroring, idealization, and twinship. Marcus's disengaged parents and his identity as a gay male in a homophobic environment contributed to failures in developing a cohesive, nuclear sense of himself that would have required the internalization of these important selfobject functions. His subjective experience of these disconnections has impaired his sense of being valued and capable of finding and maintaining meaningful connections. In addition, when the other proves to be disappointing and not able to serve the selfobject functions he needs, he becomes enraged and dysregulated. The gaps in empathic responsiveness with others lead Marcus to choose relationships that either repeat patterns of disengagement or experiences that perpetuate a lack of intimacy in a wish to finally get his needs met by someone he loves. The task of psychotherapy, then, is to implement an "exposure" therapeutic relationship to gradually allow him to mourn what didn't and doesn't happen relationally while also providing a new, safe, empathic immersion experience.

CBT

Marcus has been trapped by his inability to choose partners that can fulfill his emotional needs, and if they are available, he becomes dysregulated and vulnerable, leading to flight or disagreements. Avoidance, unfortunately, keeps this pattern in place. Individuals don't expose themselves to feared scenarios, whether they are an object, person, situation, or feeling that could lead to emotional dysregulation or overwhelming cognitive dissonance. As a result, Marcus is likely unaware of the emotions or cognitions underlying his behavior. Warding off memories of past conflicts with others, including homophobic harassment, and experiences of rejection by his father in particular, leaves him with rigid behavioral patterns that are unfulfilling and leave him depressed.

In the case of Marcus, his choosing relationships where his needs are unmet keep this cycle in place. On the few occasions when his needs are met, it feels so new and overwhelming that he behaves in a way that jeopardizes it to keep the schema of "I am unlovable" stable. This schema has a protective function: It protects Marcus against probable emotional states such as grief or loss that arise from interpersonal rejection. The goal of therapy is to help Marcus see how this schema is causing him loss and grief and has outlived its coping function, and for that he has to expose himself to newer relationship choices, including those with the therapist.

The other mechanism that keeps Marcus's relational maladaptive cycle in place is his depression and internalized homophobia. When he hears homophobic slurs, violence, debates, and political wars around his sexuality or experiences microaggressions at work, he wonders, "Why can't I be like other people?" In his mind, if not for his sexuality, his life would be so much easier. His attempts to engage with members of the queer community arouse self-hatred and shame internally, which leads to avoidance and isolation. This also deprives him of social support, which is critical to dealing with his internalized homophobia and depression (Sherry, 2007a). This also means the skills he needs to navigate these spaces become rusty with time. The schema "I am wrong and unlovable" gets triggered in these occasional interactions, which reinforces the avoidance and isolation, keeping him in the cycle of recurrent depressive episodes.

Empirical and clinical contributions to interventions

Evidence-based treatments for depression include CBT, interpersonal psychotherapy (IPT), dialectical behavior therapy (DBT), and IPT plus antidepressants (IPT-A). Borrero and Przewoski (2024) state that "[f]indings indicate that specific to the treatment of depression in Latinx youth, IPT-A is *probably efficacious*, CBT is *possibly efficacious*, and MBI and DBT treatments are *experimental*" (p. 44). IPT's focus on relationships and communication seems to have an edge while working with Latinx youth; that being said, it is essential to remember that confounding variables such as researcher bias, no long-term follow-up, and differences in how treatment success is defined contaminate research studies (see Chapter 5; Cuijpers et al., 2020; Wampold et al., 2011). Consequently, Cuijpers et al. (2020) concluded that for the treatment of depression, it is still difficult to predict who will benefit from which intervention. It can take a few trials of different modalities for clients to find a treatment that works for them, reinforcing the need for flexibility and the assimilation of different theoretical frameworks.

The minority stress model (Meyer, 1995, 2003) integrates identity theory with group relations, personality theory, and social and psychological theories of stress to show the harmful effects of stigma and prejudice on LGBTQIA+ populations. Social support and community support are protective factors against internalized homophobia in LGBTQIA+ relationships (Meyer, 2003). It is associated with lower suicidal ideation, lower suicide attempts, lower psychological distress, and lower likelihood of engaging in risky sexual behavior (Sherry, 2007a). LGBTQIA+ individuals often present for therapy because of isolation, particularly when there is a lack of social support. This sense of isolation is exacerbated when the individuals feel that they have to hide their identity. Research has shown that concealment of identity varies by age, sexuality, class, and immigration status, with African, Asian, and Hispanic Americans more likely to conceal their sexual identity than European Americans in general, and in health care and work settings in particular (Hoy-Ellis, 2021). Research on BIPOC sexual minority individuals also shows that the way they experience minority stress is different from their White counterparts (Meyer et al., 2008), with internalized homophobia highly correlated to depression and anxiety (Newcomb & Mustanski, 2010). In the case of Marcus, his avoidant attachment pattern and identities as a gay Latine male is correlated with him being less accepting of his sexual orientation. Implications of research in this area indicate that insecure attachment patterns—particularly fearful or avoidant styles—exacerbate the sense of social isolation but can be ameliorated with a secure and positive therapeutic relationship. Thus, the work of therapy in such cases includes less of a focus on symptom management and more on the connection provided within the therapeutic framework (Sherry, 2007b).

There is always appropriate curiosity around client–therapist matching on issues of gender, race, and ethnicity, and an important consideration is whether a therapist's identity is a positive or negative factor. There is data showing that clients express an initial preference for therapists who match their race and ethnicity, even perceiving them more positively, which could increase client retention. However, over the course of therapy, there is almost no benefit to treatment outcomes or client satisfaction with therapy when racial matching occurs (Cabral & Smith, 2011; Hung et al., 2023; Johnson & Caldwell, 2011). Though there is important qualitative research that emphasizes the importance of matching of sexual orientation (Jumarali, 2022), there is also research indicating that the matching depends on which identities the client believes to be most salient (Anders et al., 2021). Marcus has a lifelong disavowal of his sexual orientation identity and would likely not be comfortable having a gay male therapist, particularly if that were disclosed initially. To date, Marcus seems to have settled in with the therapist and reports being satisfied with therapy in general.

Treatment plan

Marcus has been coming to therapy to address his pervasive low mood with depressive episodes and inability to sustain enduring and nurturing relationships. While not an explicit goal, Marcus has internalized the societal rejection of homosexuality and anti-Latine racism. Marcus and the therapist joined to start work to alleviate his symptoms of depression: anhedonia, anergia, social isolation, irritability, and insomnia, and the therapist focused the first few sessions on case history taking and assessment. Marcus confessed to using alcohol to cope with the insomnia, and has had three episodes of severe depression, which were treated with antidepressants that he takes until he feels a little better and then stops against medical advice.

The therapist decided to work with the theoretical base of Wachtel's cyclical psychodynamics (2017). This means understanding the relational cycle that Marcus has of unconsciously pushing people away and then receding into isolation and depression. Consequently, when this cycle is recreated within the therapeutic relationship in the transference dynamics, the therapist works to repair the ruptures and stays with Marcus even when Marcus pushes him away. He does this by being reflexive, interpreting what has occurred for both of them and giving Marcus the agency to renegotiate emotional closeness with the therapist. Based on a psychodynamic understanding of depression and its developmental origins, the therapist focuses on building a strong alliance with Marcus to provide insight into his relational patterns as they unfold so that Marcus is aware of his emotions and can work toward their acknowledgment and acceptance (Alexander & French, 1946; Grenyer & Marceau, 2022; Rogers, 1951).

The therapist also decides to introduce (assimilate) behavioral activation in the treatment plan to deal with the symptoms of depression, such as avoidance of pleasurable activities (Stein et al., 2021). This would include daily monitoring of mood and activities to show the connection between them, identifying activities that provide pleasure and those that give a sense of mastery, and building small, achievable goals to help Marcus regain his motivation and energy levels. The behavioral activation needs to be balanced with a greater understanding of Marcus's subjective experience of these interventions.

Lastly, the therapist plans to use ACT to pivot the client back to his values. These values would be the guiding map for the activities that he finds pleasure and meaning in doing. This would help deal with experiential avoidance and increase psychological flexibility. The values also offer points of grounding/anchoring to tackle issues of internalized homophobia and meaninglessness that can accompany depression. An ACT response to internalized homophobia focuses on defusing from the self-stigmatizing thoughts and focusing on value-based action (Fowler et al., 2022; Yadavaia & Hayes, 2012).

Course of treatment

Marcus is an easy person to talk to, is always on time, and seems to be very mindful of the frame of the session. He answers questions clearly and seems more willing to have the therapist lead the conversation rather than bring up his concerns. The therapist holds off on introducing behavioral activation or ACT as yet because it seems that Marcus's internal motivation/investment is not very high, as if he is coming for therapy as a passive attempt to "check the box" of compliance. Alternatively, this could also fit his pattern of needing to be very careful about who he lets into his world—which, given his background, would represent good judgment. This apparent "passivity" was a reminder to the therapist to watch how this plays out in the transference process and in Marcus's difficulty with therapeutic interventions, if it comes up at all.

Early in the treatment, the therapist asked Marcus about his childhood using open-ended questions and later about his relationships, as well as his understanding of why he is depressed and suffering. Exploration of the assumptions (attributions) that Marcus makes for the failure of his relationships and why this keeps happening is critical. A vital dialogue occurred regarding his beliefs about how people should act and the texture of those beliefs. Marcus's comment about never being loved well was explored with respect to what being "loved well" means. The therapist was trying to understand what distortions there might be in his schemas about himself and others and elicit the feelings associated with those schemas or unformulated experiences.

When Marcus shared his story, the therapist heard that he does not feel loved, seen, or cared for in his relationships. He understood the pain and profound loss Marcus had felt growing up, as well as his loneliness and isolation. It is essential for the therapist to mirror those feelings and subjectively immerse himself in those affective states. Empathy is critical before any problem-solving can occur. However, there were fits and starts to forming this empathic immersion experience with Marcus. Marcus had developed a finely tuned "bullshit" monitor out of a lifesaving need to hide his identity and pass, particularly while in the military. He had also experienced much pseudo-support that felt inauthentic to him, particularly in his childhood and teen years. He got the message from his father that officially he was loved, but his father's avoidance of him contradicted this. The therapist recognized that, at times, he needed to acknowledge that as a young, "White" therapist he could *not* fully comprehend Marcus's experience. While the therapist and Marcus may form a strong therapeutic alliance moving forward, the differences between them must be acknowledged and explored, and it may take Marcus some time to start trusting the therapist.

To better understand Marcus's role in his romantic break-ups, the therapist elicited and listened to how Marcus may have unconsciously sabotaged these relationships. In one session, Marcus said, "He knew how I felt about us; we were committed in our hearts, but I felt hurried; I never said I wanted to break up; that is on him; he left me, he did not love me enough, maybe he never loved me, and this was all a pretense." The therapist asked him *what* this narrative does for Marcus and *how* it makes him feel, and then tentatively offered an alternative explanation for Marcus's boyfriend, leaving him suggesting that maybe the boyfriend felt insecure about Marcus's commitment to the relationship, and it made the boyfriend push harder for a commitment. Perhaps the dynamic between them was of a pursuer (the boyfriend) and pursued (Marcus), and the partner had picked up that Marcus did not want the relationship to move toward greater intimacy?

The therapist asked Marcus if he felt any aspects of the alternate explanation could also be true. He said, "Sure, some parts could be true." The therapist then followed up to ask that if some parts of the story were true, what did it mean for the story (narrative) that Marcus tells himself? This caused something to shift in the session, and the therapist decided to explore it in the next session; the therapist was trying to disrupt Marcus's narrative. However, Marcus was a "no-show" in the next session and did not inform the therapist, which was unusual. When the therapist brought this up the following week and gently suggested that maybe Marcus was upset with what happened in the last session, Marcus denied that he was upset and said that it was snowing, that he had missed the train, and things had gotten off schedule, so he had decided to cancel. This signaled to the therapist that, one, maybe he and Marcus had gone into providing alternate evidence too soon and the relationship was still tenuous, and two, when Marcus is upset, he tends to isolate and deny his emotions. This experience also signaled to the therapist his need to consider why he moved to try to "disrupt the narrative." Could there be countertransference that made him move too quickly or not explore the statement further? Was he experiencing homophobia as Marcus described the relationship and wanted him to "man up" to his role in the break-up?

The healing of this rupture with Marcus took a long time. He was disengaged but present every session, and one day said, "I don't think therapy is for me or working for me." The therapist led this discussion with humility and gentleness to explore what aspects were not working for him, including whether it was because of the therapist. The therapist also volunteered that he might feel understandably cautious after he felt so misunderstood and apologized for the blunder (empathic failure). Something about this apology seemed to soften Marcus's stance, although he said that all of this talking was not helping and that he wanted something more *active* to happen in therapy.

There can be a couple of interpretations made about Marcus's desire for action. The therapist could have perceived that Marcus wanted and needed to feel empowered in the therapy after feeling disempowered by the therapist's intervention. However, that raises the question of why Marcus is asking for this empowerment now. A more dynamic interpretation of this shift could be that he felt the therapist was "too close" to understanding Marcus's fear of intimacy in relationships. This itself was terrifying to Marcus, and he needed to retreat to feel safe again. We know from Marcus's historical behavior that feeling too close leads to a retreat on his part; with that being said, it doesn't mean that the therapist should interpret the wish to distance to Marcus at this point, since the relationship has not healed from the previous rupture. This is a point in the therapeutic relationship where it is important to listen for multiple meanings to clients' messages. In this case, Marcus had skipped a session and was on tenterhooks about therapy. The therapist heard the implicit pain expressed of how it felt to "be wrong" and "unloved." Marcus needed a safer, structured framework to allow himself and the therapist to continue working together.

The therapist shifted to understanding what values mattered most to Marcus so as to design activities that aligned with those values. Doing so fulfilled Marcus's wish for action, and dynamically for his wish to be seen and attended to. Some of the questions that the therapist asked to get to those values ranged from "What do you want your life to be about?," "What is truly important to you?," "What kind of person do you want to be?," "How do you want to show up in your relationships?," "What values are most important in your work life?," and "What actions can you take today to live more in line with your values?" (Harris, 2019). The therapist asked Marcus to imagine that it was his seventy-fifth birthday, and he was surrounded by his loved ones praising and describing him—who would be there? What would they be saying about him? What would he like them to say in addition?

In response, Marcus was quite thoughtful and said at that age he would like to have lived a fulfilled, healthier life with a partner and friends. He would not want to see himself as sad, lonely, unfit, or drinking at seventy-five. He wished people would say he was a kind, helpful man, a loving partner, and a caring son, that he loved well and was loved well. The therapist deduced that community, family/partnership, and health seemed to be values Marcus holds dear. The therapist explained (psychoeducation) how avoidance and social isolation seem like a good idea at first as they reduce the chance of having negative interactions with the world (with good reason, given Marcus's intersecting identities and experiences with racism and homophobic taunts), but that they also deprive a person of opportunities that could lead to positive feelings. The therapist also explained to Marcus how not living a life aligned with his values may be causing him not to appreciate himself and contributing to his sadness. The therapist asked Marcus what he would be doing if he lived his life based on the value of health. How does he describe health? Marcus said that he would go to the gym more often, as he feels good when he is fit and strong. The therapist then asked Marcus how he would feel about working out some goals for fitness that would be achievable and pleasurable for him. This would serve two goals: It would get Marcus out of his home, and the exercise would help elevate his mood.

The therapist also used psychoeducation to speak to Marcus's value of having a partner and a sense of community. He explained to Marcus that one of the factors contributing to his loneliness was internalized homophobia and internalized heterosexism caused by the negative societal messages, discrimination, and stigma prevalent in a homophobic social environment:

This includes a global negative attitude toward homosexuality, discomfort with disclosing one's sexual identity with others, disconnectedness from other queer individuals, and extending to discomfort with same-sex activity (Newcomb & Mustanski, 2010). The therapist provided language for the painful affect that Marcus was experiencing. By putting these experiences into the cognitive realm, it lifted them out of only being felt affectively, which left him feeling passive and helpless. He now had an explanation for his feelings, which could then lead to bringing back action or behaviors into the CBT triad of cognition, affect, and behavior that is so essential for change to occur.

Marcus was shocked to learn that he was not alone in having internalized heterosexism, and that it was more common than one would imagine. The psychoeducation served to improve the alliance in unanticipated ways: for example, he started to see the therapist as an ally and was more engaged in therapy than before the rupture in the alliance. In addition, he asked for more resources to read and experienced a mixture of lightness and curiosity as the sessions progressed. He also started pushing the frame of the sessions, wanting to meet more often and coming up with numerous questions around internalized homophobia. Sherry (2007a) said that when working with LGBTQIA+ individuals such as Marcus and those who developmentally do not have a secure attachment, the therapeutic frame might have to be held more loosely and in a more egalitarian fashion. For this therapist, given his age and experience, it was a challenge not to push Marcus to figure things out on his own or to offer too many solutions that could be overwhelming.

One of the bigger challenges in addition to maintaining a therapeutic alliance was to help Marcus engage with the queer community. The psychodynamic concept of projective identification describes the process of devaluing that occurs with Marcus. He feels tremendous shame about being gay (internalized heterosexism), which he disavows and projects onto members of other queer groups. He then rejects them as being inappropriately flamboyant. For example, Marcus asked, "Why do they have to be so loud, so colorful?" The therapist responded by asking, "And what does it mean if they are loud and colorful?" Marcus's answer was, "That means I am loud and colorful, but I am not. I am not like them."

The therapist used cognitive restructuring to show Marcus how many of his reasons for not engaging with the queer community come down to his feelings of shame and low self-worth which inhibit his reaching out. Marcus and his therapist explored different models of men who were Latino and queer; some of whom were straight passing like Marcus, and others who were not. They explored where he internalized the messages in school, family, and the military to highlight how these stereotypes are maintained and rejected through socialization. The therapist also asked Marcus to do an experiential exercise based on Lin and Israel's (2012) research study, where he wrote a letter to a young gay Latino man who realized he was attracted to men. The therapist used ACT to help Marcus defuse from the self-stigmatizing thoughts and see them as cognitive events rather than facts. Choosing value-based action and taking small risks followed, such as going to a queer event he liked or a book reading, which were introduced in later sessions. As he began to have more experiences with other gay men that did not confirm his projections, the distorted identification was lessened.

Therapeutic relationship

The therapeutic relationship started off slowly, with ruptures that led to pivotal moments of acceptance and trust. The therapist provided Marcus with the mirroring that he had not experienced as a child or an adult. The therapist became an ally in Marcus's journey of working on his internalized homophobia, which also allowed Marcus to feel a twinship in the commitment. Twinship does not mean that the therapist and the client have to be exactly alike, rather they share the experiences of "mutual finding," belonging, and sense of being human together (Togashi & Kottler, 2012). In a practical sense, the therapist could support, share, applaud, and commiserate with Marcus's attempts to challenge existing schemas, the reality of discrimination, and specific attempts to move out into the world.

There were moments in this work with Marcus where the therapist felt impatient and critical of Marcus's passivity and apparent rejection of potential social supports, thinking, "Have you been living under a rock?" The therapist, being younger, growing up in a liberal university town, and being university-educated, had seen a world where being gay was more acceptable and did not see it as a stigmatized identity, even though it was a minority. This led to a similar impasse between the therapist and the client, where the client felt that the therapist did not have time for his concerns to unfold, and it felt identical to the feeling he had with his father: "he did not want to be with me." The therapist, on the other hand, was caught in the countertransference of "How can the client be so ignorant about his sexuality?"

It would also be fair to wonder whether when the client said that this therapy was not the right fit and the therapist suggested ACT and values work, was it then that the therapist really became invested in what Marcus wanted to work on? Or was it then that the dynamic and power in the relationship became rebalanced, so that Marcus felt more of an active agent in his own life? Did the relational connection previously established lead to Marcus being able to take ownership in his life? Perhaps most likely all of those potential explanations are true; empathy matters, titrating interventions according to reactions for both therapist and client, and at some point, as Freud (1919, p. 166) pointed out, clients need to be helped to move out into the world.

Conclusion

We have discussed Marcus's case to highlight how therapy involves understanding a person as an individual, growing up in an ecology of systems with differing messages that influence that individual's sense of self and self-worth. The therapeutic space itself is one such example of ecology where these messages can be refuted or validated, whether we look at it from a cyclical psychodynamic perspective or a social learning perspective. Social justice in therapy means invalidating and refuting these deleterious messages, showing their connection to a client's health and relationships, and helping clients regain pride and joy in who they are. Social justice also means understanding a client's need to decenter power in the sessions when they are feeling disempowered and following the client's lead in setting the goals for therapy.

The therapist brought his knowledge about the intersection of heteronormativity and anti-Latine racism to hear how Marcus was affected by this and how it was related to his depression. He could hear how Marcus's upbringing, in conjunction with the world he lives in, had left him struggling with intimacy in relationships. Yet, it was the critical process of reflexivity and humility that helped repair the therapeutic alliance with Marcus when the therapist was not attuned to Marcus's need to go slower in their work together. The therapist's apology and ability to withstand Marcus pushing him away and staying in the relationship gave Marcus a corrective emotional experience of a safe relationship. The therapist provided tools and direction that the client asked for to demonstrate responsiveness and empower the client in the session. The therapeutic frame was held loosely, yet firmly (flexibly, but not elastic), to let Marcus grow, be seen, and be accepted rather than make himself invisible and smaller to fit in a world that had most times rejected him. While it is imperative that we advocate to shift the oppressive systems that impact our clients and the worlds in which we both live and practice, it is equally important to acknowledge the power of a therapeutic relationship in understanding, supporting, and transforming the internal and external lives of clients and therapists. In doing so, we can see beyond our theories and techniques as Jung suggested (Antoniou & Blom, 2006) and allow ourselves and our clients to be transformed.

References

Alexander, F., & French, T. (1946). *Psychoanalytic therapy: Principles and application.* Ronald Press.

Anders, C., Kivlighan, D. M., III, Porter, E., Lee, D., & Owen, J. (2021). Attending to the intersectionality and saliency of clients' identities: A further investigation of therapists' multicultural orientation. *Journal of Counseling Psychology, 68*(2), 139–148. https://doi.org/10.1037/cou0000447

Antoniou, A. S., & Blom, T. G. (2006). The five therapeutic relationships. *Clinical Case Studies, 5*(5), 437–451 https://doi:10.1177/1534650106292668

Borrero, E., & Przewoski, A. (2024). A systematic review of evidence-based treatments for depression in Latinx youth. *Child & Family Behavior Therapy*, 1–58. https://doi.org/10.1080/07317107.2024.2438341

Cabral, R. R., & Smith, T. B. (2011). Racial/ethnic matching of clients and therapists in mental health services: A meta-analytic review of preferences, perceptions, and outcomes. *Journal of Counseling Psychology, 58*(4), 537–554. https://doi.org/10.1037/a0025266

Cuijpers, P., Stringaris, A., & Wolpert, M. (2020). Treatment outcomes for depression: Challenges and opportunities. *The Lancet Psychiatry, 7*(11), 925–927. https://doi.org/10.1016/S2215-0366(20)30036-5

Fowler, J. A., Viskovich, S., Buckley, L., & Dean, J. A. (2022). A call for ACTion: A systematic review of empirical evidence for the use of Acceptance and Commitment Therapy (ACT) with LGBTQI+ individuals. *Journal of Contextual Behavioral Science, 25*, 78–89.

Freud, S. (1919). Lines of advance in psychoanalytic therapy. *Standard Edition, 17*, 159–168.

Gold, J. R., & Wachtel, P. L. (1993). Cyclical psychodynamics. In G. Stricker & J. R. Gold (Eds.), *Comprehensive handbook of psychotherapy integration* (pp. 59–72). Plenum Press. https://doi.org/10.1007/978-1-4757-9782-4_5

Grenyer, B. F. S., & Marceau, E. M. (2022). Helping patients master core conflictual relationship themes in psychotherapy. *Journal of Clinical Psychology, 78*, 386–395. https://doi.org/10.1002/jclp.23314

Harris, R. (2019). *ACT made simple* (2nd ed.). New Harbinger Publications

Hoy-Ellis, C. P. (2021). Minority stress and mental health: A review of the literature. *Journal of Homosexuality, 70*(5), 806–830. https://doi.org/10.1080/00918369.2021.2004794

Hung, Y., Linville, D., Janes, E., & Yee, S. (2023). Race matching in predicting relational therapy outcome: A machine learning approach. *International Journal of Systemic Therapy, 34*(2), 83–94. https://doi.org/10.1080/2692398X.2023.2169028

Johnson, L. A., & Caldwell, B. E. (2011). Race, gender, and therapist confidence: Effects on satisfaction with the therapeutic relationship in MFT. *The American Journal of Family Therapy, 39*(4), 307–324. https://doi.org/10.1080/01926187.2010.532012

Jumarali, S. N. (2022). *The impact of identity-based matching on the psychotherapy experiences of lesbian, gay, bisexual, transgender, and queer people of color* (Order No. 28966665). Available from ProQuest Dissertations & Theses Global; Publicly Available Content Database. (2704365047). https://flagship.luc.edu/login?url=https://www.proquest.com/dissertations-theses/impact-identity-based-matching-on-psychotherapy/docview/2704365047/se-2

Lin, Y., & Israel, T. (2012). A computer-based intervention to reduce internalized heterosexism in men. *Journal of Counseling Psychology, 59*(3), 458–464. https://doi.org/10.1037/a0028282

Meyer, I. H. (1995). Minority stress and mental health in gay men. *Journal of Health and Social Behavior, 36*(1), 38–56. https://doi.org/10.2307/2137286

Meyer, I. H. (2003). Prejudice, social stress, and mental health in lesbian, gay, and bisexual populations: Conceptual issues and research evidence. *Psychological Bulletin, 129*(5), 674–697. https://doi.org/10.1037/0033-2909.129.5.674

Meyer, I. H., Schwartz, S., & Frost, D. M. (2008). Social patterning of stress and coping: Does disadvantaged social statuses confer more stress and fewer coping resources? *Social Science & Medicine, 67*(3), 368–379. https://doi.org/10.1016/j.socscimed.2008.03.012

Newcomb, M. E., & Mustanski, B. (2010). Internalized homophobia and internalizing mental health problems: A meta-analytic review, *Clinical Psychology Review, 30*(8), 1019–1029. https://doi.org/10.1016/j.cpr.2010.07.003

Rogers, C. R. (1951). *Client-centered therapy; its current practice, implications, and theory.* Houghton Mifflin.

Sherry, A. (2007a). Internalized homophobia and adult attachment: Implications for clinical practice. *Psychotherapy: Theory, Research, Practice, Training, 44*(2), 219–225. https://doi.org/10.1037/0033-3204.44.2.219

Sherry, A. (2007b). An attachment theory approach to the short-term treatment of a woman with borderline personality disorder and comorbid diagnoses. *Clinical Case Studies, 6*(2), 103–118. https://doi.org/10.1177/15346501052834173450058317

Stein, A. T., Carl, E., Cuijpers, P., Karyotaki, E., & Smits, J. A. J. (2021). Looking beyond depression: a meta-analysis of the effect of behavioral activation on depression, anxiety, and activation. *Psychological Medicine, 51*(9), 1491–1504. https://doi.org/10.1017/S0033291720000239

Stricker, G., & Gold, J. (Eds.). (2006). *A casebook of psychotherapy integration.* American Psychological Association. https://doi.org/10.1037/11436-000

Togashi, K., & Kottler, A. (2012). The many faces of twinship: From the psychology of the self to the psychology of being human. *International Journal of Psychoanalytic Self Psychology, 7*(3), 331–351. https://doi.org/10.1080/15551024.2012.686158

Wachtel, P. L. (2017). Attachment theory and clinical practice: A cyclical psychodynamic vantage point. *Psychoanalytic Inquiry, 37*(5), 332–342. https://doi.org/10.1080/07351690.2017.1322431

Wampold, B. E., Budge, S. L., Laska, K. M., Del Re, A. C., Baardseth, T. P., Fluckiger, C., Minami, T., Kivlighan, D. M., 2nd, & Gunn, W. (2011). Evidence-based treatments for depression and anxiety versus treatment-as-usual: A meta-analysis of direct comparisons. *Clinical Psychology Review, 31*(8), 1304–1312. https://doi.org/10.1016/j.cpr.2011.07.012

Yadavaia, J. E., & Hayes, S. C. (2012). Acceptance and commitment therapy for self-stigma around sexual orientation: A multiple baseline evaluation. *Cognitive and Behavioral Practice, 19*(4), 545–559. https://doi.org/10.1016/j.cbpra.2011.09.002

Index

For the benefit of digital users, indexed terms that span two pages (e.g., 52–53) may, on occasion, appear on only one of those pages.

Tables, figures, and boxes are indicated by an italic *t*, *f*, and *b* following the Page number.